Why We Ride

women writers on the
horses in their lives

edited by
Verna Dreisbach

SEAL PRESS

Why We Ride
Women Writers on the Horses in Their Lives

Copyright © 2010 by Verna Dreisbach

Published by
Seal Press
A Member of the Perseus Books Group
1700 Fourth Street
Berkeley, CA 94710

Library of Congress Cataloging-in-Publication Data

Why we ride : women writers on the horses in their lives / Verna Dreisbach, editor.
    p. cm.
  ISBN 978-1-58005-266-5
  1. Horses. 2. Women horse owners. 3. Human-animal relationships. I. Dreisbach, Verna, 1968-
  SF301.W46 2010
  636.1—dc22
                        2009049393

9 8 7 6 5 4 3 2 1

Cover and interior design by Domini Dragoone
Printed in the United States of America by Edwards Brothers
Distributed by Publishers Group West

In memory of GOSLOVICH,
my first true love.

Contents

Note from the Editor
Verna Dreisbach

I have been in love with horses since I can remember. And I know I'm not alone as I remember images of that first glimpse, sensations of that first touch, and ultimately the exhilaration of that first riding lesson. As a young girl, I was hooked. But it wasn't until junior high that I found my true love.

Like dog owners who profess their breed of dog as the only one they'll ever own for reasons ranging from loyalty to intelligence, personality or "just because of the way he makes me feel," horse owners are no different. We choose a horse for her beauty, her ability, or for what we see of ourselves reflected in her. I found beauty in the racehorse, the thoroughbred racehorse—a beauty that captured my heart long before a boy ever did. Enticed by slender legs and narrow faces, I treasured the climb upon their back, the long view down from above, and the effortless movement of their strides, the sensation of the ground passing under us as if Pegasus had taken flight. But mostly, I loved their passion to run and the sweat of their bodies glistening in the sun, dripping from their bellies to the ground—a passion so intense that it seeps through every bead of moisture that tickles their skin, into every muscle that twitches. The prancing, the inability to stand still, the glaze in their eyes as they near the racetrack. *That* reveals their spirit. That tells their story.

And while a thoroughbred's passion for life, for the run, has an addictive quality that I can identify with, at times I yearn for a casual ride, to stroll with dropped reins and loose legs, to lose touch with time. Without having to light the sky on fire.

I'm learning to enjoy and appreciate the balance—what other horses, other passions, can teach me. I've learned that after the sprint, life is also about the slow parts, about the calm where we find our peace. And to that end, I bought a paint and a quarter horse to balance my blazing passion with some much-needed grounding. Sometimes my thoroughbred needs to take a nap.

But what is most true about my connection to each horse I have ever owned is that each has been a catalyst of personal exploration— each horse providing insight and revealing my hidden self, those parts that ultimately make me whole. Just as we ride through life collecting bits and pieces of ourselves, this collection of stories offers a journey through the horse lives of so many wonderfully gifted writers. There are many of us whose lives have been shaped by our horses and whose lives have been made richer for that.

Why We Ride features twenty-seven personal, heart-felt stories by women who I truly hope will transform your life as they have transformed mine. May their voices inspire you to believe that your life is a shared journey. If you've ever dreamt of that first horse, Dee Ambrose-Stahl will share with you that you're not alone. Jane Smiley offers insight into her life-long relationship with horses and the moments of unity we yearn for and sometimes capture. Jacqueline Winspear suggests that we all need to return to the basics, and it's her horse that reminds her that the simplest way is right most of the time. Michele Scott, Kara Gall, and Kate St. Vincent Vogl all speak to their relationships with their fathers and how horses were at the very heart of those relationships. Valerie Riggs, Janice Newton, and Samantha Ducloux Waltz discovered that their horses held insight into their marital relationships. And several women, (Lisa Romeo, Vanessa Wright, Dobie Houson, and myself), hold the heart of the horse so close to their own that they sometimes can't tell where the horse begins and they end. For those who yearn to push boundaries Jill Widmar, Linda Ballou, and Therese Zink share in the spirit of the horse, the horse that yearns for its freedom past imaginary fences. Many more stories in between share in the enduring and passionate experiences with our horses—horses that have helped us become better women and, most importantly, better people with richer lives.

Animals can endear themselves to almost anyone's heart, but horses—and specifically the bond these women share with their majestic creatures—tell a special story. May these stories remind you of your strength and insight in knowing which paths to choose. May these stories show you that your journey with horses is more than the sum of its simple parts. May these stories help you to see that in the end, why we ride and whom we choose to take along to enlighten our journey become not just a part of us but make us who we are. We are all horses of a different color as Penny Porter tells us. And yet our colors melt into others along the way, turning life into a never-ending kaleidoscope of wonder. This is what makes life such a thrilling ride, and what better way to experience life than through the pastures you cross, the hills you climb, and the fences you jump. What better way to journey through life than on the back of a horse.

foreword

Number One Son

Jane Smiley

 Back in 1996, I fell off my horse and broke my leg. After I was set up in my hospital bed in the dining room of my two-story house, I didn't have much to do, so I subscribed to *The Bloodhorse*, and sometime in December, they sent me their annual Stallion directory. I was still lolling about, unable to ride, so I taught myself how to decipher the various coded messages attached to the pedigrees, and one of these was "dosage." Dosage is a way of analyzing whether the bloodlines of a given Thoroughbred make him or her more of a sprinter or more of a stayer. Since I was a big fan of *National Velvet*, I only looked at the stayers (hmm, that word still gives me a thrill), and the sire with the most stayer dosage was a big brown horse, then almost thirty years old, named Big Spruce. I pondered his picture every day. He was completely unrelated to my adored gray gelding (also a stayer, imported from Germany), but there was something about his look— kind, muscular, large—that appealed to me.

Then my leg was healed, I was back on Mr. T., and we had all moved to California. My subscription to *The Bloodhorse* followed me, and of course I could not help perusing the classified horse-for-sale ads in the back of the magazine, and of course in February, those words "Big Spruce" popped right out at me. The mare was in California, about three hours from my new house. I had no idea where I was going, but I drove there. The woman who owned the mare was dispersing her band. The mare was not very large, but she had a certain air that could only be called stylishly self-possessed. She could have been in a fashion show. On top of that, of course, when the woman put her back in her stall after showing me how she moved, the mare turned and looked me in the eye, not omitting to rest her chin on my shoulder. I was, as they say, done for.

A year later, my firstborn foal was on the ground, and looking at him, energetic, beautiful, the spitting image of Big Spruce, I thought, *That was easy.* He was so big that the farm manager where I kept the mare called him Lumberjack, and "Jack" stuck, though now his show name is Little Jack Horner, who said "what a good boy am I." This is a bit of wishful thinking on my part.

Since I've detailed Jack's early life in my book *A Year at the Races*, I don't plan to repeat that in this essay but, rather, to ponder the strange day-by-day enmeshment that is possible when you have known a horse all his life, when he is your dream horse, and when you become so aware of his idiosyncrasies that you feel them in your own body as if they were your own feelings, especially when this is a learned behavior, hard won on your part, not the result of any inherent talent or sensitivity.

I rode Jackie today, in fact, as I do five times a week whenever I am not on the road earning his room and board. We had a jumping lesson. Here is how it went: I drive down to the arena and leave the tack there, then drive back up the hill and park the car. I can see Jackie in the far aisle, beyond the near horse and through the bars. As soon as I pronounce his name, his head goes up and his ears flick forward. He starts watching me. He always starts watching me as soon as he sees my car. His life-companion, Essie, is not so attentive—she recognizes my advent but is not as passionate about it. For Essie, life goes on, day after day. For Jackie, everything is a drama.

I groom and halter both the horses and lead them down to the arena. Jackie goes slightly ahead of me, casting his gaze here and there. He has been watching the horizon since he was a day old. One of my trainers, Ray Berta, calls him a "sentinel horse." This is not necessarily a good thing. In the arena, I unsnap Essie's lead rope and she wanders away. Jackie gets tacked up and goes on the lunge line. After he has lunged for a while and my jumping trainer, Samantha Reid-Scanlan, has commented that he seems quiet today, she turns him toward a two-foot fence along the railing and invites him to jump it. He's cautious, but he jumps it three times in each direction, increasingly self-confident each time. His form is perfect—lovely bascule, legs neatly tucked, always right in his choice of the take-off spot. After he does this job, Sam walks him around the arena, over

Jackie

lots of cross-bars, some with flowers set underneath them. Jackie
seems confident about these, too.

But he is not like Essie, who starts every jumping lesson looking
for the next jump, who is never bothered by any fence or, if she is,
would rather jump it than contemplate it. Jumping is Essie's delight.
For Jackie, jumping is an existential dilemma—he loves the energy
of it, the way it appeals to his pleasure in forward movement, his
pleasure in galloping, his pleasure in using his body, and even his
pleasure in showing off. But jumps change size, change shape, change
position in the arena. Jumps are untrustworthy and suspicious. If you
do not get over them perfectly, something bad could happen (though
nothing bad ever has). You could make some sort of wrong move, and

then, God knows. Essie feels that whatever happens, she can put it together somehow. (Once, Essie spooked at a strange man emerging from the shadows. She took off and within three strides was faced with, in a row, the back end of another horse, a four-foot-wide jump standard, and a 3′ 3″ jump. I tweaked the rein, she jumped the jump. No problem.) Jackie is as perfectionist as any human I've ever known. His confidence depends on everything going just right and being predictable. Once he's done it his way for a while, he thinks quite well of himself. Do I sound crazy, shamelessly anthropomorphizing my horse, making him unique, treating him with a dose of psychotherapy? If I do, it is because thinking of him in these terms is the only thing that has worked to make him useful and reliable. He is a personality. I have to give him credit for being a personality, for showing the effects of nature and nurture, in order to train him. It wasn't until I attributed to him the psychology of perfectionism that I began to be able to work with him in a productive fashion and, in fact, to manage to reassure him and get him to trust me.

After he has lunged for ten minutes and walked over the flower fences, I take him to the bank and mount. As I walk him over there and as I set him up to be mounted, I fend off my own anxiety, which is a habit I got into at the beginning of 2007 and have yet to completely master. In our neighborhood, the few weeks around Christmas are wet, cold, and busy, so sometimes I don't maintain my riding schedule. In January 2007 I got on Jackie after a week of rain and took him into the indoor arena for a jumping lesson. All through 2006, he had been reliable and fun. When he was hard to get along with at the beginning of the jumping lesson (bucking, jerking his shoulder away), I got off, untacked him, and let him run around so that he could let off steam. This time, when I got back on, he was limping in the right front. There was no way to know what had happened, and I knew that even if we did know, the vet would prescribe stall rest. We had tried stall rest before, and less than a week of stall rest had resulted in so much anxiety and resentment that Jackie had tied up within a half an hour of being brought out of the stall. Long-term sedatives, which work for some horses, had no effect on him, and so I took a chance. I turned him out with his mares, and I said, "It's up to you to get better." I gave him four months. He got better. But at the end of four months without being ridden and regularly taken out of his comfort zone, he was spooky. One day, I walked him through the gate of an arena he had been in hundreds of times. He was on a loose rein. He spooked at something up the hill and was out from under me in about five seconds. I landed hard on my hip. I still have a bump there. Some horses are happy to get rid of you (I've seen those and had one, too), but Jackie is not happy to get rid of you. He saw something scary and he thought it was his job to get us out of there. He was worried and anxious that I had been left on the ground in the danger spot. He came back immediately and sniffed me. I came to wonder, over the next couple of days, whether I would ever trust him again.

Every time I mounted up, my heart started to pound and my

hands tightened on the reins. And he did not trust me, either—he took it upon himself to spook at every little thing—water stains in the wall of the indoor arena, rustlings on the hillside, strips of sunshine—and while he didn't get me off again, he came close. I was all too aware of our relative degrees of athletic talent. For a horse, he is quick and strong and agile. For a person, I am none of these, so he was ahead of me by several dimensions. I had to make myself conscious of the position of his shoulders, because where they were, he was about to be. But his body worked faster than my mind (not to mention my body). We spiraled downward. What had once been a pleasure that often gave me a sense of exhilaration now became a torment that at best produced a sense of relief. The worst part was the feeling that I had when I rode him; fear paralyzed me and made me unable to think about what we were doing in the course of a ride. We went around the ring like zombies.

As soon as I am on Jackie today, I sense that he is in a quiet and cooperative mood. Did I not used to notice this? I can't remember. All I remember is getting on him day after day and riding off up the hill onto the trails, down to the arena. These thoughtless days would be punctuated once a year by big spooks and sudden falls. Sometimes, I admit, he had good excuses—once he spooked at two dogs leaping out of the long grass and another time at the plastic Liverpool jump rising up in the wind. But once he spooked at the shadow of his own head preceding him over a trot pole, and several times at nothing discernible to me. The mood of going to work—of expecting to do lots of changes of direction and pace that will culminate in jumping jumps—is one that is good for me as well as him; it breaks through feelings of paralysis (but that is not the word—the word is "trance"; my fears have entranced me and made it hard to think and move).

My third instructor, my dressage instructor, cautions me against conceiving of Jackie's spookiness as too mental. Her theory is that all horse feelings begin in the body, with stiffness along the spine and in the hind end. A horse who is stiff is a horse who is ready to react when stimulated to do so, by bucking or spooking or rearing. The way to smooth his performance is to get rid of his stiffness by flagging him and working him in the round corral. When his body is soft and relaxed, he will forget about his fears or his resentments and do what is asked. This is certainly true, and I have known horses in whom resentment predominated and horses in whom fear predominated. It's taken me a long time to feel residual stiffness in my horse and even longer to act on my feelings. Too many times in the past, I have been too lazy to get off and work the horse through his stiffness. Now I know, as I did the day before yesterday, when I walked Jackie down to the arena and his head was high, that untacking him and letting him work it out is the best policy. But today, I sense nothing—no sudden interest in events outside the arena, no overflowing energy that has to be galloped off, no impatience.

There are horses who can be warmed up the way we warmed up horses when I was a teenager—a few circuits around the ring this way, a few around the ring that way, walk, trot, canter, but Jackie has to be warmed up like a dressage horse—turns on the haunches, turns on the forehand, shortenings, extensions, transitions, shoulder-in, haunches-in, leg yield, serpentines with flying changes. He has, in fact, had a lot of dressage training and enjoys everything about it, including going to shows and warming up (or blowing off steam) by galloping—once he had to go into the main ring at the Pebble Beach Dressage Show, which was full of flags and flapping tents, and the only way I could settle him was to let him gallop on the lunge for the half hour ahead of my ride time (he got a decent score, too). He also likes to work off the tension of jumping with some beautiful extended trot. This reminds me that a few months ago, a woman I know ran into the woman who sold me Jackie's dam. She asked me, "Did that mare ever settle down?"

I thought, *Nature strikes again.* But I don't remember her as agitated; I remember her as interested.

Sam doesn't correct him, she corrects me—heels down, heels down, heels down. She is the soul of patience. I work on looking up, raising my hands slightly to shift my balance back and down, keeping my weight in my outside heel. Almost fifty years of this, and I am still reminding myself how to ride. As for him, I can feel his body relax and start to float. This is his particular talent. Once I saw a small suspension bridge across the Delaware River, and I realized that some horses have that architecture—the spine and the muscles of the neck and the back are constructed in such a way that the horse is especially light on his feet, and when Jackie is really together, he hardly seems to be touching the ground. My job is to be balanced and light, too, but never to get ahead of him. This is the hard part of his perfectionism—it extends to me, and I am more of a "whatever" sort of person, like Essie.

Jackie was orphaned at a month old—the mare had colicked in the night and died by morning. After that, he was put in with a miniature horse and then with a weanling filly who was a month older than he was. But I encouraged him to attach to me, by visiting him and brushing him and rubbing him down with a chamois. He did attach to me in a way that my non-orphaned foals never did, and his attachment to me is a constant pleasure. But it also means that because he is attentive to me, I have to do the right thing. If I abdicate my responsibility, he gets nervous. According to Ray, my responsibility with regard to spooking is the most important one—if he spooks, I am to keep steady contact and not let him run away. He can't help spooking, but it is not having the spook controlled that really scares him. My job is to control the spook. Does this seem utterly simple? Yes and no. No other horse I've had has been so quick. If the spook happens in adagio or even allegro time, I can sit it and contain it. If the spook is presto, that's a challenge. My responsibility with regard to jumping is to sit up, sit still, and be resolute. Flowers? Still got to go. Jump a little higher than last time? Go anyway. The black box is on the right this time when it was on the left last time? Don't look at it, and jump anyway. That's the key—he is as apt as any other perfectionist to stare at the horror, whether it is flowers or boxes. If I sit up and raise my hands, he looks over the jump rather than at it.

Why I bother to do this is certainly a good question. I don't know many other women my age who still jump. We are never going to go to the World Cup or win a championship. We are never even going to realize his talents. He was good at dressage, but my back was killing me. I wanted to keep riding. But I have Essie—Essie is as safe and reliable and steady a jumper as you could ask for; why am I not obsessed with her?

In part, I am sure that it's because he's the complicated, beautiful one, the "character." Horses, like people, have charisma. People notice him and compliment him. Mares notice him and attend to him—I've never seen a mare reject his advances. Other geldings recognize him as a rival, and the more self-confident they are, the more they can't stand him. In part my obsession follows the law of intermittent rewards—since Essie is always rewarding, I don't think about her as much. I ride her, I show her, I'm grateful and adoring, but I don't have to worry about her. Jackie has me trained to pay attention and to work hard on doing the right thing. The reward may be a blue ribbon (he got two blues at the last show). But the real reward is something I feel in my body, though not often. Today, in our lesson, I get several rewards: The first is relief—no spooking, getting the job done, galloping down to the fence and over, getting the changes, riding a well-behaved boy. The second is pleasure in the movement and in my own sense of being balanced and in sync with the horse. The third is the teacher's knowledge (mine) that the student is improving, getting consistent. The fourth is the student's knowledge (myself as student) that I am putting my riding together more consistently. The fifth is riding through adversity—no, he doesn't get every change, yet he gallops down to the fence and jumps it anyway; yes, we come into a couple of the fences a little slowly, but he opens his stride and does fine. The sixth is that old temptation to love the horse I created, the temptation I've been feeling since I first laid eyes on his twelve-hour-old grace and beauty. But today we don't get the real reward, and I've only gotten it two or three times. This is the real reward: The course is set, six or eight jumps, and I know it. We've been around it once already and it is fixed in my mind. Jackie seems to know it, too, because after the first jump, he is already attending to the second one. He makes tight but steady turns, in perfect rhythm, jumps every fence in stride, is alert and on his hocks the whole time. He's happy; I'm happy. When we finish this course, it has been a single thought with different aspects that are all connected and a single feeling from beginning to end, counted out by the rhythm of his strides. It is like a piece of music or any other art object that presents itself as a whole rather than a bunch of separate parts—it has a defined beginning, a defined end, and a sustained dynamic in which every good stride builds on the last good stride and all the strides are good. Unlike other works of art, though, it cannot be re-experienced. In a few seconds, it has come and gone.

Maybe professional horsemen get this feeling all the time. I once heard Chris McCarron describe a horse race he had just been in, which to me seemed chaotic and hard to understand. For him, that minute unfolded systematically and understandably—it took him longer to describe it than it had for him to take part in it, and his description was cogent and eloquent. For me, though, this experience is rare and unlike any other human experience. In fact, it makes most other human experiences seem abstract, reliant on one sense or the other, but not all senses (surely including smell, if not taste), as well as that sixth sense, rhythm, that seventh sense, body orientation, and that eighth sense, the feeling of being in unity with another living being. That is the upside of the downside of his relying on me—he is better able than any other horse I've known to be with me.

I have spent twelve years asking of this horse, "Who is he?" Theories abound, most of them fairly simple—he's a horse, which means he's not very intelligent, not very complicated, pretty much an opportunist (a carrot and a stick kind of guy), someone with simple emotions (fight, flight) and no ideas. Someone whose *perspective* is easily ignored. In the course of those twelve years, crows, whales, non-human primates, rats, bluejays, squirrels, elephants, and many other animals have been reconceived as having intentions, ideas, projects, and points of view, but no one (as far as I know) has studied the horses that are all around us, being required all the time to engage in a multitude of tasks that we present to them in our necessarily flawed and inconsistent fashion ("Here, take care of my ten-year-old daughter and do it at the gallop"). Primacy in this research seems to be given to wild animals, uninfluenced to human culture. But let's say for once that there is an intermediate category of animals, those whose culture interacts with ours, who have been found by us to be similar enough to us that they can be put to use by us millennium after millennium. If they are similar enough to do every job we ask of them, then they are similar enough to have a psychology and intelligence that mirror ours. It's time to give them some credit for having an inner life, and past time to study it.

The Racehorse

Verna Dreisbach

The nights were most restless, anticipation not of the rising sun but of the hustle and scurry of the pre-dawn hours. I, too, felt this tension, a keen ear for the sounds of the night. The sound of defiant kicking against a wooden barricade, accompanied by screams of frustration and fear, frequently awakened me. I, too, felt this fear as I bolted from my bed, awkwardly attempting to find my shoes without stepping onto the cold, dust-covered concrete floor. My brother, who slept above me, never woke to the sounds of the night, oblivious to this entire other world. The single window near the door, covered with dust and a metal security barrier, filtered light into the room, enough for me to fumble with the lock on our tack-room door. Our bedroom opened to what seemed to be a limitless shedrow of horses, monstrous robotic hot walkers, stacks of hay and coiled-up water hoses. I listened for the sound of the kicking, for the horse who had found himself bound by his own legs and body against his stall. After many months of living among the horses, I was able to discern which horses had the most trouble with the night. I talked them through their fury, the sound of my voice calming their fear. Occasionally, I slipped into their stall and pulled their legs over their trapped body to freedom. As a girl of ten years old, I felt quite heroic and brave dealing with such monstrous animals, moving their entire bodies with my small frame. A kick of their legs at just the right moment could send me hurling across the stall. Once freed, we would both stand in silence, calming our fears, and then find our way back to bed.

Only the sound of the horses prancing by or whinnying with delight would ever awaken me—never the clatter of the cars driving by, the brightness of headlights shining through my window, or the sound of voices increasing in number. It was always dark when I slipped from my warm bed, somewhat startled by the coldness of the room; morning seemed so far off. On days that I didn't have to go to school, I was part of this fast-paced adventure. I loved to watch the excitement of the horses that passed by who could neither bear to walk, nor trot, but simply pranced and skipped sideways with uncontrollable anticipation as they neared the track. They waited all night for the chance to run as fast as they could around the racetrack, and to feel the cold, misty air race past their faces and against their sweaty, heated bodies. I would sit on the edge of the railing that separated me by only inches from the horses. The darkness prevented me from viewing the entire track. I was close enough to feel the ground vibrate with their approach as their bodies seemed to beat aggressively into the earth. Clumps of dirt kicked up from their hooves would nearly hit me. A slight breeze as they raced by would stir wisps of hair across my face.

They returned exhausted yet revived, with sweat dripping down their legs, foam oozing from their mouths as they chewed on their bits, froth clinging to their buttocks where their legs met, and their necks sodden where the reins had rubbed. Most returned with their rider, although some returned with an empty saddle, reins flapping against their neck and irons beating against their sides. I would hear them approaching from a distance, the sound of their gait resembling that of complete freedom and momentary triumph over their controlled world.

Generally, they acted compliant and were washed down with a cold water hose before they were fastened by their halters to the methodic, circular hot walker. Others, however, either in playful gesture or defiant outburst, would singlehandedly pull the entire hot walking machine over onto its side. This was when I was able to become a participant rather than a spectator, and I willingly took the job of "hot walking" these difficult horses. They intrigued me the most in their quest to be themselves, insolently refusing to comply and assimilate to their masters. They had extraordinary personality, energy, and zeal. In no way did I attempt to tame or control their manner. They pranced and hopped about, walking sideways as their bodies moved in every possible direction. At times, they completely

Chicklet

lost control. One particular horse would rear up so high and with such force that I simply had to let go of the lead rope and wait for him to fall over backward onto the ground. He would stand, startled, and shake off the dirt that clung to his wet body, waiting for me to pick up the rope from the ground, and then we would return to our walk.

The rising sun signaled the end of the chaos. The heat of the sun intensified the musty smell of the wet horses, the urine-soaked ground, and the piles of manure being carried away, one load at a time, by the tractor. Owners, trainers, and jockeys had already left or were in the process of departing. Horses were returned to their stalls, propped high with clean, fresh straw. Buckets of warm bran, sweet grain, and fresh flakes of hay were waiting for their return. The horses did not know whether to eat first to satisfy their hunger or to roll in their fresh, soft beds, the hay scratching against their clean, shiny coats. Life slowed down, and with the final load of the tractor, silence settled in. The people were gone, and only the horses and I remained. This was the most peaceful time of their day. Not a single head stuck out from its stall, and they were all at rest, finally.

Looking back at my childhood, I felt most at peace during these quiet, lethargic afternoons at the racetrack, sitting near the stall of a favorite horse reading a book or finishing my homework. I was far from being alone, the solitude welcome. In this unspoken world, a mutual appreciation and understanding existed, and I felt as if I appreciated the horses more than anyone. It was not solely because I lived with the horses that I understood their world, but because I chose to be a part of their world. Too often, we live or visit places yet never really feel as if we are there. They are easily forgotten or we leave in some manner unsatisfied. We might come to the realization that we act as spectators in life rather than participants, discovering how removed we are from the experience of place, time, and our connectedness to others. Relationships with people are full of the spoken language, with the ability to express feelings and desires in words, yet they seem to be the most difficult to attain and maintain. With the horses, I developed authentic relationships without any verbal communication. Innately, I knew the desires and feelings of the horses I lived with.

The horses were my family, and the racetrack was my home.

Owning Clydes

Kate St. Vincent Vogl

 Growing up, I didn't have a horse. I had thirty-six. At least, my dad did. He started on a whim—just to rent a pony for my sister's birthday, but the horseman said it'd be seventy-five dollars. It was, in 1970 dollars, much too much for only a few hours' fun. My dad had to ask. "So how much would it cost to *buy* the pony?"

"Seventy-five dollars."

And so Dad brought Toady home in the back of his convertible Cadillac. I was four and didn't know that horses don't usually travel with hooves planted firmly in the back footwells of a car. I'm not sure my dad knew either.

Our first barn went up within the week, my dad readying it to fill with horses, and not just any horses.

Clydes.

Clydesdales represented everything Dad had ever wanted—ever

since he was six. That's when Mr. Coqueterra pulled him up onto the beer wagon on Main Street in Norway, Michigan. Dad still remembers the courses of reins the beer distributor held gathered in his hands, the power of connection between what the old Frenchman held and the broad backsides of the Clydes before them, gleaming studs dotting the leather breeching and a golden horn crested on each horse collar. And beyond the pair of wheel horses stood another matched pair with that same impossible gleam, and beyond that another set, and even beyond them, to where the boy thought he could hardly see, stood the lead pair. An eight-horse hitch. The boy—he would become my father—reached an arm around the Dalmatian next to him and gave a squeeze, a secret resolution that, in the years to come, he would be sitting atop his own beer wagon, that course of reins in his own hands.

It was his destiny.

Coqueterra had, after all, pulled no one else up onto that wagon, maybe because no one else had made the effort to go down to the river to see how the horses bowed their heads like swans beside the water.

Secrets border the paths to obsession as well as to inspiration, and Dad's secret bridged both. Over the years, he developed a knack to make things happen, a means to achieve this end. And so, as a man of means, he made his first trips to Toronto, to find what the experts looked for in a Clyde. Who better to ask than the top judge at an international fair? A judge who lived right in Toronto on a farm.

A simple place, as if austerity could guard against the howling winds. The farmer-judge was old country, the kind who lugged buckets of water up from the house for the horses to drink. Not because he couldn't afford to plumb the barn—he'd made plenty when the city bought up most of his land to build its airport. But he was the kind of horseman who cared more about the heart of the horse than his convenience. Just the kind of teacher Dad was looking for. The farmer-judge had a mare. "Good bones," he said, "but she ain't broke."

Dad understood what that meant as the car bumped along in the field, close enough so the mare would turn on her fine haunches and gallop away. Only a two-year-old, but she had the makings of a true brood mare. Feminine, elegant. Never mind she was shaking out her mane as if to prove that someone even as strong as my dad would have to fight to tame her.

Her name was Duchess, and she was regal and wild as the borealis woods Dad hunted in as a child in the Upper Peninsula of Michigan. The kind of mare who could breed a champion.

She was the first of many at our Double Tree Farms. At first I could name all our mares, and I can name these still: Duchess and Marie and Flossie. Great bays with soulful eyes, blazes on their faces, and Clydesdale hearts big enough to break. That was junior high, and I could get the popular girls—Betsy and Christine and once even Dawn—to come on overnights with me to our farm. We'd chase the Shetland ponies in the fields until we could wrangle ourselves on and ride bareback along the abandoned railroad tracks.

Some weekends, Dad herded our family into the Cessna, which

Earl the pilot would fly up to Canada. We'd stay in a sprawling ranch, with green diamonds mowed into the lawn. Dad was looking for even more Clydes to complement the stable, and this is where we went to find them. I'd tag along to the barn to watch as Dad sidled up to a gentle giant and ran his hand down a leg to get the mare to lift up her hoof. He knew now what to look for.

He also knew he wanted more.

Before long, Dad had up to eight mares in foal at a time, and I couldn't keep track of the names anymore. At least when Christine—or was it Betsy?—came back for more overnights, I could name which one was in the birthing stall. First Duchess, then Marie, then Flossie. We'd stand with our chins resting on the rail, our faces pressed between the bars. Dad would be inside, one arm around the foal's neck, the opposite hand holding on to a bottle. Harold the trainer would stand quietly to the side, only one button holding his overalls together even in winter. From time to time, old Harold would offer up another suggestion, but foal after foal refused to take, even though the vet would come to cajole it into living.

"Damn Clydes," that old trainer would say. "They don't ever suck titty."

And so we lost them, one after another. Hard enough, but looking back, I suppose at least these babies arrived in the world fully formed and alive, one step further than a stillborn child, which was the closest my mother—my adoptive mother—ever came to carrying a baby full term.

Those days of foals-almost-with-us were marked by plastic horse nipples drying on our countertop. My family was a sunny-side-up family, the kind to find possibilities even as they seemed to be shriveling up. Maybe that's why Grandma Verne would make light and tease me in front of my junior high friends by slipping a horse nipple underneath her apron, upon her pendulous breast. "Kate," she'd say, to get my attention, and she'd laugh to see me turn red.

"Mom," my mother would chide her, but I could tell she, too, was suppressing a smile.

And Dad, he resolved to show the world, even if those damn foals didn't know enough to live. The problem, according to him (and probably according to that farmer-judge), was that the horses had been bred that way. The Scots didn't weed out the mares that didn't foal strong like they did for Belgians and Percherons at the land grant colleges, like Michigan State and Purdue. The Scots loved the horses as pets and kept whatever foal came along. The Clydes were known as Gentle Giants, but only because they were big babies.

And babies had to be taught everything. Dad would be back in that birthing stall, holding the foal's head and prying open its mouth up by the mare's teats, all too aware of the power in the haunch of the new mother beside him, while Harold reached in from the other side to work the teat until the milk let down and he'd try and squirt it into the baby mouth Dad kept pried open. A weekend exercise as tenuous and frustrating as a work-a-day job, but this one had life-and-death consequences.

I don't know what it took for that first colt to remain among the living. If only I knew, if only I could remember why he did and not the ones before him. Maybe that colt drew upon the wild strength of his dam the Duchess, or maybe he just had the stubborn urge and vision like my dad to make it through. Either way, I remember how the blue roan clambered up that first time, how he nudged his mama's fine shoulder as if that could be a source of milk, until Harold gently urged the newborn to the backside of the mare, where life and its sustenance could be found. Feeding was touch-and-go enough for Dad to send him down to Ohio State, but by then it was more for him than for the colt. For all his criticism of the Scots for treating their Clydes as pets instead of as a bloodline, Dad had come to view these animals not as stock but as babies—his babies. And just as he'd taken on a special duty to care for my sister and me because our birthmothers couldn't, so, too, would he see that these foals got the care and attention they needed if a connection couldn't be made between mare and foal.

Dad named him Baron, an improbable name for a gangly colt. Within the year, Baron had warts blossoming upon his forehead, so I would not want to show even my best friend. We ran straw-bale races instead and built forts by rearranging what had been stacked so neatly in the loft behind the apartment that Dad had built above the barn.

By the next summer, the warts were gone and Baron began to look like he could live up to his name. He would measure nineteen and a half hands high, and with his mother's fine bones and elegant moves, he would show well in halter class; he would breed well for years. Dad would celebrate his move into shows by making it a family affair: He'd submitted my older sister's photo to the *Draft Horse Journal* so she could be queen, but when the draft classes showed at our county fair, she begged off sick.

She'd done this before. I had to stand in for her when she ran off to the parking lot as the band at D'Amicos started singing her "Happy Birthday."

This time, though, I had to do more than pretend it was my birthday. I donned the *Draft Horse Queen* sash and walked through sawdust in the ring to hand out awards for halter class and hitches. The Grand Champion went to Baron. A reporter took a picture of me in my sister's tiara as I held Baron's lead rope, and we made the front page of the *Medina County Gazette*. My sister's honor, my glory. Baron's back hoof was tipped, but Dad still blew up the picture and had it framed for our den.

Showing became serious. Baron was ready for the Ohio State Fair next, and Dad brought in reinforcements. We had Harold, of course, and also a trainer from Canada for the six-horse hitch, and Smokey Bear was there to braid all the manes. Really, her given name was Smokey—and she was all that, with long chocolate hair and a halter top that my mother would never permit me to wear. Smokey seemed to live perched up on a stool, fingers making noble order of the shaggy and coarse black manes. She slept on a cot in the tack room, and Harold slept in the trailer, both dovetailing their lives into the circadian rhythms of a show, along with all its trappings: sulfur

Baron

strewn across the halls to whiten the horse feathers, leather on the back of a currycomb cracked or broken from use. Dad had arrived in Columbus a newcomer, but he'd come in with Baron and he left with a string of blue ribbons and more than that, the respect of the showmen.

By now, my sister and I were past riding bareback on a Clyde for the neighborhood parade. The Bicentennial for our town, a six-horse hitch in a red wagon, was behind us. Baron was earning his keep as a prize stallion at all the state fairs. Dad was selling horses as much as he was buying them—his wheel hitch had gone to Budweiser, a better life for a horse, with Astroturf lining the halls at their St. Louis barn. Bud's trainer had driven us along the back roadways to the working stables, and he'd stopped to roll down his window and talk to Augie Junior, who was driving the grounds in his personal Mercedes.

Augie was only fifteen at the time.

That kind of privilege I understood to be part of an American dynasty, even if I didn't recognize until college that what we had as a family was not so commonplace either. It took my boyfriend from Beverly Hills to point out that middle-class families did not own more than two dozen Clydes or jet away in their own plane on weekends.

Baron was unforgettable, looking down from on high with those haunting moon-eyes, white-blue and seemingly so empty you could fill them with anything you wanted. I was too young to have dreams weighty enough of my own to offer, and so I found his gaze brutally unsettling. I would have to turn away before the young stallion would catch my eye, as if questioning whether I, too, had it in me to be a champion.

My father, though, burst with dreams of his own and saw only possibilities when he squared Baron in the eye. That included possibilities already being realized by the other stallions Dad had to keep separate—something I didn't understand until I saw the golden Belgian emerge from the century barn on his hind legs, ready to mate.

"My Christ," Harold would say, "that one's trouble."

What was trouble was Baron, whose thinned Scottish bloodline was showing as Dad readied him to breed. Baron had less experience and less instinct than a teenaged boy. Hooves caught on the mare's back. A ton of horse not knowing where to lean its weight. On the advice of Augie's trainer, Dad sent his best Clyde up to Lansing, to Michigan State, to learn how to be a gentleman.

And, oh, what lessons he learned. When Baron came home, he trotted off that trailer and sired one prize-winning foal after another. He knew when it was time to be gentlehorse; he knew when it was time to be a gentleman. Harold had the key, bringing him down to the century barn when it was time to do business. And so with my father's guidance, the last of the wild from Baron's mother had been tamed.

As fine a gentleman as Baron was, the Belgian stud was growing meaner by the pairing. Dad called in the vet, and Dr. Barth pulled the barrel-chested sorrel into the middle pasture to jab him with his needle, *West Side Story*–like. The stallion dropped, deadweight, and the vet sweated over that tonnage for more than an hour. The Amish, Dad said, could geld a horse standing up, fifteen minutes easy. But not this one. There is regret in Dad's voice as he tells the story today, a lament over fatherhoods lost and prices paid in that middle pasture.

Risks and losses are part of the horse business, I suppose, and so too must gambles be sometimes made in the business that makes owning horses possible. My father started his own company when I began senior high. Dad rolled the Caddie and the Lincoln out of the garage, and set up makeshift shelves in their place, sharpie markers noting the parts numbers for concrete mixers on cardboard boxes. Money was tight, but Dad still found a way to bring his stable to the Royal.

Baron, of course, and a filly he'd sired. And a six-horse hitch, the kind that inspired a little boy on his way to owning a barn full of Clydes.

For the Royal, we had the trappings of the professionals. A beer wagon painted red with white trim. Harnesses, signage, and ribbons. And most of all, horses. Little Holly had everything of her grand dam in her, and though she was an April foal, she measured up against the January born. The judges lined her up second, then thought better of it. A last minute decision in an arena of international spectators, and the judge moved the little filly into first to the roar of an approving crowd.

Holly's father was next. And Baron, our Baron, would not disappoint. As if he'd seen what his little girl could do, he would prance his way into a solid first as well. In the Grand Champion lineup, father and daughter would compete against each other. And the father—our father, our Baron—would win. A silver platter for a prize, and on it the world was handed over to my father.

Victories may last time for time immemorial in our memories, but not in reality. Over time, in real time, a recession hits.

The horses had to be sold, and were. First the ponies, then George, the dapple grey Dad purchased for a detour on his way to the glue factory. Each pink slip and each Coggins handed over was made carefully, a fostering of care for each of the horses. Baron's Holly was adopted out into a good family, one that would ensure her bloodline would continue to make its mark at the Royal. My family didn't talk about it much, but when Dad began to sell off the first of the twenty-seven Clydes, dinners were quiet. Dad didn't eat much, just made a sandwich out of the baked chicken. He'd eat only half, then turn, tip his chair back, and put his feet up on the counter, his glasses pushed back on his forehead, chewing the inside of his cheek.

He would not sell Baron.

By now I was a senior in high school; I'd taken economics. I had thoughts to share, words to say. At least I could press my mother on the issue. "It's an opportunity cost," I said, using my vocabulary word of the week. "Dad needs to get rid of Baron, too." But I didn't yet understand what was a fungible good, what wasn't.

"That's your dad's baby," Mom said. "That's the first to survive."

So.

Dad was sentimental.

And more than that—loyal.

That's when I learned there's a certain respect to be had for surviving, even when making it merely means doing what so many others take for granted. Who knew, starting out, what an effort it was to merely do the instinctual, to suckle? Who knew that the first of our horses to figure that out would be the first to become Grand Champion at The Royal Agricultural Winter Fair? Baron had been Dad's first colt, and the pride of his later winnings was nothing compared to that first hardscrabble victory.

Baron would stay with us; of course he would stay us. Only him and his mates.

There would be other losses, ones Dad could not escape. It would come after I'd been through college, after law school even. All the years we'd been in horses, you'd think I'd see this coming. Baron was one of our last horses left, and he was barely hanging on. Weekends I'd visit and see him out in the pasture, but he was leaning up against the barn for support. It was the most the old stud could do.

The next time I was back, it was a muted dinner, and out of respect for Dad's red-rimmed eyes, I didn't dare ask him directly about his grief. There was only one reason for my dad to have that kind of sorrow. While we were cleaning up, I asked Mom if Dad had decided to sell the rest of the horses.

"He will now," she said. "Baron died."

I've heard there's no greater grief than burying your baby. But what if you're charged with arranging the death? Dad had dug out a hole in the back field with the front end loader. And he and Harold and the vet who'd cut that Belgian walked the limping Baron back to the large open wound in the earth. Dad stayed for the vet to jab another needle, a more lethal one, into his baby's flank. And this time when a great draft horse dropped, he would not later struggle to his feet. And Dad had to turn his back, and he walked a slow walk back to the barn. His baby would be gone, his baby he'd made into a gentleman.

He'd had to ask Harold and the vet to do the rest, to jerry-rig that ton of horse into the hole. Because sometimes that's what it takes to survive.

Growing up, I didn't have a horse. My dad had thirty-six.

And one of them had him.

A Horse of a Different Color

Penny Porter

 "When it comes to horses, what you want and what you get are often two different things." Bill, weary from building a new hay barn, kept up his warning to me even as he fell asleep that night.

But I'm a dreamer, and foaling season is a time for dreams. After years of raising Hereford cattle, we'd just become Appaloosa breeders, and I was dreaming of precious foals, blue ribbons, and eager buyers.

That first year, the dazzling hair-coats of nine little Appaloosas had already transformed our pastures into a landscape of color, their tiny faces bright with stars and blazes, their rumps glittering with patches and spots splashed over them like suds.

Bill and I were sure our tenth foal of the year, due before dawn, would be the most colorful of all. That's because its father was a white stud with chestnut spots over more than half his body, and a multi-colored tail that touched the ground. The mother was covered with thousands of penny-size copper dots. I already had a name for their unborn treasure: Starburst.

Normally, I would have been awaiting this new arrival in our freezing corral, numb fingers clutching a flashlight. But tonight was different. Bill had bought me a closed-circuit TV, which he set up on my side of the bed. That way, I could watch the monitor in comfort and observe the mare's progress. Then when she reached her last stage of labor, if help was needed, I'd rush to her side.

Now, on the screen, I could see the spotted mare's hide glistening with sweat. White-rimmed eyes betrayed her anxiety, and dust-devils swirled like headless ghosts in the wake of her pacing hooves. Suddenly she stopped cold. Nostrils wide, ears twitching back and forth, she listened for dangers in the night. *It'll be a while yet until she foals*, I thought, and I dozed off.

I awoke with a jolt. Three hours had passed. A glance at the monitor revealed the mare flat-out on her side, steam rising from her body in the frosty air. The birth was over. But where was her foal? I sat up fast, studying the screen and searching the fuzzy shadows and distant corners of the corral. It was gone.

"Bill! Wake up!" I shook him hard. "Something stole the baby!"

Wild dogs, hungry coyotes, and bobcats raided my imagination. I was the one who walked the night when we had calves or foals being born, and I remembered catching a raccoon slaughtering my chickens in the moonlight. I remembered a bobcat, daggers glinting from his eyes as he slithered across the roof of our rabbit hutch. One midnight, I'd even seen a bear lumbering past our mailbox.

Moments later, after leaping into my jeans and sneakers and grabbing a jacket, I was on my knees in the dimly lit corral, stroking the mare's neck. "Where's your baby, mama?" I called, almost crying in panic. "Where'd it go?"

Suddenly a plaintive whinny rose from behind the water trough. Then I saw a face pop out of the shadows—thin, long, dark, ugly. The ears hung like charred potholders from a rusty hook. Right away, I realized why I hadn't seen this newborn on my TV. No colorful spots. No blazing coat. The foal was brown as dirt.

"I don't believe it!" I said as Bill crouched down beside me for a closer look. "There's not a single white hair on her!" We saw more unwanted traits: a bulging forehead, a hideous, sloping Roman nose, and a nearly hairless bobtail.

"She's a real throwback," Bill said, standing up. I knew we were both thinking the same thing: *This filly will be just another mouth to feed. She'll never sell. After all, who wants an Appaloosa without color?*

By now the spotted mare was on her feet eyeing this trembling little stranger with contempt. The foal staggered toward her and tried to nurse. The mare wheeled and kicked, knocking the baby to the ground in a scrambled heap. It cried out with fear and surprise.

"Whoa, Mama!" Bill shouted. "Stop that!" He lifted the foal back on her feet. "I'll get the mare some hay," he said. "She needs to be by herself." I knew he was right. Nature would take care of bonding if

Angel and Spotted Bear

we left them alone. But after Bill tossed some alfalfa on the ground, hoping to quiet the mare, the filly tried to nurse again. This time the kick was so violent it sent the baby skidding under the fence.

"Oh, Bill," I pleaded, wrapping my arms around the shivering foal, "help me stand her up—just one more time." Once she was on her feet, I stayed with her a minute, steadying her. "You'll be OK, little one," I murmured. "Just keep on trying." I hated to leave but knew it was best.

The next morning when Scott arrived for work and saw our newest addition, he minced no words. "What are we going to do with that ugly thing?" he asked.

By now, the baby had nursed but it looked like all the

nourishment had gone to her ears. They stood straight up in the air. "She looks just like a mule!" Scott said. "Who's going to want her?"

Our younger girls, Becky and Jaymee, now fifteen and twelve, had questions of their own. "How will anyone know she's an Appaloosa?" Becky asked. "Are there spots under the fur?"

"No," I told her, "she's what's called a 'solid.' That means no breed characteristics at all. But she's still an Appy inside."

That's when Jaymee came up with the glorious wisdom of a twelve-year-old. "That means she's got spots on her heart."

Who knows, I wondered. *Maybe she does.*

From the beginning, the homely filly seemed to sense she was different. Visitors rarely looked at her, and if they did we found ourselves saying, "Oh, we're just boarding the mother." We didn't want anyone to know our beautiful stallion had sired this ugly foal. After all, mare owners seeking an Appaloosa stud want to be convinced he produces only quality babies with small heads, straight legs, neat little ears, long flowing tails and, above all—a coat of many colors.

When the filly was two weeks old we turned her and her mother out to pasture with the herd. Being the newcomer, she was afraid to romp with the other foals because their mothers bared their teeth at her. Worse still, her own mother now seemed to sense her offspring needed all the protection she could get. So she angrily charged any horse that came within fifteen feet of her little one. Even if another foal ventured too close, the mother lashed out with a vicious snap. Little by little our bobtailed filly learned the world was a place to fear.

Before long, I started noticing something else—she relished human company. She and her mother were first at the gate at feeding time, and when I scratched her neck and shoulders, her eyelids closed in contentment. Soon, she was nuzzling my jacket, running her lips over my shirt, chewing my buttons off, and even opening the gate to follow me so she could rub her head on my hip.

"Mom's got herself another lame duck," I overheard Scott say to his dad one day.

Bill sighed. "Oh, God. What is it this time?"

"That jug-headed filly. What else?"

Unfortunately, her appetite was huge. And the bigger she got, the uglier she got. *Where will we ever find a home for her?* I wondered.

One day a man bought a beautiful two-year-old "leopard" gelding from us for a circus. Suddenly he spied the brown, bobtailed filly. "That's not an Appaloosa, is it?" he asked. "Looks like a donkey."

Since he was looking for circus horses, I snatched at the opportunity. "You'd be surprised," I said. "That filly knows more tricks than a short-order cook. She can take a handkerchief out of my pocket and Rolaids out of Bill's. She can crawl under fences. Climb into water troughs! Turn on spigots."

"Reg'lar little devil, huh?" he said.

"No, not really. As a matter of fact, I named her Angel!"

He chuckled. "Well, it's eye-catchin' color we need at the Big Top," he told me. "Folks like spotted horses best!"

I knew he was right, but as his truck and trailer rattled down the dirt road, I pictured our homely filly jumping through flaming hoops with white poodles in pink tutus clinging to her back. *Why couldn't a plain brown horse do the same thing?* I wondered.

As time passed, Angel—as we now called her—invented new tricks. Her favorite was opening gates to get food on the opposite side. "She's a regular Hoodini," Bill marveled.

"She's a regular pain," said Scott, who always had to catch her.

"Maybe two chains and double clips'll work better than one," I suggested. It made no difference. Angel's hunger for anything edible on the other side of the fence persisted, and the jingle-jangle of horse teeth against metal chains on corral gates never stopped as she honed her skills.

With Angel's huge appetite, I tried giving her an extra flake of hay before bed. Her affection for me grew. Unfortunately, so did her appetite. One morning Scott found her in the hay barn. She whinnied a greeting. Broken bales littered the floor. Her sides bulged. Scott was disgusted.

"You've got to be more patient and give her some attention, Scott," I told him. "You spend all your time grooming and training the other yearlings. You never touch Angel except to yell at her."

"Who has time to work with a jug-head?" he grumbled. "Besides, Dad said we're taking her to auction."

"What! And sell her for dog food?"

I corralled Bill. "Let her grow up on the ranch," I begged. "Then Scott can saddle-break her when she's two. With her sweet nature she'll be worth something to *someone* by then."

"I guess one more horse won't hurt for the time being," he said. "We'll put her down on the east pasture. There's not much grazing there, but . . . ." He was keeping his options open. Still, Angel was safe—for now.

Two weeks later she was at the front door eating dry dog food from our watchdog's bowl. She'd slipped the chain off the pasture gate and let herself out—plus ten other horses as well. By the time Scott and Bill had rounded them up, I could see that Bill's patience was wearing thin. He turned to the girls. "You two, give her some attention. School's out now. Maybe you can even make her pretty."

That summer, they groomed her, bathed her—and looked for spots. They even rubbed mayonnaise and Swedish hair-grow into the stubbly mane and tail. This folk remedy worked with some horses but not with Angel. When they tried to brush her teeth, she simply ate the toothbrush. That was on top of all the cantaloupes and watermelons they fed her. She ate everything. Angel loved all the attention, and perhaps to show it, she even stopped opening gates.

Then school started, and Angel lost her playmates. Scott came into the kitchen one morning, fuming. "That filly's gotta go, Mom," he said. "She got into the tack room last night, pulled bridles off the hooks, knocked saddles on the floor, chewed up a tube of toothpaste the girls left on the sink. She's gonna stay in that east pasture if we have to build a wall around it."

Fortunately, the rains came. The grass grew. Angel stayed in without a wall and now she got fat as a buffalo—and her assortment of tricks grew. When Bill or Scott drove to the field to check on the herd, she'd chew the side-view mirrors off the truck, eat the rubber off the wind-shield wipers, or bend the aerial. If they left a window open, she'd poke her head inside, snatch a rag, wrench, glove, or notebook off the front seat, and run away with it.

Surprisingly, Bill began forgiving Angel's pranks. In fact, we soon found ourselves looking forward to her best stunt of all. When an Appaloosa buyer would arrive, Angel would come at a gallop, slide to a stop about thirty feet away, and back up to have her rump scratched. "We have our own circus right here," Bill told buyers. By now, a small smile was even showing through Scott's thick mustache.

The seasons rolled by. Scorching sun brought rain, and flies by the millions. One day, when Angel was two and a half, I saw Scott leading her to the barn. Her rump was raw, bleeding and crawling with maggots from the hopeless thwacking of her hairless bobtail. "She gets no protection at all from that stupid tail," Scott told me as he treated Angel with antibiotics. "I'm gonna make her a new one." That's when I realized Scott's feelings for the horse were starting to change.

I smiled as he cut and twisted two dozen strands of bright yellow baling twine into a long string mop and fastened it with adhesive around her bandaged tail. "There," he patted her and stepped back to admire his handiwork. "She looks almost like a normal horse."

When Angel recovered, Scott decided to break her for riding. Bill and I sat on the corral fence as he put the saddle on. Angel humped her back. "We're going to have a rodeo here!" I whispered. But as Scott tightened the cinch around her plump middle, she didn't try to lie down and roll on the ground as some young horses do. She simply waited. When he climbed aboard and applied gentle pressure with his knees, the willing heart of the Appaloosa showed. He ordered her forward, and she responded as though she'd been ridden for years.

I reached up and scratched the bulging forehead. "Some day she's going to make a terrific trail-riding horse," I said, taking a moment to admire her tail. Every new shipment of baling twine came in different colors, red, orange, yellow, black. Today her tail was blue.

Scott seemed to know what I was thinking. "Blue's for winners, Mom," he said. "With a temperament like this, someone could even play polo off her. Or she could be a great kid's horse."

Now, even Scott was having a few dreams of his own for our plain brown Appaloosa with the funny-colored tail.

Angel was soon helping Scott train young foals. Riding her, Scott would clip one end of a rope to a yearling's halter and wrap the other end around the saddlehorn. Angel would then pull, even drag the younger horse along, but always with care.

At foaling time, she whinnied to the newborns as though each one were her own. "We ought to breed her," I said to Bill. "She's four. With her capacity to love, imagine what a good mother she'd make."

"Hey. That's not such a bad idea. People often buy bred mares," he said. "Maybe we'd find a home for her." Suddenly I saw Scott frowning. *Could he really care?* I wondered.

For the first nine months of Angel's pregnancy, Scott kept her busy exercising yearlings. For once, she seemed to forget about escaping from her corral. Also, winter offered only dry, parched fields, so the temptation to get out was gone until a heavy rain came and our fields burst to life. She was getting closer to her due date, and I tried not to hear the jingle of a chain, because in my heart I knew Angel would once more start slipping through the gates in quest of greener pastures.

One morning we awoke to an unseasonable cold snap. I was starting breakfast when Scott opened the kitchen door, his hazel eyes looming dark beneath the broad-brimmed Stetson. "It's Angel, Mom," he said. "You better come. She got out of the corral last night."

Trying to hold back my fears, I followed him to his pickup. "She's had her foal somewhere," he said, "but Dad and I couldn't find it. She's . . . dying." I could hear the catch in his throat. He never got this close to animals. "Ate too much new grass, or maybe a poisonous weed." Suddenly his voice broke. "She's halfway between my house and here. Looks like she was trying . . . to make it home."

I scarcely heard him as unbidden memories rolled through my mind: the jingling of a security clasp, the rattle of chain, the creak of an old wooden gate being swung open. And now, last night, silhouetted against the rising moon, nostrils wide, testing secrets in the wind, our horse that nobody wanted had escaped for the last time.

When we got to Angel, Bill was crouched beside her, his boots sinking into the mud. "There's nothing we can do," he said, nodding toward the lush green fields, an easy reach for a hungry horse through the barbed wire. "Too much fresh alfalfa can be a killer."

I pulled Angel's huge head onto my lap and stroked the worn softness that the halter had left behind her too-big ears—those same ears that had made me think of charred pot-holders when I found our dirt-brown filly hidden behind the water trough four years before.

Tears welled in Scott's eyes as he knelt beside me. "Best damned mare we ever had, Mom," he murmured.

Angel! I pleaded. *Please don't go!* But I felt our mare with all those "spots on her heart" slipping away. Choking back my grief, I ran my hand down the gentle darkness of her beautiful warm, brown fur and listened to the heavy, labored breathing. The long legs strained, and her neck arched desperately backward, seeking one last breath of air. She shuddered. I looked into eyes that could no longer see. Angel was gone.

Then in a cloud of numbness, I heard Scott call out only a few yards away—disbelief in his voice. "Mom . . . Mom! Here's the foal. I found the foal!"

Deep in the sweet-smelling grasses where Angel had hidden him lay the foal of our dreams. A single spot brightened his tiny face, and a scattering of stars spangled his back and hips. A pure, radiant Appaloosa. Our horse of many colors. "Starburst," I whispered.

But somehow, all that color didn't matter any more. As his mother had taught us so many times over, it's not what's on the outside that counts. It's what lies deep in the heart. That's where Angel's spots and beauty were. It's that way with all animals—and it's that way with people too.

It's All in the "T"– or Perhaps the "D"

Jacqueline Winspear

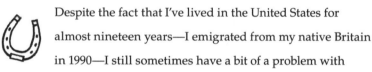 Despite the fact that I've lived in the United States for almost nineteen years—I emigrated from my native Britain in 1990—I still sometimes have a bit of a problem with pronunciation and with "hearing" what is being asked of me. For example, in American English there is less of a distinction between "T" and "D." If I ask for water in a restaurant, it's not unusual to be met with, "Pardon me?" Oh, yes, I should have said, "Waader." So, I sometimes give the wrong answer when a friend calls and asks, "How's the riding going?" I respond that I have just finished a chapter, or there's a deadline looming. "Oh, no," says the friend, "I said riDing, not wriTing." They know, my friends, about my two passions.

I fell in love with books when I was a toddler, which was about the same time that a black stallion caught my attention. Each day he held vigil over all he surveyed from atop a hill close to our home, and in the evenings as dusk fell, he ambled down the hill toward his stable. On Saturdays, when my mother walked the two miles into our local town to do the weekly shopping, I'd wriggle in my pushchair calling out to the horse on the hill. As soon as my mother stopped alongside his paddock, I was already running on unsteady legs toward the fence, clutching a hastily grabbed handful of sweet clover grass. The horse would look down the hill at me in an imperious fashion as if I were a little pilgrim come to pay homage and steadily make his way to the fence, his big black head arching over to take my humble treat. By some miracle, I kept my fingers, and from the first touch of his velvet-soft nose across the palm of my hand, I felt a love that would last a lifetime.

Later, when we'd reached the town, our first stop was the library. It was just a small room set alongside the council offices, a magical place where I was allowed to choose my two books for the week—just two books, because at barely three years of age, I was the library's youngest patron. On the way home I'd have to sit on a rickety pile of library books, because Mum took care of the reading needs of the elderly people on our street, choosing books according to their expressed likes and dislikes.

"None of that blood and swearing for me, Mrs. Winspear."

"Mr. Kilby does like his westerns."

"I do like a bit of romance, dear. It takes you away from it all, doesn't it?"

She followed their instructions to the letter and never made a mistake.

A few years later I was on my way to school, and as the bus rumbled along the road I looked for my black beauty, and he was gone. I continued to look for him until I realized he would never again return to his pasture, and my heart ached for days.

My path to owning a horse was as long and winding as the journey to being a writer, and once again it seemed the two passions were on a parallel trajectory. Though I was raised in the country, it wasn't easy to learn to ride. Horses were associated with wealth, with those of a certain station, and in our family there was no disposable income to spend on such things. I was always one to leap at the chance of a ride if it crossed my path—and needless to say, I tried to associate with people who might throw such an opportunity in my direction—but it wasn't until I'd completed college that I kept a promise to myself, that when I had the money, I'd learn to ride. And though it would be years before I owned a horse, I rode several times each week, sometimes hacking out across the fields and through the woods, but more often immersed in dressage, which I had come to love. There was something about the way the training connected horse and rider that engaged me completely, as if in the practice of this ancient art of horsemanship we were channeling each other's thoughts. It was a feeling akin to meditating in unison.

Every vacation from work, every weekend and day off was spent on horseback, yet at the same time I drew back from owning a horse because I thought I needed to learn more before I took on the responsibility. My writing followed the same path. I managed to land work in publishing, my dream job because it brought me closer to books, to literature, though I only spent one year working in general books before moving into academic publishing—a very different animal! Despite the fact that I wrote each day and had more ideas for books than I knew what to do with, the more I learned about the business of publishing, the more I thought, *I don't stand a chance.* And my literary efforts remained in drawers, never seeing the light of day, let alone ever being sent to a magazine or book publisher.

It was after emigrating to the United States that I decided to take my writing in hand. I began attending workshops and with my heart in my mouth sent out my essays and articles to magazines. My work began to appear in print and on the radio, and after ten years—was it really so long?—I began to write my first novel. But all too soon that old friend, Doubt, assailed me once again, so I put away the manuscript until a 2001 riding accident resulting in six months at home, and a year's worth of physical therapy led me back to the book. Faced with living in a rural area with no public transport and unable to drive, I couldn't bear the thought of so much time alone and nothing worthwhile to show for it by the time I was well again. I'd had to find a new home for my horse, and I was unable to use my right arm—and I was trying hard not to feel sorry for myself. Then one day a friend said, "Why don't you finish that novel you started ages ago?" It was a long shot. Until then, I was non-fiction writer, working around my day job to find the time to write. Now I'd just had major surgery on my right arm—and I'm right-handed. I pointed out this physical limitation to my friend, who said, "You've got a left hand, haven't you?" So I began to write again, with my left hand on the keyboard. Three months later, I had a finished manuscript. Six months later, a book contract.

Five years ago, soon after publishing my second novel, I started riding again, having found a dressage trainer at a barn just five minutes from my home. Six months later I bought Serendipity— "Sara"—my Dutch Warmblood/Thoroughbred mare. And then last year I bought my own black beauty, a young Friesian named Oliver. Sara is a workhorse, a true professional who lets me know in no uncertain terms if I am not reaching her high standards. Oliver is still very much a baby, and if Sara is a taskmistress, then Oliver is my teacher—and not only in my riding.

The more I endeavor to raise the bar for myself, both in the equestrian sport of dressage and in my work as a writer, the more I see them reflecting each other, with a breakthrough in one heralding a nudge up from the plateau in another. They require a similar mindset on the path to mastery, an appreciation that achievement is like the search for the holy grail, where the learning is all in the pilgrimage, and there's no end to the road ahead. It is through the practice of dressage that I have acquired many of the lessons that stand me in good stead as a writer.

Dressage teaches us that foundations are important. At any event

Oliver

where top riders are competing, you will see them in the warm-up arenas going through the same motions, the same moves that a raw beginner might be challenged with in an early lesson. And when you hear those same riders interviewed, or read about their daily training sessions, it's all down to basics. Whether novice or master, we all work on transitions to ensure the equine partner is listening, on the same page. We walk, halt, trot in circles, and circle again in canter. We strive—and ache—for that perfect sitting trot, buried treasure, and then we go into our core to create impulsion.

I recently used that word, "impulsion," in a conversation about writing, and another writer, herself a show-jumper, said, "I've never heard that word outside the equestrian world." But that's what I strive for, that harnessed energy, that control, to create prose that is alive, that has an immediacy, that is engaging, compelling for the reader. I'm doing that with language, with pace, with rhythm—ah, that's something I know from my dressage training, *rhythm*.

After I'd published my first book, I lost confidence as a writer and thought the dream of being able to practice my craft full-time might slip through my fingers. Following days in creative limbo when I wondered how I might ever drag myself from a dark abyss where a half-written second novel threatened to die on the vine, I looked to my dressage training for direction. Clearly, it was back to basics, to the literary equivalent of the lunge-line. I found a teacher and joined a class. Dressage has taught me the value of a good trainer, and that no matter where you are on the rung of success, the lunge-line is a safe place to be while you're working on your balance—and without balance, rhythm remains elusive.

I've come to know that few people have the perfect body for dressage, and just as I learned to use my left hand to finish my first novel, so I'm constantly working to accommodate those aspects of my physique that are not suited to dressage. Sometimes I ache, but I know that each twinge in my back, or pull at a hamstring, is proof that I'm developing the muscles I need to communicate with my horse. And I'm inspired by those who overcome physical disability to ride a horse—how can I complain about the way my feet turn out duck-like in the stirrups, when I see someone who cannot walk trotting around an arena? I've learned in my riding, and in my writing, to watch, digest, and learn from the masters. I scan training DVDs, travel to clinics and competitions, knowing I can use even one timely observation to bring change to my dressage training. And I've a bookshelf full of dressage books. I've a writer friend who says that money spent on a book is always worth it if he finds just a single snippet, one word, one comment he can employ in his writing, whether that book is for research, for craft, or for reading enjoyment. So for my writing, I go back to the classics, to Dickens, to Austen, then on to Hemingway and Fitzgerald, to be inspired by the greats, and I scan the book reviews for new authors to watch and learn from—just as I turn the pages of magazines and books on riding, looking for those ideas, tips, and stories that will make me think, teach me, and help me reach up toward that bar I've just raised on myself.

Sometimes I feel that, with the reins in my hands, it's like playing a concerto, each muscle in my body teasing out the melody. And there are days when my fingers glide across the keyboard, words I've never even spoken before tumbling out onto the page to create a scene, an image, a stepping stone in the story that I know really works. But as my dressage trainer said on a particularly challenging day, "You can't expect yesterday's ride today. It's another day, the horse is the same horse, but different today, and you're different too."

Until Oliver came home, I'd never had much experience with young horses, but I've learned that with a young horse it's crucial to lavish praise for any small improvement—such things rarely come in big doses; we get better incrementally. I've also learned that most of the time he's trying really hard to do the right thing, and it's important to make much out of doing the right thing. New concepts are introduced to him gradually, in stages, as if constructing a house. First the foundation—we warm up readying ourselves for the task at hand, and at the start of each lesson we confirm that we have "go" and "halt" and that he is paying attention. Then we get to work, breaking down every part of a given move—a leg-yield, for example—into its constituent parts. One deliberate step at a time we make progress, confirming his understanding along the way. Then we put it all together, one brick on top of the other, in the same way that I string words to form images, develop character, enliven dialogue, and create story. I made a few mistakes with Oliver in the early days before I met my new trainer, and I thought those errors could never be put right, that I had ruined a good horse forever. But I discovered that the process of correction could be seen as a metaphor for rewriting—I had to go back in, rework the words, and put the piece together again.

Because I work for myself, from home, I know I have a habit of pushing to get it all done, and now, immediately. As writers we have deadlines, contracts to meet, book tours to work our way through, emails, etc., etc., etc. I know I am not alone in trying to push the envelope and do more today than I did yesterday, and I will sit at my desk until I meet or surpass my word-count goal for the day. Heck, I will sit here, paralyzed bum and all, until those words are written. It was Oliver who reminded me of a lesson I should never have forgotten.

Last summer, we were working with my trainer and coming to the end of the session. Young horses—even strong breeds like Friesians—have to learn to be balanced, have to build strength to carry a rider, and they can tire easily, especially if they are jet black and it's summer. On this occasion we were having a bit of trouble getting something right. We tried several times. I was tired, he was tired, but I had a bee in my bonnet about perfection and I wasn't going to stop until I had conquered that move. I was so weary, I didn't do something that can be quite important with young horses—with any horse if you're being careful—which is recheck the integrity of the girth a couple of times in a training session. The net result was that, eventually the saddle went one way, and I went the other. Ollie, fortunately, stopped without treading on me with his big Friesian feet. And me? I realized why the comic books show stars around the heads of characters who have been knocked out, because I couldn't see out of my left eye and my head was popping like fireworks—and I was wearing a helmet. My trainer ran up and asked me what month it was, and I said, "Probably November." Then she asked me the year and I said, "Two thousand six." I was two years out. The next thing I knew, I was in her car and she was telling me that if I wanted to throw up, just try to do it out the window.

Now when Oliver and I are out together, I work on putting into practice my new mantra—whatever we do, be happy with the best we can do today. Oliver just turned five in June. He could easily live until he's thirty, which means we'll probably pop our clogs at the same time. We have many, many more years for us to get better at what we do, and I promise we will have a lot of fun along the way, even when we're working hard. And as for my writing, okay, so today I met my goal, and I had a great time. I enjoyed writing every sentence, and I knew exactly where I would go back and work the words—a bit like a potter kneading the clay once it's on the wheel. Yesterday I only wrote a couple of paragraphs. They weren't great paragraphs, but they moved the story along and for the most part I liked them; they brought me to where I needed to be. They could use more work, and they'll get it, but they were good enough for the day. I'll give myself a treat.

Back in October, Oliver and I went along to our first show. He was a bit of a dingbat at first; I had to run him around to get the overabundance of excitement out before we went into the arena. He made the onlookers laugh with his high-pitched whinnying as we walked past the judges—young horses like to shout out loud to see who's out there. Made me laugh too, which took away the nerves. And because he came in with ribbons—first place in one class and second in another—he earned extra treats, which he would have had anyway, because he tried hard and we enjoyed ourselves. But here's what the judge said in her notes: Horse and rider show great potential. I stuck that on the wall, for the days when I forget that we're all just trying our best, whatever the outcome.

It was at the end of another lesson, when Sara and I had completed a perfect series of transitions, that I trotted alongside my trainer, rivulets of perspiration running down my back, and said, "Some days it's like breaking down a wall to find a door." A bit like that other passion, the one with the "T" in the middle.

Getting Back
on the Horse
Kara Gall

I will not ride a horse.

The last time I did, I was ten. We endured a wintry March, days from spring equinox, and the beginning of calving season: one hundred fifty head of my father's Red Angus-Simmental crossed herd gestating as one. Though a solid half-foot of snow stubbornly claimed the ground of our fallow fields and pastures, it was time to drive the cattle home.

They had overwintered in a cornfield seven miles south of our homestead, among stalks that jabbed out of a flat, treeless horizon, empty of the sheltered draws and soft, grassy pockets of the loess canyon pastures to where we would be moving them. Two cows had already birthed their calves in the sharp stubble, which meant we were already behind schedule.

We drove them on foot. A cold but frozen ground made for

easier traveling than the mud that would accompany the spring thaw. My mother led the herd in an old rusted Ford, the new calves bawling in crates in the pickup bed. My sister, five at the time, rode with our mother. I could see her round face peering back at me from where I nestled into the warm John Deere 4020 tractor cab with my grandfather. We rolled along not more than fifteen miles an hour, a bale of alfalfa hay hooked to the hydraulic lift behind us to entice the expectant mothers homeward. The two new mothers led the herd, anxiously jogging toward their baby's cries.

Behind the cattle, my father rode Streak, a feisty, purebred Arabian. A horse with a reputation for intelligence, spirit, and stamina (not to mention a proclivity for dumping my father in the irrigation reuse dam whenever possible), Streak wound back and forth behind the herd, keeping any wanderers in check.

At predetermined locations, my mother or I would jump out of our vehicles to stand as border patrol in open driveways or fence lines, shooing the cattle forward with our arms and the "Whoop, whoop, hey boss!" holler my father had taught us. Most of the time, however, we in the front were the incentive, my dad and Streak the enforcement.

The trip was unremarkable. We met no oncoming traffic. No tourists, lost on what they initially hoped might be a pastoral shortcut to a major highway, drove recklessly through the herd. Not a single cow defected into the neighbors' spring wheat. There were no major mechanical failures, no arguments between my father and grandfather about the best possible way to do any number of things,

Streak

and no sprained ankles or blown-out knees—all of which have happened on various drives before or since. It was just us and the cattle on a cold, hard country road under a slate-gray sky, catching shy glimpses of upland game—pheasants, mourning doves, quail, turkey, and chukar—all on their own migrations. I watched as a family of whitetail leapt over a fence line on a ridge to the west. Even at ten, I recognized a kind of peace in our collective, silent movement and, further within this peace, a longing to be even closer to it.

Suddenly, the tractor felt stuffy. The need to guard a washout that dropped sharply toward a creek bottom was cause enough to jump from the cab. Once I was out in the crisp air, my yearning kept me afoot, distracting me from returning to the warm tractor cab.

After the cattle passed, I caught up to my father, whose bright yellow stocking cap raised objections to an austere sky; he had never been one to wear a cowboy hat.

"I want to ride," I said. He reached down and pulled me up with one arm, the other arm relaxed on the reins. He wouldn't let me ride alone, not while we were still driving the cattle, but he promised I could ride Streak up the hilly driveway to the barn once the cattle were safely closed in their pasture.

I can't tell you what we talked about, or if we even talked at all, those last few miles back home. But I know we felt that same longing within the tranquility of the ride, an unspoken desire to melt into the natural world, to simultaneously recede and solidify. To have it be more than enough, and to mourn the ephemeral. Whatever else has come between us since then, whatever else might, I know we share this.

My mother parked the Ford a couple of hundred feet beyond the gate to the pasture and stood in the road. The cows filed in through the narrow gate with little fuss, ambling eagerly toward the bale of alfalfa my grandfather was now unrolling into a finger of pasture sheltered by Eastern Red Cedars. I stood on Middle Canyon Road, holding the reins as Streak champed and shook his head, his breath foggy with cold. My father backed the Ford into the pasture, hauled the calves from their crates, and set them down near their nervous, grunting mothers.

My father gave me a boost into the saddle, then waved and smiled before he turned and crossed the ditch toward the old Ford. I squeezed the reins more firmly as I nudged my heels against Streak. We started across the meadow at an easy pace. Even so, I had a startling hunch that something was missing when a flurry of wind stripped my stocking cap from my head and threw my slender body off center in the saddle. Just as I tried to correct my slippage to the right, some unseen change of topography, a break in the ground masked by the smooth cover of snow, caused Streak to stumble and trip. I lost hold of the reins, sliding down backward over the saddle, headfirst. Like a backstroke swimmer in her last five yards, I couldn't see the wall of ground, but I knew it was coming. Suddenly, my hips jerked upward as my right foot snagged in the stirrup. Spooked, Streak took off in a gallop across the meadow toward a washout. I threw my elbows up over my head, scraping the ground with my hands on each downbeat of Streak's cadence. My right hand struck a branch buried beneath the snow; the tip of the branch caught a stitch of my knitted mitten and scored a wide gash across my palm. And then there was the blood.

My dad always said that Streak was the sort of horse that never quit, that he'd keep going until he died. I heard Streak scream, something I didn't know a horse could do, and farther away I heard shouting as my father barked, "Stop screaming! You'll scare 'im more!"

I suppose my own screams were lost to my ears in the trauma of the moment. But by some miracle, my foot released from the stirrup, and I lay sobbing on the ground until my mother picked me up. We walked back to the pickup truck as my father ran off to recover his horse. On the ride up the hill, my sister, who sat on her knees on the old canvas seat cover, pet the wispy windblown strands of my hair and wiped away my tears. I sniffled and glared out the window. Through the cracked side mirror, I could see my father following us on Streak, rough with the reins, riding him hard up the hill. When he cut ahead of us, dangerously close to the front of the pickup, my mother slammed on the brakes, causing us to skid toward the jagged edge of the driveway. I thought I heard her curse, something that scared me even more than my two-hundred-yard drag.

At the top of the hill, my father was waiting with Streak in front of the barn. He motioned to my mother to stop the pickup and beckoned to me to get out.

"You need to get back on the horse. Come here. Take a ride on Streak."

I was horrified. "I'm not getting on him. I'm hurt!"

My father had no intentions of letting me off so easily.

"You're not hurt that bad. C'mon. If you don't get on now, you'll never get on again."

And at that moment, fear, raw and primal, gripped us both: fear for my safety and a deeply disturbing sense of being lost from each other. But he remained relentless.

"You'll be fine. C'mon. It's now or never. Get on that horse."

They say a horse can sense what a person is feeling to the degree that he's unable to distinguish his rider's fear from his own. I suppose that is what happened between my father and me that day, in that moment; neither one of us realized the other felt the same thing, our own small fears amplifying the other's until there was nothing but the thundering footsteps of an emotional stampede.

"I'm not doing it," I whispered. "Please, Mom, tell him I don't have to do it."

I attempted to climb back into the pickup, but my father would have none of it.

"This is *not* your mother's decision to make. I told you, Kara, if you don't do it now, you'll never do it." And with one quick motion, he grabbed me under the shoulders, lifted me completely off the ground, and set me down on top of the horse. As if there were nothing to me, as if all that defined me were that inconsequential.

Getting back on the horse marked the first time I time I consciously stuffed my hurt so far down that it made no noise. I wanted to scream. I wanted to keen and screech, but I knew that such hysterics would only alarm Streak, causing him to dash off again and break the thin veneer of amity I had with the horse, if not my father. Tears fell silently down my cheeks. I held my sobs the entire circuit: across the yard, behind the barn, over to the quoncet, behind the windbreak, and through Grandpa's sunflower patch—such menacing dead stalks! At intervals I could see my father through the haze of tears—hands on his hips, back to the barn—measuring my resilience.

When we got back to the barn, my father laughed, not at all connecting with my true state of mind. "There! Was that so bad? Good job," he said and set me down on the ground and patted my back.

I was surprised at the stillness of my body; inside I vibrated like the old-time threshing machines the local elders fired up during the annual Fair and Corn Show. I looked up at him and, in a voice much too deep and controlled for a ten-year-old, firmly said, "I did what you wanted. I got back on the horse." And then I looked at him with all the steel I could muster and said, "And I will never ride again."

That's when the thrashing inside me snapped loose into my lungs and my legs, and I screamed, "Never!" I sprinted the hundred yards back to our house.

Time tested, I was as good as my word. Twenty-two years later, I still haven't mounted a horse.

It is a hot, dusty Saturday in May, and I'm standing in front of an empty corral, cold beer in hand, the fleshy smoke from branding burning my eyes. My shoulders are sunburned, despite cumulative layers of sunscreen and dust. We've just "worked"—vaccinated, castrated, and branded, as needed—three hundred head of cattle. We've sorted them back into cow-calf pairs and driven them to grassland pasture where they will fatten over the summer. Dozens of neighbors, friends, and family sit around the chute, celebrating a hard day's work.

My mother's cousin Jeff calls to me from across the yard. Not unexpectedly, his skilled horsemanship helped him gain favored status in my father's eyes in the fifteen years since I left home.

"C'mon, let's go for a quick ride. Cool these ol' gals down," he says as

I limp toward him. I've been sitting for only ten minutes, and already I'm starting to stiffen up. He tries to hand me the reins of his old sorrel mare.

I lift my hands in defense, backing away. "Oh, no. Not me, Jeff. I don't ride horses."

"You grew up on a farm, and you don't ride? What the hell is wrong with you?" he asks.

I raise my eyebrows. "You've never heard of my infamous horse grudge with Dad?"

He scoffs. "This has nothing to do with your dad. C'mon, get on."

I feel myself resisting and then suddenly not. There is no stealth equine specter waiting in the paddock to knock me on my keister. All that stands before me is a man with a horse.

The story of Kara Who Will Not Ride, so ingrained in my history of self, suddenly seems so petty now, hardly worth explaining even, let alone holding on to. And after a few embarrassing misses, trying to hoist my no-longer-slender body on top of the horse, I find myself settling in as if time has taken me back to the land of confidence, just before that fateful event years ago.

I look tentatively at Jeff. "The last time I did this I was ten. You're going to have to remind me how it's done."

Fortunately, Jeff is a patient teacher, something my father has never been. As we ride, he teaches me to lean my weight up onto the stirrups and to keep my heels down, which will not only make me more secure and the horse more comfortable but will stop my foot from being caught in the stirrup should the horse spook.

"I wish someone had told me that twenty-two years ago," I mutter. Still, I try this simple change of posture. With my heels in place, and my center of gravity shifted in the stirrups, it occurs to me that I am absorbing the shock of the ride rather than being abused by it. It also occurs to me that my father and I have never learned this skill in our relationship. We've always reflected the other's fears, anger, stubbornness, and pride like a series of solar-power mirrors, intensifying and concentrating the energy with each successive pass. I wonder if it might be possible to absorb my father's feelings instead of shooting them back at him.

We ride down into my favorite draw, just a half-mile west of the house, where as a child I picked many a plum with my mother and grandmother. I am unable to lose myself completely in the riding. There are simply too many unresolved thoughts and feelings standing between me and that unbounded joy that other women seem to come to so easily with horses.

"You're too tense," Jeff says. "Let up on the reins a bit. The more you hold 'em, the harder it is to control her." I relax my hands, instantly fearful, but Jeff's old mare moves gently forward, as if she has all the time in the world. The idea that letting go will give me more control seems incredibly counterintuitive, yet it is obviously working. I realize that the control I found in refusing to ride, the only small measure of control a scared ten-year-old could assemble, wasn't control at all, only a barrier to moving forward. It was my choice to allow a horse to stand between me and my father, and my father to stand between me and my horse. It was my choice to let both father and horse stand between the scared girl I was and the confident, composed woman I had the potential to become. I could hold on to these choices, let them define me as they had for years, or I could let go.

I look up to find Jeff stopped at the bottom of the canyon. I let the sorrel step up beside him.

"I think equestrian grace has eluded me," I quip, to which Jeff simply replies, "Hey, you're doing fine."

And I realize that I am, indeed, doing fine. Sure, I have to work at it, this laying to rest of fear and pride, this conscious letting go, but underneath the fear and anxiety, I feel a vivacity and exuberance long missing from my life. My legs are quivering, and my muscles buzz in time to the dusky hum of summertime insects. Inside my body and out, everything feels more distinct.

On top of a ridge, the cool black silhouette of a shelterbelt against a sapphire sky stirs me to wonder if there isn't a kind of grace in the clumsiness of my actions. Maybe grace isn't only about beauty in form or movement. Perhaps grace is a first step, the sharp breath taken before daring to say "I forgive you" or "I trust" even when everything inside screams otherwise. Maybe grace is simply getting back on the horse even though it would be so much easier not to. And for me, getting back on the horse wasn't about my dad at all in the end. It was about me. It was about longing to be closer to an internal peace, a peace that was daring to emerge.

And in that peace, which I am still learning to embrace, I now have the capacity to love—better yet, *see*—the man who was both protector and betrayer exactly where he rides. I now know his center of gravity lies in an open field or pasture, happiest when moseying along a slow-moving current of pulsing cycles and seasons. I know this because it is mine, too. Had I not been so stubborn, I would have seen; the prairie is expansive and giving, and there is room for both of us to ride.

Painted
Christmas Dreams

Dee Ambrose-Stahl

*Deirdre awoke early, just like every December 25. She tiptoed
downstairs, hoping against hope that this would be the year her
dream might come true. Her parents were already awake and
seated at the kitchen table; that fact alone gave the young girl pause, as they
were never downstairs Christmas morning until much later.*

*"Morning, sleepy head," Ben, Deirdre's father, said. "'Bout time you
roll outta the hay!" When Nancy, Deirdre's mother, tried to hide her giggle
behind her coffee cup, Deirdre knew something was afoot.*

So began the short story—or some variation—that I wrote every
year growing up. It was my dream to walk downstairs Christmas
morning and find a Paint Horse tied outside the picture window.
I, like most other girls, was obsessed with horses. Usually that
obsession passes like any other fad. My obsession didn't. In fact, it

set down roots so firm that not even marriage to a "non-horse" man could pull them up.

Every year I wrote a similar story, "Dreaming of My Paint Horse," and gave it to my parents, hoping that they would get the hint. It seemed they never would. Every year I looked out the picture window to find an empty yard and disappointment, a vacant space where my horse ought to be.

We were never deprived as kids, far from it. But I'd have gladly relinquished every toy, every item of clothing, even every horse statue and book for that Dream Horse.

My childhood passed as did many of my interests. Tennis? Too much like work. Knitting? Knot! Horses?—now that was the constant passion in my life. I read about them, wrote about them, even joined a 4-H club that taught about them, and of course I dreamed about them. My own horse, though, was always out of reach.

My older two sisters each had a horse when they were younger, but, in the words of my parents, "They lost interest in the horses as soon as boys came along." How was that my fault? I didn't care about boys. Boys were dumb, and this was my mantra even through my teen years, until, of course, the unthinkable happened . . .
I met Ron.

Ron and I came from similar, working-class backgrounds and became best friends shortly after we met. Ron was perfect in every way, except that he barely knew the head from the tail of a horse. This, I thought, I could deal with. I might even teach him a thing or two. We were engaged within six weeks and married a year later. Some things you just know.

We marked our fifth anniversary, then our tenth, then suddenly we were looking forward to our twentieth anniversary of marriage, and through all the years my obsession with horses lived dormant, below the surface of other life goings-on, but it was present nonetheless. Ron dealt with this "quirk" of mine the way he dealt with most things—with a quiet smile and an "Oh, well" shrug of the shoulders, thinking I would get over it someday. But someday never came.

The Internet, however, did, and its "information superhighway" allowed me access to horses. A voyeuristic approach, I'll admit, but one that at least gave relief to some of my desire. I discovered a myriad of websites that listed horses for sale, and I haunted them all. I searched for Paint Horses, torturing myself looking at horses I knew I'd never own. One day, though, I found a website owned by Sealite Paint Horses in Ijamsville, Maryland. I immediately searched the "Foals" page. There, my pulse quickened from a minor trot of anticipation to a full-blown gallop at finding so many Paint foals, from weanlings to long yearlings. Three in particular I was drawn to—two yearlings and a weanling, all beautifully marked and all fillies. My heart dropped into my shoes.

On impulse, I phoned Kim Landis, the owner of Sealite, although I felt as if I were doing something illicit. We chatted for nearly an hour about horses in general and her Paints in particular, and I was thrilled when she invited me to visit. I told her about the fillies that had caught my eye. She said that they were all three still for sale. My heart ascended back into my chest and it filled with a kind of joy I'd never known. The news was both a blessing and a curse.

As much as I wanted to be horse shopping, Realist Ron made an excellent point when he asked, simply and softly, "How can we afford a horse?"

"So we'll just go for a drive," I said, "look at pretty horses, and that's all. We'll come home right after. I promise." I knew the truth, though.

A few days later, we loaded our two corgi dogs into the back of the Jeep and began the three-hour drive to Maryland, the home of my dream. It's important to say that Ron has a gift for keeping me "leveled," so to speak. I am impulsive; Ron is pensive. It's been this way between us since we first met. I can see how this difference may cause grief in some marriages, but for us, it created a balance.

While we drove, I chattered on about how beautiful these foals were, how much I couldn't wait until I saw them in person, how exciting it would be to raise and train a baby, and how sweet a Paint's disposition is. Ron nodded a lot and spoke little.

When we arrived, I was breathless, either from my incessant talking or overgrown excitement. We met Kim, her husband, Chris, and the Sealite gang. I felt like I'd found the Holy Grail, or like a sixteen-year-old who gets a brand-new car for her birthday—all my senses were on overload as I tried to absorb each of the dozen or more Paints all at once. Then I saw her. "Oh, my God, Ron! Look at her!"

Ron followed my gaze with his own. Off beside the run-in shed stood Sky, one of the black-and-white Overo fillies I had seen on Kim's website. "Wow," was all Ron could manage, and I had to agree.

Large brown eyes looked at us from her blazed face. The side closest to us sported a white patch that nearly covered her ribs, and on her neck was what could only be described as a bleeding heart! Her four white socks were of varying lengths, but best of all, she seemed to be very well balanced in her conformation.

As we stood looking at Sky, some of the youngsters became curious about the newcomers and warily approached us. Among them was Lacy, who promptly decided she could fit in my back pocket. I gave her a pat and told her how pretty she was, all the while keeping an eye on Sky.

"She wants things on her own terms," I whispered to Ron as I dipped my head toward Sky. "I like that."

"You do?"

"Uh huh . . ." Without seeming too obvious, I walked over to Sky. "Hey, sweetheart," I whispered as she smelled my proffered hand. "How are you, baby girl? Over here all by yourself. You're not anti-social, are you?"

Sky's ears flicked back and forth like an air traffic controller's paddles as she assessed me too. I scratched her withers, a favorite itchy spot of most horses, and saw her head lower and relax. I was hooked. Sky was independent and refused to pander for a scrap of attention from us mere humans. She was not spooky or skittish; she just approached new situations on her own terms. This was a familiar quality, as I, too, tended to set and adhere to my own terms in most situations. I wanted to see how she might do on her own.

We took Sky away from her herd mates so that I could watch her move in a round pen. Her tail became a flag and her nostrils air horns as she floated around the pen, head held high. Sky lifted effortlessly from trot to canter to gallop, allowing me to take in every muscle, every pointed look she flashed my way. Her eyes were animated but not wild, a thing I loved about her. Sky was so full of joy in all her horseness.

I talked with Kim about Sky's price, and I could tell Ron was not, at this moment, loving life as much as Sky. He went off with Chris for a few minutes, then casually called over to me, "I'm going to check on the corgis." That was Ron's cue to me that he wanted to go, *now*, before I did something foolish like put a deposit on this horse.

It's fair to say Ron would never say these things aloud or embarrass me; living with him all these years, I've learned how to read his nonverbal clues. But this private message between us provoked me for some reason, even though the tiny voice of reason was knocking inside my head. Usually I'm good at ignoring that voice, but I overrode it and began to talk not just price with Kim and Chris but transport, shot records, farrier care and the myriad other details concerned with a new horse purchase. Ron stayed at the Jeep during this exchange, eying me warily. Eventually, I bid Kim and Chris farewell with the promise of "being in touch."

Ron, predictably, didn't say a word as we started our drive home. "Tell me what you're thinking," I asked.

"What I'm thinking?" he said. "About what?"

"The weather, Ron! What do you mean 'about what?' I mean about Sky!"

"Oh, she's nice, I guess. I don't know. . . ."

"Nice?! She's gorgeous!" How could he not see this?

However, my pronouncement was met with more silence that lasted many more miles until I once again broached the subject. "But she's special, Ron! And I know Kim and Chris would deal on her price."

In typical, Sensible Ron fashion, my husband pointed out what I already knew in my heart but did not want to hear: "We can't afford a horse."

I couldn't really argue with this. The purchase price of a horse—any horse—is the easiest expense to meet. Maintaining an equine for the twenty-five years or more of its life is where the economic strain comes in. Ron was right, as he usually is in all economic matters. We could not afford a horse, period. I tempered this acceptance by adding silently, "Not now, anyway."

"I'll take the coward's way out and email, rather than call, Kim tomorrow to tell her." These last words caught in my throat.

Later that evening, we stopped for dinner along the interstate. I don't know if it was the country decor of the restaurant or the Christmas section of the attached gift shop, but suddenly I was transported back in time. It's Christmas morning. I race down the stairs and offer the brightly lit tree only a quick glance, for just past the tree is the picture window. It can't be! I shake my head and rub my eyes, certain that my mind is playing tricks on me. I look again, and it—she—is still standing there. Sky is standing in the front yard of my childhood home, her glistening black-and-white coat a stark contrast to the glimmering white Christmas snow. Before I can react, my husband's voice brings me back to reality.

"What? I'm sorry, what did you say?" I said.

"I asked what you were thinking about. You've been really quiet, but you smiled just now," Ron said. That's when I realized that in nearly twenty years of marriage, I had never shared the story of the Dream Horse with him. Over dinner, I recounted the tale, with a bit of sadness in my voice that I just couldn't hide. Ron's normally brilliant blue eyes clouded over.

"I know exactly what you mean," he said with a sigh as he reached across the table for my hand. Like me, my husband grew up in a blue-collar family with never quite enough money. He, too, knew firsthand the feeling of The Dream, but his Dream was on two wheels, not four hooves—the iron horse.

The rest of the drive we remained silent, arriving home just after dark. Exhausted and disappointed, I climbed into a hot shower and then managed to read a few chapters of a book. I fell asleep imagining my beautiful new filly cantering across the field to greet me. She offered me her soft, pink muzzle, and I wrapped my arms around her glistening neck and buried my face in her mane, breathing in her heady smell. I felt the level of contentment I'd been searching for, but it was only a dream.

"Are you going Christmas shopping with me on Saturday?" I asked Ron. It was December 18, and we had yet to do any big shopping for family and friends. With our work schedules, that Saturday was looking like our one and only hope of accomplishing any shopping together.

"Oh, um, well. . . ." Ron stammered. "We can't go anywhere Saturday."

"What do you mean we can't go anywhere? We've got tons of shopping to do!"

"Well, I'm expecting a delivery, and we have to be here when it comes. You know how FedEx can be," he said.

I was furious with him, as he would now have to wait until the last minute to do any Christmas shopping. Fine. I left him to his FedEx worries and did the shopping myself that week. I was not at all gracious about this scenario.

I barely spoke to him that week, and when I did speak, it was a short, clipped answer to something he said first. My Christmas Spirit was obviously going to be absent in the Stahl home this year. I made sure this fact was not lost on Ron.

Saturday morning came and I was in the den wrapping presents. I had a perfect view of the driveway through the picture window. I would certainly see the FedEx truck when it arrived.

My anger with Ron collided full force with my eagerness to catch a glimpse of the delivery. Eagerness was winning out. Would the shipping box offer any clues? Would I know what it was from the box that it was in? Damn!

I wasn't paying attention and cut the wrapping paper too short. As I reached for a new roll of paper, Ron's thundering feet on the stairs made me jump. What startled me even more, though, was his voice. "He's here!" Ron shrieked, hitting a pitch I hadn't heard from him in all our twenty years together. I had no idea Ron loved the FedEx guy this much.

"Come here, come here, come here!" Ron chattered. "You've gotta come here . . ." and he pulled me by the hand to stand in the doorway facing the driveway.

"Look!"

And then I did, but what I saw didn't register. White SUV. *SUV?* Pulling something. A horse trailer. *A horse trailer?* A horse trailer with "Sealite Paint Horses" painted on the side!

I staggered backward into Ron's arms, and he kissed me on the head as he draped a coat over my shoulders. "Let's go," he whispered in my ear, gently pushing me out the door.

As my brain spun circles trying to wrap itself around this image, the driver's window of the SUV rolled down as the vehicle came to a stop. "Merry Christmas, Dee!" I heard the driver yell— wait, that's Chris!

I remember Chris getting out of the vehicle and giving me a hug.

sky

I remember holding my breath as he dropped down the window of the trailer. And I remember thinking, *She's home,* as her familiar white face popped out from behind the window. She looked at me and her soft brown eyes reflected, "I remember you."

And as I stroked her beautiful white face, I said something brilliant to Chris like, "You were supposed to be the FedEx guy!"

So how did Ron do it? How did he make my dream come true?

Apparently, the night we returned from Sealite, he had called Kim and Chris and made the arrangements, all on the sly. My sad story of yearning and Christmas disappointment had moved him to action.

I stood wrapped in Ron's arms, watching Sky become

acquainted with her new home. I turned and looked into Ron's eyes. My question was simple. "Why?"

"Because you wanted her from the beginning. I wanted to be the one who made your dreams come true."

Somewhere, in the deep, dark recesses of my memory, I felt the curtain drop down on an old yearning and a new kind of contentment fill every bit of those years of wanting and waiting. Then I felt another curtain rise above a thousand new dreams as I settled my head against Ron's chest and looked into the eyes of my new Paint dream.

Ron and I smiled, laughed, cried tears of joy, and talked well past midnight about our new dreams and how we might make them come true for each other.

Great-Grand-Mare

Vanessa Wright

Her name is Mafalda, but you'll have to know her for twenty, maybe thirty years before she'll tell you that. Until then, just call her Mickey. She first fell in love with horses as a young girl in Italy, riding with glorious, dauntless abandon along the gleaming emerald ridges of the Apennine Mountains, among the storied palaces of Genoa, to the warm, white shores of the Ligurian Sea.

Perhaps she would have become a kind of girl-*eques,* a knightly guardian of the ancient heart of Rome, or a modern-day Epona, protectress of horses, and first among those who gallop into the great mysteries. But the shadow of World War II began to spread across her country. So she and her family set sail for America, and, sadly, the grim, gray Atlantic would prove too wide for even the greatest of her beloved mounts to leap.

Not even an ocean, though, could quench her horsewoman's spirit.

Drawing upon the determination of the dedicated rider, she became one of the 4 percent of American women who attended college in the 1930s and was one of the first women to join the factory workforce when America joined the war. Guided by the open heart of the true horse-lover, she married for love instead of duty, raised her three daughters to seek fulfillment in both family and career, and, when her husband passed away shortly after her retirement, she took their shared dream upon her shoulders and traveled the world for nearly twenty years, alone.

Returning home at last, she acquired a new job and a brand-new sports car, complete with 200 horses champing and stamping under the hood. To this day, she drives that car faster, farther, and with more flair than I drive my frumpy four-door hybrid, and when she does resign herself to riding with me, she tells me I drive like an old lady.

"How would you know?" I always reply.

I tease her because I love her: she is my grandmother, my Nonna. But when I laugh, I am laughing at myself, because she is ninety-two. And because, at ninety-two, after an eighty-year hiatus, she decided to get back into riding.

As a riding instructor, of course, I knew it was impossible, and I had told her so two years before, when she drove down with my mother to meet my horse, Pegasus.

The mist hung thick as wool that morning. Yet even from where Pegasus and I stood, at the top of the high hill in the farthest corner of his pasture, we could see Nonna's little red racer piercing the rosy haze, speeding through it like a sunbeam eager to best the dawn.

The car winged to a stop at the pasture gate in a purposeful flourish of golden-tipped gravel. Pegasus, a full seventeen hands and 1,200 pounds of Thoroughbred speed and Lipizzan power, responded with a shrill, welcoming whinny. He craned his neck and pricked his ears in the hopes of discovering the kindred spirit behind the wheel.

I patted his shoulder and murmured soothingly. But as my mother opened the passenger door, Pegasus arched his neck and flexed his muscles. And when Nonna climbed out from the driver's side and joined my mother at the gate, he began to prance in place.

Without a halter, without a bridle, I couldn't hold him any longer. So I whistled, he whickered, and, side by side, the two of us ran down the hill.

In the valley, I knew what my mother and grandmother were seeing: a hurtling ball of brightness, like the sun rising too fast, or a star sweeping too close to the earth. Reaching the fence, Pegasus wheeled and reared, churning the mist into a whirlwind around him. Plunging to his feet, he dipped his head and snorted like a dragon. Fire blazed in his eyes, and steam jetted from his nostrils.

My mother gasped and sprang back from the fence. Nonna, though, reached out and chucked him under the chin, as if he were a kindergartner toddling in from play.

"May I ride him?" she asked lightly.

My jaw dropped. "Are you serious?" I replied. "It would be much too dangerous." Her face fell, and I fumbled for softer words. "He's still learning to be a proper riding horse. Right now, my instructor is training him; it will be months before she lets me ride!"

Nonna nodded politely. "May I run with him, then? Like you did? If I remember rightly, I outraced you up Federal Hill not too long ago."

I remembered. On a blistering August afternoon, Nonna had charged up Baltimore's fabled fifty-foot, near-vertical staircase, leaving me, the rider, my husband, the runner, and my mother, the treadmill queen, panting in her wake. Still, a horse is slightly less predictable than a set of granite stairs. Pegasus especially was a fountain of equine exuberance—more than one of his handlers bore the mark of a pistoning shoulder, a wayward hoof, a whipping tail.

Thankfully, inspiration struck. I snatched a halter and a fifteen-foot longe line from the fence. Haltering Pegasus and grasping the line close to his chin, I asked Nonna to stand to my left and gave her the rest of the coils.

"Lead the way," I said.

Nonna closed both hands around the line with the keen gladness of a jockey picking up the reins of her favorite mount. She piloted us back up the hill, to the topmost ridge of the summit. She breathed the cool, fresh air in deeply and surveyed the hills, cantering endlessly toward the glowing horizon.

"Let's run," she said.

She jogged a few steps, then surged into a sprint, running faster than I thought she could. I held Pegasus tightly by my side, but it didn't matter: His eyes, ears, and hooves weren't following me but her.

All was well until we reached the foot of the hill. From the gate, my mother started shouting, "Wrong there! Wrong there!"

Alarmed, I glanced at Nonna, at Pegasus, at the ground around us and the track ahead. I couldn't see anything wrong, and I dared not risk a sudden stop.

We ran on to the gate. As soon as I caught my breath, I said to my mother, "What do you mean, 'Wrong there?'"

She laughed. "Not 'Wrong there,' *grandmère*! Don't you remember your French?" Nonna and I looked at her blankly.

"*Grandmère* is French for 'grandmother.' That makes me Pegasus's grand-mare." She turned to Nonna. "And that makes you his *great*-grand-mare."

Flushed and maybe blushing, Nonna tousled Pegasus's forelock. Smitten, he nuzzled her hand.

"He certainly agrees," I said. "Great-grand-mare indeed!"

Nonna grinned and kissed Pegasus's forehead. She looked so content, I felt sure the experience had satisfied the horse-longing in her heart.

I could not have been more wrong.

The following year, my mother brought home a 13.3-hand Haflinger named Snickers, a pony—ahem, a horse—who proves that his breed's golden color is not a reflection of genetics but of the halo that shines perpetually above their ears.

When our extended family came together at my parents' house for a belated Christmas dinner, my mother regaled us with true tales of the good and gallant "Sir Snicks." He had carried my mother, a novice rider, on three-hour trail rides through the trail-less local forest. He had stood calmly while her companions' horses spooked or bolted at ATVs, off-leash dogs, and chaotic contingents of high-speed bicyclists. His kindness, honesty, and plain horse-sense had enchanted even the barn's expert riders, who now invited my mother and Snickers to ride with them and asked them to lead the way.

"Horses are so magical," my mother's older sister, Donna, sighed. "I hugged a horse once, in Ireland. She hugged me back, too. She curled her neck around me and pressed her cheek to mine. I've never ridden, though." She flashed a wicked grin. "Because my sister got all of the riding lessons!"

It was an old joke, older than Snickers, older than me, though I knew it well, having heard it at least thirty-one out of the last thirty Christmases. Yet rather than retorting with the seemingly endless list of childhood advantages that Donna had, which she did not, my mother said, "You could ride Snickers."

Her words lit the room like fireworks. Immediately, though, I envisioned Donna's glittering memory of hugging a horse dissolving into the gritty reality of riding one for the first time.

"What a great idea!" I said over the hubbub. "Donna, I'll even give you the riding lesson."

"I'd like to see that!" crowed Nonna from the head of the table, and the siblings, spouses, children, and assorted beloveds seated around us enthusiastically agreed.

An hour later, our family was gathered in the barn's icy indoor arena. Watching Donna, though, no one noticed the cold. Dressed in my mother's boots and sweats and riding helmet, Donna looked like a cloaked Titania, resplendent, ethereal, yet mantled in earthly joy, circling the starlit plain upon her noble pony-throne.

As she and I passed by, Nonna touched my mother's arm. "Please take a picture," I heard her say. "This is too special to forget."

After pausing for pictures, Donna rode to the mounting block and dismounted. She hugged me, pouring out a hundred gracious words of thanks, then hugged Snickers, whispering a hundred more, and then hugged each member of our family, all of whom had stampeded over to hug her back and to celebrate her courage and her triumph.

Smiling inside, I extricated myself from the hug brigade and slipped to Snickers' right, running up the stirrup, loosening the girth, and brushing the dust from his legs. As I fussed, the group slowly broke up, until I could see only my mother's helmet bobbing above the saddle. With a lighthearted "Last call" on my lips, I circled to Snickers' left—and froze in my tracks.

It was my mother's helmet, all right. Except it was perched atop my grandmother's head. From under its brim, her face shone with a clear, pure, utterly ingenuous hope.

My heart died in my chest. As her granddaughter, I wanted to say yes, shout yes, cry yes. Riding Snickers would make her so happy, and seeing her proud and uplifted on his burnished, fairy-tale back might renew my own enduring, passionate hope that she was and

Snickers

always would be unstoppable, unbreakable, and, most of all, immortal. I would do anything to sustain her inner brightness; I would dare anything to prove that her beautiful, clear light was not paling, that I did not see in her a growing otherworldly translucence, a kind of fading at the edges that struck terror into a place infinitely deeper than my heart.

For a riding instructor, though, there is no such mercy. Every instructor knows that the only place for wishful thinking is the unforgiving distance between the saddle and the ground. My duty was not to my dreams or to hers but to her safety, however harsh my judgment might have to be.

I forced myself to see her advanced arthritis, her debilitated left side, the tenuous, fragile web underpinning her health and strength. The unaccustomed stretching and the post-ride soreness alone could cripple her, and if she fell—

—oh my God, if she fell—

No. I couldn't allow it. It was impossible. Reckless. Criminal. A thousand excuses vied for place at the tip of my tongue.

Yet before I could choose one, before I could speak, time itself shuddered to a halt. For in that moment that I had declared it impossible, I also saw what else was impossible. Our far-flung family was gathered together. The arena was completely empty. The horse was small, kind, and steady, her own daughter's trusted friend. Even her neurotic granddaughter was present to be her guide.

As quickly as it had risen, my panic drained away, and a cool, crystal stillness welled in its place. Finally, I saw how Nonna had, throughout her life, proved all conventional thinking wrong. Finally I understood, forever and without a doubt, what she had always known. Whether it be orchestrated by coincidence, a higher power, or the sheer might of the human spirit, *anything* is possible.

I pushed the mounting block almost under Snickers. Nonna put her foot into the stirrup and swung her leg over his back.

It didn't even brush his rump.

There she sat: strength, beauty, and truth in a saddle. Yet I sensed in her a lingering, private shadow—one of those dark, tender places that all of us have—and in that shadow, a trickle of anxiety, a creeping fear that she was not as invincible as we both believed.

"Breathe, Nonna," I said softly. "Breathe into your feet, into your stirrups."

She did, in and out deeply—until some long-forgotten muscle loosened, pitching her sharply, swiftly left.

My right hand shot out and clutched her leg. Bracing her side with my arm, my shoulder, and feeling her weight flow down my spine, into my heels, I thought fleetingly of the flying buttresses of Notre-Dame, of the architects who decided that some achievements are transcendent, are consummate, are timeless enough to be worth the ultimate risk.

That decision, though, wasn't mine to make.

"What do you think, Nonn?" I asked, no longer as teacher to student or even granddaughter to grandmother but as rider to rider.

"Let's go," she replied, and she bumped Snickers with her heels.

Holding Snickers in my left hand and my grandmother in my right, I began our circuit of the arena. Snickers swiveled one ear back and fixed his eye on me, sliding it occasionally back to Nonna. Though they had never met before, he placed his feet so carefully that night that I believed he knew whom he carried, and I believed he cared.

The three of us walked, whoaed, and counted hoofbeats; humble but powerful exercises that helped us reach beyond our separate fears and touch the harmony that resonates between all living things. I felt my heartbeat slow, heard Snickers chewing, and watched as Nonna's spirit explored and returned to the places it had retreated from. The silent symphony of our journey, of the partnership of women, horse, and family, slowly swelled to a deep and thrilling crescendo. Somewhere along her newly glowing edges, an aria began, and, flooded by the rising, streaming radiance of her heroic soul, all of our secret shadows were swept away; all of our fading edges began to sparkle and fill in.

At last, we rounded the final turn and paused on the straightaway for pictures. I felt so calm, so profoundly connected, I wasn't even startled to hear myself say, "If you feel safe and confident, you could let go of your reins and wave."

Of course, she did. Not only did my ninety-two-year-old grandmother—Mickey, Mafalda—wave, she blew a few beauty-queen kisses, and, as my mother snapped one last photo, she stuck her tongue out at the camera.

As we returned to the mounting block, my mother held Snickers, I held the stirrup, and Donna's husband, Michael, stood at Snickers' hip to help Nonna dismount. But as she rappelled her leg over Snickers' back, my worst fears pounced: Nonna lost her balance and toppled forward, too quickly for us to react.

It was blessed Saint Snickers who swung his neck out and caught her. He stood rock-steady as Nonna, her arms knotted around his neck, supported by my mother, me, and Michael, slid her legs down his side. Watching her intently, Snickers waited until her feet touched the mounting block. When the heels of her borrowed paddock boots finally rested on the step, he curled his neck around until his cheek brushed hers and gave her the gentlest of nudges with his nose— relieved horse-hug and a parting horse-kiss.

Nonna chucked Snickers under the chin and gave him a kindly farewell pat. Then she straightened and tottered with a proud bronco-buster's straddle down the mounting-block steps.

She may have been wobbly, but I was shaking. I offered her my hand, as much to steady myself as to steady her.

Nor was I the only one affected. As we walked toward our family, everyone—youngest to oldest, male and female, related by blood or by marriage—stared at her, with eyes as big and wondering as foals'. Together we saw what Pegasus, Snickers, and every other good steed had seen for nearly a century: a woman with the glorious, dauntless soul of a horse, the leader and mother of a herd that thundered from Italy to America and on around the world. Truly, a great grand-mare. That night, once again, Nonna blazed a new trail for us and reminded us that we can run as far, as fast, and as near forever as we wish.

As this understanding took fleet, four-legged shape in my mind, Nonna leaned toward me confidentially.

"I wanted to trot tonight," she whispered, "but I was a little too scared." Then her gray-green eyes, still as clear and sharp as the spires of the Apennines on a bright spring day, twinkled.

"Oh, well," she shrugged, smiling. "Maybe next year."

A Man Like My Horse

Valerie Riggs

In my traditional Spanish-style home, where I have lived for ten years with my second husband, I awaken at dawn feeling discouraged, exhausted, and deeply sad. This is the day my second divorce becomes final. I knew it was coming, but I had fought against it with all my might, and now there is nothing left to do but face it.

My petite gray cat, Willow, wakes me up at 6:00 AM on the morning of my new divorced-again status by stomping around on my shoulder and hip while I lie alone in my too-large ex-marital bed in the fetal position. For about five seconds after I open my eyes, I feel at peace. Then, as Willow's pokey feet roam over my body, the realization comes pouring into my consciousness that I now have to deal with life alone again and handle all of the fallout, anger, and rejection of another divorce. It seems easier to just turn over, cry, and go back to sleep.

But when you are a horse owner, this is never an option.

My now ex-husband, Robert, has been so determined to divide all our material possessions exactly down the middle that I have feared he would want to own half of Cruz, my hardy, handsome two-year-old quarter horse. But Robert resents Cruz, intuiting (probably correctly) that I love Cruz more than I do him. So he took some extra equities from our portfolio to make up for *his* half of *my* horse. I admit that I love Cruz an unreasonable amount and tend to him with what could be perceived as a neurotic amount of care and protection. But the sight of Cruz's finely chiseled head, wide forehead, and sturdy legs makes my heart feel as soft as whipped cream every time I look at him.

I throw on my riding clothes in the pale light of this unfortunate day, feed my cat, load my two enthusiastic Australian border collies, Sam and Sally, into the back of my white Ford pickup, and start the six-minute drive downhill to the New Market Riding Club, just like I do seven days of the week. On this day, however, my heart feels like a heavy piece of black stone sitting in my chest, and my head is pounding slightly from all my recent crying jags. I feel like my energy tank is at zero, and it crosses my mind to just complete my basic chores at the barn, then return home to climb back into bed. Yes, I think, that sounds like an excellent plan.

But my grief and depression lift as I see Cruz moving swiftly to the front of his corral like he always does when he hears my truck door slam. He is consistently demonstrative of his delight in seeing me. The sound that he makes, an expectant whinny with a gleeful

Cruz

blustery exhale at the end, makes me laugh every time I hear it. What a gift he is! I, Adrianna, a two-time divorcée who woke up today just this side of being a total emotional wreck, am now lighthearted and laughing after one look and two sounds from my beautiful Cruz. My healing miracle—that's what I call him.

Now that Cruz has elevated my emotions, I have lost the desire to climb back into the womb of my bed sheets and feel sorry for myself. I want to enjoy my time with my horse, my dogs, and my friends at the riding club.

As I place Cruz into the cross-ties and begin his pre-ride grooming, I concentrate on the joy this ritual brings me. I rest my cheek against the flat profile of his warm face and keep it there as he playfully tosses his head from side to side. Then I roll his lips up just for fun because it makes him nicker and snort. Then to finish our cross-ties play, I blow on his nose, he blusters back at me, and I giggle. Where have all my negative emotions gone? The darkness inside of me has been replaced with a bubbling spring of delight. I start to work on brushing his chestnut coat and his black mane and stockings as the sun makes its grand appearance over the golden-beige hill behind me.

As I lean my shoulder into Cruz's much larger, well-muscled shoulder and run my hand down his leg to encourage him to lift up his foot, it strikes me that it is a uniquely comforting, solid feeling to press my weight into Cruz and have him trustingly and predictably respond. I have no man to cuddle up to now, but I love the feeling of sinking into Cruz while he lifts his foot into my hand so that I can use the hoof pick. There is nothing quite like it. I finish off his grooming by rubbing him down with a towel to make his coat glisten in the freshness of the early daylight. Just as I finish tightening the cinch on his saddle, I hear my three riding girlfriends approaching our corral.

"Good morning, my friends!" I call out as I step into the stirrup and mount.

"Hey, Adrianna," Julie says. "How are you doing today?" She knows what *today* means.

"Terrible at first, but now that Cruz and I are together, pretty good!"

"Is it final?" Paula asks, trying to be delicate.

"Yep—I'm a single woman once again," I tell her.

"I'm sorry about that," Michelle says.

"Thanks. Let's forget about my troubles for now and go enjoy our ride."

People think there are no seasons in San Diego, but I am acutely aware of every change that takes place in my canyon throughout the year. It is fall, and I can taste it in the air. I know it means the holidays are coming—will I be able to face them without a man in my life?

The four of us chatter about the different conditions of our horses, how their gaits feel today, and what our plans are for the afternoon. Cruz feels strong and stable beneath me. If he ever has the slightest inflammation in his feet or joints, no matter how subtle, I am able to detect it instantly. But on this beautiful autumn morning, with Cruz 100 percent whole and healthy, and my three best friends with me on the trail, the disasters in my personal life seem like a subplot without much meaning. Here I find my meaning, one rocking, clomping step at a time. My dogs, Sam and Sally, are trailing behind with their pink tongues hanging out and their fluffy tails wagging.

After our rides, my girlfriends and I always meet at the local Starbucks for our wrap-up coffee. I tell the women I am going to pass on our ritual today because I need some solitude—just Cruz, my dogs, and me in the natural beauty of our canyon—to sort out some issues in my head. The women are kind and understanding, say some reassuring words that don't really sink in, and wish me well.

I continue my morning ride. At first I try to let go of all thoughts and just relax into the saddle and the rhythm of Cruz's gait. A sanguine mood settles over me, and I somehow know that, despite my difficulties, everything is going to be okay. I have my horse, my dogs, my cat, my family and friends, my home, my riding club and my canyon trails. Plus I can enjoy the awesome weather and seasons of San Diego. Nobody has it all. That is a myth. I have a life that brings me joy, laughter, and love. I am a lucky, blessed woman. So what if I am going to be waking up on Christmas morning without a husband this year? I'll survive.

I halt Cruz underneath a shady oak tree with a water tub and we both have a long drink, Cruz from the wooden tub and I from my canteen. I lean forward and place the side of my face on his dark mane and gently stroke the side of his neck. Then I dismount and let Cruz graze on the last of the green grass from the summer rains. The dogs happily flop down in the dirt underneath the oak tree and pant. I sit on top of a time-worn, moss-covered picnic table with my feet on the bench below. I feel like taking stock of the past and planning my future, so I rest backward on my hands and look up at the cloudless azure sky.

Why had I lost two husbands through divorce? Did I have terrible taste in men or was it *me*? Was I difficult to get along with? I am willing to take responsibility for my situation, but I want to be clear about the exact nature of my errors.

Husband number one had been a tanned, blond-haired, blue-eyed yachtsman. I had been spellbound by his outdoorsy good looks and his wealthy lifestyle. Also, his robust way of coordinating a crew on a sailboat and his vigorous competitive spirit had won me over. He told me that I would always come in second to his love of sailing, but the glamour of it all was irresistible. Unfortunately, after a few years of marriage, I discovered the intense loneliness of being a yachtsman's wife. He would go away to compete in sailing races for weeks and months at a time. I realized I wanted a day-to-day husband to have by my side, so I left.

Husband number two offered me the daily attention I craved. But his magnetic jocular personality, white-white teeth, and slender, lithe body had distracted me from discovering his mean streak and his wandering eye before it was too late. My second marriage was even shorter than my first because being hurt and humiliated was worse than being lonely. I tried to change him, so he left.

It is obvious I had repeated an error. I had not been fully aware of what I was getting myself into when I said "I do" to these seductive men. I will never make that mistake again. The next time I am fortunate enough to fall in love with a man, I will take my time, be clear about exactly who he is and what our life together will be like.

So what kind of man do I want? A thought comes into my head that makes me laugh out loud. I want a man like my horse! I can imagine a man who would move swiftly toward me when I arrived home and who would consistently demonstrate his delight in seeing me. He would be playful, cheerful, and make me laugh. He would make my insides feel like butter melting on warm toast because he was so good to me. He would be trusting, loyal, and reliable. What a fantastic mate my horse/man would be!

But I know this is just a fantasy. Men are so much more complicated than horses. Yet I believe I will look for some of Cruz's best qualities in my next lover. I will also do my part and make a romantic partner feel like a high priority in my life and not always put my "horse time" before him, like my first husband did to me with sailing.

The truth is I don't need a man at all. I live an independent life and function fine on my own. But I have a vision for my life that includes a fiftieth wedding anniversary with a loving husband and is filled with the joy of children, grandchildren, and great-grandchildren. I am going to pursue my dream as I pick up the pieces from the mistakes that I have made. My heart feels bruised, not broken. I won't give up. I know that an alluring future is my destiny.

Suddenly, Sam and Sally jump up and begin barking in the direction of the dusty hill that rises to the south. I hear the sound of hooves on the trail and then spot Ian, my riding instructor, coming down the hill toward us on his dappled gray-and-white mare, Amelia.

"Hello, Adrianna!" Ian exclaims, definitely displaying delight in seeing me. I feel buoyant as I watch him push his sandy-colored hair out of his attractive green eyes. It occurs to me that he makes me laugh during my riding lessons and that he is a solid, reliable sort of guy, just like my horse/man would be. Too bad he is married to my riding friend Julie. But there have to be other guys like him out there—men who have some of the best qualities of my horse and a passion for riding. Yes, that would be the best of all worlds.

"Hey, Ian. How are you?" I reply.

"Good," he says. "Are you heading back to the club? Want to join me?"

"Sure. Love to."

I mount Cruz and we head back to the riding club together. I glance over at Ian and see his kind eyes crinkle at the corners as he smiles at me. I wonder: If I date a man like Ian, is it possible for that guy also to have the qualities a horse could never have? Would he be romantic, compassionate, and committed? Would family come first with him?

The clarity I now have about what I want in a man is giving me confidence. I want a man like my horse, but better, like only a fine man can be.

I woke up this morning feeling like a dismal failure and dreading the thought of facing my life alone. Now, with the guidance of my magical horse, and with the luxury of solitude in nature, I have some perspective. Everyone makes mistakes. Life is long, and errors can be corrected. I have a clear plan and a fresh chance at love. Armed with hard-earned wisdom, I am determined to achieve my goals. A man cannot be expected to give me the unconditional love that my animals do, but he can love me in a way that will help make the vision I have for my life a reality. I picture myself and a dedicated, kind husband playing with our children and animals throughout the decades, and having my past divorces stand as a small and distant footnote in the total saga of the happy life I plan on living.

It Always Happens One Summer

Lisa Romeo

"There is always one moment in childhood where a door opens and lets the future in." –Graham Greene

My oldest child is fourteen, and he is heading off to sports broadcasting camp. He's nonchalantly excited and also poised, not in the sense of being mature but in the way of being ready, ripe. I wonder if, at camp or any other moment now, something will come along, and in the very best sense, he will be gone. I'm wondering because he is just the age when everything happened for me.

It happened in a barn.

I should have been at theater camp in upstate New York all summer, but hours after arriving on the bus, I was calling home: There was a hole in the stage, I found strands of hair in the dinner of cold stew, and I was beginning to doubt that Robert Redford would direct the finale. My father took me home the next morning, called his lawyer, and I went back to my usual summer routine—hanging about reading a book a day and writing terrible poetry on a noisy manual typewriter.

My mother said it to my father out loud: *Maybe you should just get her the horse she has always wanted.*

Money was not the issue, but a horse was still a big deal for a kid in split-level New Jersey suburbia where girls usually got puppies and hung up *pictures* of horses. The dozens of times I had actually asked for a horse, I only heard, "Are you crazy?" No crazier, I thought, than occasionally flying first class to Florida simply to escape the cold in New Jersey.

Later, I realized "crazy" wasn't about what a starter horse would cost but what my father sensed might happen afterward. He pictured me riding a few times a week, then every day, and then lessons, trainers, horse shows, custom boots, and eventually another horse. He was used to knowing a lot about almost everything and usually being right.

When it came to buying a child a horse, however, my father knew less than I, a teenager smitten with photographs of Princess Anne steeplechasing across Britannia. I suggested we go to a large training stable two towns over, where I'd often seen rings full of fancy horses ridden by teenage girls in sleek breeches and tall black boots. He had other ideas.

His brother, my Uncle Nunzio, who worked at the textile factory my father owned, knew a guy, as he frequently did, who worked at the track, who had a brother. From there, the web stretched to a small stable twenty miles from our house, where we found Ralph. Ralph glanced at me for only seconds, then showed us Poco.

"He's registered, papers and all. But he's just green broke," Ralph said to my father, who looked at me, eyebrows raised. I nodded confidently. Purebred I understood, but which breed? And, what did *green* mean? I decided that didn't matter: My father was going to buy me a horse and my mind was made up. I would take any one he was willing to consider.

Poco was the one.

Poco was chocolate brown, gorgeous, and velvet under my fingers. Before I even saw him trot, I was disproportionately and naively in love. Royal Pocoa (his papered name) was a Quarter Horse, from sturdy ancestors bred for the rugged old West, with good-natured and sure-footed reputations, calm, hearty and hale.

A Quarter Horse in fact is an ideal first horse—that is, a trained, experienced Quarter Horse, say one about ten years old. Poco, as you might imagine, was two.

Ralph sent Poco around the paddock in circles at the end of a longe line, then rode him three times around a small ring. No one suggested I do anything but watch. Between Uncle Nunzio, Ralph, and my father, there was a good deal of head nodding, backslapping, and a promise of next-day delivery. Poco would live at White Oak Stable, a small ten-stall barn, one of only two places in Cedar Grove where I'd ever seen horses living, tucked behind a meandering ranch house at the less-developed end of town.

The next morning, my mother drove me twenty miles down the Garden State Parkway to Eiser's to procure all things horsy. With a list from Karen, who managed White Oak, we serpentined the aisles, happily loading a basket with unusual-sounding and strange-looking objects—a shedding blade, hoof pick, Absorbine liniment, a flysheet, salt lick, and curry comb. An older woman with skin the texture of the leather surrounding us fitted me in a saddle, and I pictured myself cantering across the heath, even though I knew that's not what riding in New Jersey would be like.

Mom, whose only Depression-era toy was a second-hand doll, was enjoying herself.

"How about getting his name on the side of one of those nice head things?" she suggested, fingering a deeply tanned, whip-stitched leather halter with engraved brass nameplate.

Sold.

Later, I'd learn that what we really needed were a couple of cheap halters made of durable nylon, but for now I was still stunned. Five days earlier I was riding a bus to drama camp, and now I was cast in a new show but didn't know any of my lines.

That afternoon, when Poco inched cautiously backward off the trailer, Karen asked about the outcome of the vet check. Turns out, before money is exchanged, intended four-legged purchases should be carefully checked, forelock to haunches by an equine veterinarian. Who knew?

Karen shrugged. My father jumped to other, practical matters.

"How much for you to take care of everything?" he asked. He was a man accustomed to flashing cash at a maître d' and hiring "a guy" to take care of anything.

Karen told him the monthly board fee, which even I knew was enough to buy lobster dinners for eight. "That's a weekly lesson, feed, and stall cleaning. The rest, the kids have to do themselves."

Karen turned to me. "You need to come every day to groom him, ride, clean your tack, and help with barn chores. Got that?"

I only got that I was somewhere I already loved. Someplace maybe where goofy boys, mean girls, and frizzy hair might not matter. I waved at my parents as they drove off. I was ready to go.

Karen clipped the crosstie lines from either side of the barn aisle to both sides of Poco's fancy halter. She expertly lifted his right foreleg and, guiding the hoof pick in smooth arcs, scraped out shavings, pebbles, and bits of manure from the bottom of his shod right hoof. It looked easy.

I stood next to my horse (my horse!) and ran my hand down his soft brown neck to the top of his leg. My heart thumped, wild and excited. I slid my hand down one of Poco's front legs and turned, crouching, toward his haunches, lightly touching his foreleg, expecting him to instantly bend and lift his leg as he did for Karen. Instead, the hoof remained anchored to the floor.

I tried again, and a third time, scared I was doing everything wrong, that I might hurt him, certain I would never get the right feel.

"Use pressure, squeeze in a little," Karen said and placed her hand over mine, pressing my fingers into Poco's flesh so that I could feel his bone under my thumb and middle finger. My other fingers nudging the tendon, I watched as his hoof rose up off the dusty cement floor and came to rest, more heavily than I anticipated, in the space between my bent knees. Weeks would pass before I could pick out a hoof without Karen's graceful assurance.

"Tack him up," Karen said. I looked at her and did not move. "Put the saddle on!"

"Finally," I said.

"Wait—you didn't even ride him?" Karen shook her head. "Well, what kind of bit did they use?"

I knew a bit was the metal piece passing through a horse's mouth, attached to the reins on either side. But what bit for Poco?

"They just told me to buy a bosal," I said, pulling from my Eiser's bags a tear-dropped-shaped, over-the-nose contraption I would learn was a rudimentary training device for very young mounts.

"You mean he's not bit-broke?" Karen asked.

Apparently, my father's check for $2,500 (around $10,000 in today's dollars) purchased a perfectly delightful toddler, the equine equivalent of a floppy-eared puppy. Poco's bloodlines were unblemished, his papers bona fide, his conformation pleasing. But experience as a riding horse? As a horse that could teach a nervous bookworm teenager how to be a horse person? Not so much.

He was greener than an inch-round tomato in July.

But if Poco was the wrong horse, Karen never said. Maybe at

twenty she still remembered that giddy, confused, overwhelmed feeling that engulfs a young girl the first time she runs her hand down a horse's face, kisses his silken snout, and knows he is hers.

"Be prepared," Karen warned. "This is all going to be new to him, too, and two-year-old horses are, well, challenging."

During my first lesson, Karen emphasized two things—sitting still and looking where I was going. Both seemed unlikely. I jiggled and jerked, lolling side to side like a half-empty feedbag. I constantly checked that my feet were securely positioned in the stirrups and the reins were threaded properly between the correct fingers.

"Look where you're going," Karen warned.

I was glancing down at the small rocks Poco was kicking up, watching his hooves flash under me as the ground moved by.

"Eyes up, Lisa!" she shouted.

But I was already in the dirt, lodged between Poco's right foreleg and the side of the barn. My right pinky and ring fingers were squeezed by tightening reins to a throbbing red. Poco stopped, quiet and still beside me.

Karen moved slowly from her perch on the mounting block to chase what she assumed would be a spooked and galloping Poco around the ring, through the barn, up the driveway, and down Ridge Road. But Poco only stood serenely by as I disentangled my aching hand and slowly stood up.

"You are one lucky girl," she said. Then she patted Poco on the neck, her expression appraising.

"And this is one sainted two-year-old," she said.

Saint Poco was not skittish or flighty like most other horses his age. He did not spook at empty feed bags blowing across the ring or at the boy next door who raced noisy toy cars every afternoon. He didn't even startle when he stood tethered in the aisle and the hayloft ladder, too loosely tied up in the corner, came crashing down inches from his nostrils. Had Poco galloped away, bucking that first day when I nearly slammed him into the wall, or had he just been a more typically unpredictable colt, prone to high jinks and equine ADHD . . . well, who knows?

I pulled myself from the dirt and walked Poco back to the mounting block. As I got back on and headed again out to the rail, unsuccessfully concealing the tears puddling in my upturned eyes, I caught my reflection in the cloudy barn window. My new black velveteen riding helmet was sprinkled with dust. The picture of an Olympic jumper on my new T-shirt was smudged over, and I worried my fingers might be broken. I was embarrassed and frustrated and wondered if I'd fit in here after all or whether the entire episode would turn out just like cheerleading tryouts and glee club—another hopeful idea crushed in the dust along with what was left of my dignity.

But I looked at Poco, who was getting his first chance to belong, too. Despite the dreamy long lashes, muscled chest, and sweet brown eyes, Poco seemed the wrong dark, tall, and handsome creature for me. As partnerships go, ours was hardly ideal. Yet somehow he and I together worked.

My father was right, not about Poco but about one thing leading to another. Over the years, more horses, better stables, and tougher trainers followed. I would learn to sit still and not take my eyes off the jumps that grew higher and wider each year. I would learn to take days, weeks even, to decide on each new equine partner.

Before buying my next five horses, I would hire the vet used by the United States Equestrian Team to X-ray, palpate, and evaluate. I would insist on taking multiple test rides and seeing videos of past show-ring wins. Eventually, I would buy only the right horses, horses who could win at major shows and were finely tuned, thoroughly trained, and completely knowledgeable about their jobs.

During those scrabbly, early, flailing-around-together days with Poco, however, I grasped enough to know that a green horse was helping to turn my awkward gray days into blue sky. When school started again that fall and the bell sounded at 2:45 every afternoon, I knew where I belonged.

That was thirty-four years ago.

At 2:45 these days, my fourteen-year-old son is walking in the back door, and I drive off to fetch his ten-year-old brother. Later, I make the rounds: Cub Scouts drop-off, pick-up at baseball practice, and along the way I pass the gravel driveway leading to the crumbling White Oak Stable, empty now and awaiting tear-down. I often can roll right past without even gazing down that rocky lane, hoping only for a scant whiff of horse manure and at the same time certain I won't catch one—just as certain as I am that horses are now gone from my life. Most of the time, that's just fine.

Sometimes, however, I am reminded it isn't.

Like when I recently saw something unnerving in my house. There's nothing so unusual anymore about finding a jumping event on cable television, maybe an Olympic selection trial or a Grand Prix. But this time was different, a reality show of equestrian life both *in and out* of the show ring. There were teenagers in brushed caps on shiny mounts at horse shows but also unbraided horses with dirty saddle pads, and kids in jeans and torn T-shirts, together getting flecked with mud during riding lessons back at the barn, sweat running down their necks.

I sat down on the couch, a little weak and a little excited, and was aware of a rare but not altogether unprecedented feeling of mixed nostalgia. My gaze wandered to a photo on the family-room wall, me in mid-gallop, mid-jump, in formal show attire, in Florida (or maybe California?), astride Cool Shoes, and I wondered—that *was* really me, right?

It was. Not the me who stumbled around with Poco but the me who emerged, slowly, over the next decade, a me who morphed from recreational rider to competitor, horse lover to horse person, trail rider to equestrian. Remembering that girl, I find myself telling my younger son about the horses—five of them; the shows—hundreds; the trainers—a half dozen, on two coasts. He likes hearing about Poco and the hay-ladder story, not so much about Tara (Tara's Theme), the exquisitely lovely retired race horse, uncannily twitchy in the show ring. There was Mitzi (Measure for Measure), the reliable competitor who taught me more about quiet preparation than any trainer; Waylon (Press Agent), who was the big gamble, a lavishly talented jumper prodigy with an equally prodigal temperament and, ultimately, a severe nerve disorder; and then Cool Shoes, an elegant and accomplished show-ring veteran, purchased during my senior year of college, who was the cause of a slipping GPA, a boyfriend left behind, and my entrée into the higher levels of competition.

I haul out the few remaining show-ring videos and head to the basement where our old VCR is still hooked up, and I stare, slack-jawed, at my younger self, delighted and also a little depressed to encounter this slim young woman with nothing on her mind except gauging the distance to the ideal take-off spot. She's moving fast, in control, and knows where she is going, or at least that is how things appear on film.

I like remembering that, at one point, life seemed manageable that way—learn the course, take all the obstacles in order, ride straight ahead. I like remembering this especially now, when life seems far too meandering, obstacles appearing out of nowhere instead of at measured intervals, interrupted strides and shifting footing the norm.

I want that certainty back, the feeling that—blue ribbon or none—the ride is what counts.

Horses gave me a sure, solid footing I couldn't find elsewhere, certainly not as the bookworm brain with rubbing-together thighs who fell at cheerleading tryouts while the cool girls snickered. In the dusty hay loft at White Oak, or at any stable or show, I belonged. I

Cool Shoes

knew what to do about a colicky horse and why horses are measured in hands and how, without appearing to move a muscle, I could signal a horse to canter on the correct leading leg. None of that depended on knowing whether The Who were cooler than Cream or if dating a prep school boy your own age was better than making out with a senior after a football game.

Falling, or failing, was even okay in this new club, as long as I got right back on.

Keeping my horse cool on a humid day was more important than wearing the right halter top to the mall. What books and clichéd television movies say about a young girl and her horse—all true. Boys, and then later men, did matter, but in a more peripheral way, and only if they felt like trailing along while I spent weekends at horse shows and, over the summer, 24/7 at the stable.

Partnering a half-ton animal over four-foot fences without breaking stride or landing in the dirt was electrifying and, at times, erotic even, holding the reins and all the cards, bonding through shared exertion, a muscled mount between my legs. My parents joked that I lived in the barn, but the truth is, the horses lived in me.

For all that, though, I also recall understanding that the thing that lures you to a life you love is not necessarily the thing you do better than anything else. In fact, riding was never easy for me, and quitting often seemed like the smarter idea. I was no natural in the saddle. I just worked damn hard. I signed up for all the extra lessons we could afford, then mucked stalls in exchange for more. I went to clinics three states away, studied show-ring videos instead of watching *Saturday Night Live*, and asked my cousin the gym teacher for exercises to strengthen my jelly-like calves.

That directed and fulfilling kind of pursuit, that passion, longing, love, grit, and desire are what I want now for each of my sons. For them, the moment won't happen on horseback, I know, and if either of them is anything like their mother, the moment will matter only to him. Perhaps I won't even understand, or notice, and that is fine.

Their own passions, their individual and unknown turning points, may show up tomorrow, or in five years. I only know the power of the turning, and its power to sustain. I am reminded every time I see the cache of ribbons packed away in a corner of the attic (not because of the ribbons themselves but because of how they got there, or because 90 percent of that happened outside of the show ring) of that now-gone, horse-infused life, a life I occasionally bump up against with a tart and sweet longing.

Most of the time I know for sure that exchanging martingales and jumps for motherhood and a twenty-year marriage has been a trade-off worth making. I know, too, that I need not have made a total swap, that I could have continued being involved with horses, albeit at a dimmed intensity, all through my early marriage, motherhood— even up to today. I could head out this very afternoon for a lesson at a major training center six miles from my house, but I know, in the end, I would be disappointed.

For me, the intensity was my thrall, the day-in, all-day, everyday blind commitment, the difficulty and challenge of becoming an equestrian duo. Horses and riding, at the level at which I was finally able to play, were about adrenaline at the in-gate, losing and being able to figure out why, packing up and moving on, totaling points, chopping ice from the tops of water buckets, and trusting my horse and my trainer and myself enough to jump without stirrups, without holding the reins, without fear. Mostly, I loved the overarching desire to put everything else aside for hours, days, years.

Being a horse hobbyist holds no comparable appeal, and when I tried, when I signed up for lessons a few years ago just to get back in the saddle, something—everything—was missing.

As for my current interests and hobbies—gourmet cooking, long walks, gardening—I could give up any of them, all of them, and not feel as if I'd sold my best friend. Failing at any or all of them would be fine. Failing any of my horses—misjudging the distance and having to make Cool Shoes stop short and maybe crash into the jump, or forgetting to pick the tiny pointy stones from Poco's hoof—would have been, or was, unforgivable, though of course the horses always forgave.

The day I saw that TV program I was caught unprepared, letting myself peer, at first tentatively and then with wildly lavish and unsated hunger, at my own onetime reality, a past passion fulfilled and also slightly deferred, still fulgent and not forgotten.

My sons ask me why I don't ride anymore. I can't explain it in a way that would make sense to kids who have yet to imagine a time when they will *not* want to ride their bikes down our hill at top speed, a time when something—or so many things—will take on the same importance and urgency as they now feel for next weekend's camping trip or tomorrow's rock-climbing party.

"I've got so much else to do," I say.

And I do. And I do all of those other things. And some times, or all the time, when I am doing them, I am thinking about horses.

Stop and Eat the Flowers

Kathryn Hohmann

My mother takes great joy in telling about the perfect spring day when she drove with her friends from nursing school to the Pennsylvania countryside. They stopped at a riding stable and rented horses for an afternoon trail ride. Mom initially felt nervous but soon settled into the saddle and began to enjoy the rhythm of the walk—until the idyllic afternoon took a sharp turn. Mom's horse wandered away from the path toward a farmhouse. Her horse climbed the porch steps, devoured the potted geraniums, and trotted into the adjacent cemetery, where he proceeded to chew his way, grave by grave, through the memorial bouquets.

"At a certain point," Mom says, "I just slid out of the saddle and walked beside him, back to the barn." Although she's philosophical about the ordeal, she has never been tempted to ride another horse. For many years, I tried to convince her to ride again but never succeeded. Given that we're unusually close and share so many qualities, her attitude toward riding mystified me.

That was before I moved to Montana and found Gilligan.

He was a running-bred quarter horse, a rangy chestnut three-year-old when I first saw him. Even though he stood out from the other young horses, I told his owners that I'd need a week to think about the other prospects I'd seen during months of scouring Montana for a suitable horse. But as I headed away from the property, I glanced over my shoulder at the corner of the pasture and saw that red gelding with the blaze and knee-high socks. Moving with an easy grace, he swung his head around and cocked one hip, as if standing alongside a highway, thumbing a ride. I don't usually pick up hitchhikers, but in his case, I made an exception.

I called him Gilligan for his gangly build, wide blaze that reminded me of a sailor's cap, and his endearing expression. The name on his registration papers, Judgin' Me, didn't seem suitable for an event horse, and it made me think of that biblical admonition *Judge not, lest ye be judged.* Whether he was cut out for the three rigorous phases of eventing—the intricate patterns of dressage; the cross-country jumping over ditches, logs, and water; and the tricky obstacles in the stadium jumping phase—remained to be seen.

On the longe line, he quickly grasped the fundamentals, learning cues for walk, trot, canter, and basic bending. Adding the saddle and bridle presented no problems. Yet the more I worked with Gilligan during that first fall season, the more something struck me

Nip

as unusual. It wasn't his conformation—he had enough height and an uphill build—it was his disposition. He lacked a certain edge that event riders seek in their partners. That's when I remembered reading advice from a top eventer, who suggested that riders should disqualify any event prospect that rested its leg while standing in the cross-ties, a habit that he believed signaled a lack of keenness. That advice made me doubt my choice, but I was a Montana amateur and not a national-level competitor, and making a firm decision about Gilligan was premature. Why be so judgmental?

Spring started to melt the snow from the foothills of the Bridger Mountains near the barn. Thinking that the sight of open country might awaken in Gilligan some inborn motivation to run (after all, he was race-track bred), I decided to try him on the trails. To ride the steep hills, I bought my first stock saddle and traded my English breeches for Lee jeans. I bought a hand-made western belt, a massive strap with a heavy-duty, primitive brass buckle, from my landlord's son. The belt wasn't my usual style, but I made the purchase to support the boy's brand-new leather-working enterprise, and besides, it completed my transformation from English eventer to western trail rider.

On the trails, Gilligan went forward at an easy walk, swinging his head to take in the views, and he proved unflappable even when we flushed a bull moose from sparse winter cover. Gilligan never bothered to lean into the slopes and run; he kept to his slow, implacable rhythm, regardless of the grade. One morning when I rode him away from the barn, he gathered himself and offered a half-hearted buck, insufficient to unseat me but nevertheless a genuine buck. Because he turned slowly and tried to amble back to the barn, I couldn't exactly describe his behavior as a show of keenness. Hauling him around, I realized that Gilligan had acted like the endearing character from an old television show and I was quickly becoming the infuriated, exasperated Skipper.

The hulking dirty snowdrifts finally receded from the foothills, replaced by shoots of grass. Thanks to the lush pastures, Gilligan grew into a robust gelding, well over sixteen hands. Each afternoon when I approached the property, I spotted him grazing on the north slope of the biggest hill, usually alone. I watched him stroll from place to place on the hillside, as if he was carefully choosing what to eat. Never a fussy eater in the past, Gilligan now grazed selectively on a certain plant that had started blooming, going from flower to flower, chewing with a look of deep contentment on his face, yellow petals sticking from his mouth. They must taste sweet, I figured, these flowers that bloomed in profusion across the foothills, but should they make up the bulk of my horse's diet?

When the veterinarian arrived for the spring herd health check, I made sure to bring up the flowers. The vet was mystified and could only suggest that they might contain alkaloids, powerful substances capable of crossing the blood-brain barrier and causing psychoactive effects. Then I mentioned Gilligan's food preferences to a friend, who told me the story of her brother's dog, a beloved family pet that had been diagnosed with cancer. Just as the end seemed near, the dog left the house during a rainy spell and was found days later, sleeping under an old oak tree. He seemed pleased to see his family but refused to leave the spot. He remained there for more than a week in gloomy weather, lapping up the root-beer-colored rain water that collected in the bowl at the base of the tree. When he finally returned home, his cancer had vanished and he lived for three more years.

I didn't know what to make of my friend's story, and I'll never know whether my horse was healing himself or getting high. I just continued with the rides.

Here in the north country, spring turns to summer so suddenly that each moment deserves to be savored. My trail rides with

Gilligan made me wonder whether the afternoons might really be endless and, if they weren't, whether I could lasso and tie down the improbable shades of blue in the cloudless skies. My horse's leisurely pace did prolong our rides, and I didn't mind when mountain bikers and joggers passed us on the trail. But it was also true that we were falling behind. My friends were already hauling their horses to competitions, and my trainer was asking pointed questions about my event prospects. So I went back to training, and as we proceeded through the exercises, I found the harder I pushed Gilligan, the wider the gulf grew between what I wanted from him and what he offered. We had tried only the smallest obstacles, and already Gilligan seemed indifferent. Regardless of how much I wanted to develop my horse into an eventer, he seemed to want to be nothing more than what he already was.

My trainer offered to help, and after a week's worth of sessions with him, she came up with a new nickname. She labeled him Ferdinand, from the children's book about the bull who would rather sit quietly under the cork tree, smelling flowers, than snort and fight in the bull-fighting ring. After reminding me of the story, she showed me another horse that was ready for competition, and she put me in touch with someone searching for a calm, steady trail partner, the perfect home for Gilligan. I meekly voiced misgivings, but my trainer reminded me forcefully that the show season, like spring in the Rockies, didn't last forever.

The prospective buyer turned out to be a sensible and sweet

retired nurse. She didn't need to come right out and say that she would dote on Gilligan; that was obvious from the beginning. I drilled her about his care, and she said she'd board at a nearby ranch, known for its natural springs and extensive trail network. And then she turned the tables and posed two simple questions. First, what was the worst thing he had ever done? I told her about the half-hearted buck, which I'd easily foiled. And then: What's the best thing?

It took me a moment and then I said, "Nothing." I probably had a strange expression on my face, because I was recalling a certain spring day.

We had climbed the steepest pitch of the trail, and I decided to dismount and watch the sunset. Years of riding in a flat English saddle had taught me to merely kick my feet from the stirrups, swing my right leg over the back of the saddle, and lower my upper body, sliding to the ground in a casual dismount. Forgetting that I'd made the switch to western tack—and forgetting about the heavy-duty, hand-made western belt—I tried my usual maneuver. Somehow I managed to catch the sturdy brass belt buckle on the saddle horn, and I was suspended, out of the saddle and yet far from the ground, hanging with my feet kicked from the stirrups, arms flailing for reins that were long gone. I dangled helplessly against the side of a 1,000-pound animal and prayed that the hefty leather strap that joined us would break, prayed that my horse would prove as laid back as ever.

Gilligan waited patiently, doing absolutely nothing, then swung his head around and nuzzled my hip, as if to say, there's really no rush. Time bogged down, and my arms trembled violently as I tried to chin up into the saddle again and again. I remember kicking frantically, and I remember how good the worn stirrup tread felt when my boot finally found purchase and I could swing myself astride.

I'd like to say that I was quick to learn the lessons that Gilligan eventually taught me, but years passed before I really appreciated what might have happened on that particular day if Gilligan had been another sort of horse—the keen, competitive kind. It took even longer before I fully understood the story of Ferdinand the Bull, the lesson about being yourself and refusing to be bullied into being someone you're not. If I'd understood those lessons, I don't think I would have sold my big red horse, not for any price.

But on that afternoon, I knew enough to linger and watch the sun set behind the mountains. And then at a certain point, I just slid down from my horse, more carefully this time, and walked slowly beside him back to the barn, making sure to let him stop and eat the occasional flower.

Horse Crazy

Diane Mapes

Like roller rinks and Chick-O-Sticks, I'd always assumed my horse-crazy years were a thing of the past.

They'd come on me back when I was nine with the fury and suddenness of a violent tropical storm. One minute I was reading Nancy Drew mysteries and collecting Creepy Crawlers, the next I was racing across a windswept island surrounded by a retinue of powerful horse-gods bearing weather-inspired names.

Misty, Stormy, Brighty, Thunderhead—I loved all of these horse heroes of literature. I loved their flaring nostrils, their quivering hindquarters, their wild manes and free spirits. I loved the fact that they were high-strung and misunderstood and unfathomably deep, like me. It wasn't so much that I wanted to *ride* them—I'd been trampled enough times by the family's Shetland pony to be past that—it was more that I wanted to *be* them. They were my brothers, my soulmates, my kin.

For an entire summer, I reveled in their box canyon adventures, their high plains' shenanigans. I read their stories, watched their movies. I even scoured the Sears catalogue for dresses made of National Velvet.

And then one day, as suddenly as it had arrived, my horse craziness disappeared. Or so I thought.

As soon as the car exited the Pacific Highway south of Seattle and started winding through the rolling fields and ramshackle farms that led to the Emerald Downs race track, I felt a long-dormant flutter, a delicate pattering in my chest like the distant hooves of a palomino galloping across a wide, grassy field.

My horse craziness was back.

Pulling into the parking lot, my friend Renate and I grabbed our sunglasses and followed the sweet smell of horse droppings toward the stadium, where a set of escalators transported us into the thrumming heart of Emerald Downs.

The track had just opened for the season, and seduced by a spate of late-night TV commercials and the recent opening of the movie *Seabiscuit*, I'd talked my buddy into joining me for an afternoon of equestrian lust. I sold it as a Saturday adventure, a harmless urban outing, a hoot; I didn't mention the carrots tucked into the side pocket of my purse or the sweet trace memory of horse breath against my neck.

Nor did I tell her I'd spent the previous evening re-reading *Misty of Chincoteague.*

Once inside, I saw betting counters lining the walkways

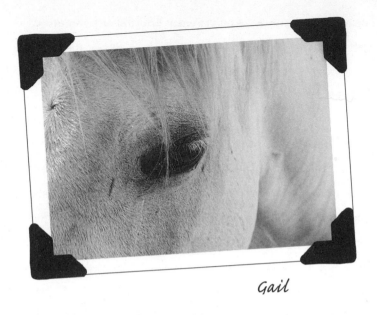

Gail

like troughs; the smell of beer, cigarette smoke, and kettle corn wafted by, lazy and thick as barn dust. While Renate went to find a program, I wandered past glass display cases of horseshoes and diagrams of Thoroughbreds, trying to acclimate myself to the strange, restless atmosphere.

Around me were all manner of people: young couples with babies, old men with cigars, gangs of backslapping husbands, groups of high-fiving wives. Many of them had racing forms clutched in their fists, pencils jabbed behind their ears. I stared at a diagrammed tote board, trying to absorb its secrets. A jumble of numbers and letters and fractions stared back, inscrutable as mud.

Just then I heard a familiar trumpet riff—*Parade to the Post*—and the flutter in my chest began to pound anew. The first race was about to begin.

Hurrying past the betting counters, Renate and I burst outside into what seemed like pilfered Pasadena sunshine and slopped down on a metal bench not far from the edge of the dirt track. Off in the distance, I saw the colorful silks of the jockeys; behind them pranced their horses. While I gazed out at the magnificent animals, Renate scrutinized her program, calling out horse names as saucy as retired vaudeville queens—Ragtime Ruthie, Vodka Martini, Spicy Stuff, Swing Baby.

Apparently, weather patterns were out these days. Attitude was in.

I peered down at a clutch of hieroglyphic statistics, puzzling over the strange terms that shouted up at me: exacta, trifecta, claiming race, lasix. The first race was five furlongs and, according to the program, would be run by maidens. Before I could make sense of this, a bell sounded, the crowd murmured, and a voice high in the stands shouted, "And they're off!"

I scanned the track ahead of me but saw only the tote board, bright numbers peppering its face. People began to jostle around me, shouting out horse names, but the track remained still. I saw a rabbit, peacefully hopping about the manicured lawn inside the rail. Then suddenly, exploding from the left side of the board, I saw a convoluted knot of silks and numbers and flashing hooves coming around the track toward me.

Dangerous Woman was in the lead, sang the announcer.

Followed by Peeps, number 6, ridden by Sandi Gann. Lovem and Leavem was jockeying for position. And Byeairmail, the favorite, was moving up.

As the horses grew closer, I could hear their hooves thundering against the track, mixing with screams of encouragement, pleas for speed, desperate cries for divine intervention. And then they were in front of me, flying by in a tangled blur of dark brown, bright blue, white polka dots and wind. The crowd let loose a final roar, the announcer shouted incoherently, and, just like that, it was over. The horses disappeared down the track and then reappeared out of nowhere, out of breath, out of luck. Peeps stepped into the Winner's Circle, the crowd sighed and shifted, and a phalanx of green tractors began to flatten the field for the next race.

Slowly, I took a ragged breath.

After a while, the herald trumpeter sounded again, the horses made their way to the starting gate, and the second race came and went, an easy victory for Knight in Silver, a three-year-old who had never won two races, a tidbit that the program felt compelled to proclaim in ALL CAPITAL LETTERS.

I couldn't stand it any more. I had to have a closer look.

An animated crowd pressed against the fence surrounding the paddock, where a handful of sleek racehorses in white tube socks paced around their stables like expectant fathers in a 1950s sitcom The air was thick with perfume, cigar smoke, horse manure, and sweat. Bad horse-themed jewelry was the order of the day.

"Are you tired, baby?" a man crooned to a black horse wearing a mask with eyeholes like some kind of equine superhero. "Tell me, are you tired?"

Teenaged boys in slouching jeans leaned against the fence, staring stoically. Sixtyish women in bridle-patterned scarves cooed nervous encouragement. I began to realize I wasn't the only one who had gone a little horse crazy. The stadium seemed full of excited nine-year-old girls, or at least people acting like nine-year-old girls. Even the ones in Madras shorts and bad toupees.

Overhead, the announcer was discussing the breeding status of one horse, the ability of another to dominate on a sloppy track. So-and-so hadn't run a mile before; somebody else's half-sister was a multiple stakes winner. I wondered how the horses felt having their bodies, their families, even their breeding capabilities dissected as zealously as an absent black sheep at a family reunion. I wondered if they realized a misstep, a muddy field, a mercenary owner could mean the end of their racing career, the end of their life, even.

Suddenly, the crowd pulled apart like a bad seam, and a line of men strode down a walkway into the center of the garden. Their jaws were pure granite, their eyes glinting steel. They moved with the unmistakable grace of heroes despite their tiny statures and penchant for garish pastels. I felt my heart begin to flutter as the jockeys snatched up their horses' reins, waltzed them once around the court, then headed for the track. You could taste the mettle in the air.

"Those guys are so brave," Renate said in hushed tones.

"Yeah, riding's pretty dangerous," I answered.

"That's not what I mean." She opened her program and pointed to a page. Listed beside each jockey's name was his weight. I noticed most of them weighed the same as I did—back when I was a horse crazy nine-year-old, that is.

We watched them go, then made a beeline for the counters, practicing our wagers every step of the way.

"Third race. Emerald Downs," Renate whispered behind me.

"Don't they already know we're at Emerald Downs?" I whispered back.

"You have to say where you are," she hissed. "It says so in the book."

"Next." I looked up. A bored blonde with inch-long press-on nails stared back, expectantly.

"Two dollars to win on Ragtime Ruthie," I stammered. Seven dollars and one exotic wager later (according to Renate, who had mastered the jargon by then), I was an official gambler. One race and seventeen minutes later, I was an official winner with $3.80 in my pocket, half of which I promptly slapped down on Cup o' Fries (the snack, not the horse).

We devoured our fries in the hot sun, then milled about the stadium, taking pictures of placid helper horses, fiery Thoroughbreds, wiry jockeys clutching saddles the size of shoulder pads. We talked to the herald trumpeter. We chatted with a pair of hot walkers. We got assurances from the woman guarding the Winner's Circle that she and other Emerald Downs employees were not weighed at the end of their shift like the poor jockeys were. We strategized, we bet. We flew out of our seats, delirious, as our pick for the sixth race furiously pounded down the home stretch—we sat back down, dejected—sans rider.

The afternoon loped along, and I sat in its saddle, content.

Around me swirled bad rock music, screaming cell phones, the wailing of babies, the drone of overhead planes, but I was immune to it all. All I could hear was the wild music of hooves and the excited burble of other nine-year-olds—some in denim cutoffs, others in serge suits—discussing horses past and present, their every syllable rife with hopeless infatuation.

Man o' War, Seabiscuit, Secretariat, Funny Cide. Horse names were whispered over and over like magical incantations, and for a moment, I was transported onto a windswept island, surrounded by a retinue of powerful horse-gods, running, running, running. Only I wasn't alone. Businessmen in suits and teenage boys in slouching jeans and sixtyish women in bad horse jewelry were running with me.

I had stumbled onto a portal of sorts. A portal into another world—horse world—where, for an instant, I could once again thunder over the earth, dirt clods stinging my muzzle, wind tossing my mane. But unlike the small town library that had transported me here thirty years ago, this portal was still around. It was only a half-hour away. There was even a bus.

As I headed for the exit, I turned to watch the horses—my brothers—line up for the next race, noting their flaring nostrils, their quivering hindquarters, their wild manes and free spirits.

Then a bell sounded, the crowd murmured, and we were off.

Irish Mist

Linda Ballou

Rain splattered on the windshield as the red-faced driver swerved his van around hairpin curves. I swayed to and fro, bouncing a foot off the seat as we careened through narrow country lanes. I'd heard that the Irish drive like they ride, with abandon, over rugged terrain in inclement weather. Those romantic rock walls I dreamed of jumping on the back of a solid Irish Hunter took on a foreboding presence as we came breathtakingly close to the scenery. My palms were wet and my mouth was dry with anticipation as we spiraled our way to horse heaven.

Terry Fergus-Browne, the owner of Stracomer, a riding school on a bluff overlooking windswept Donegal Bay, had come highly recommended by three major horse tour companies. I linked up with the other riders for breakfast—kippers, ham, sausages, and eggs.

The group was composed of about a dozen well-dressed

Italians, two teenage girls from Switzerland, four older Americans in western garb, and a couple from Dublin, all out for a weekend in the country. Broken English bandied about at the breakfast table. The consensus was that we were all eager to ride and meet our mounts for the day.

By 9:00 AM, I was aboard Marshal, a handsome black gelding with noble carriage, a lovely forward stride, and the will and power to jump anything put in his path. Massive muscles rippled beneath his glossy coat damp from the drizzle. Twice the size of my sweet little mare at home, he set a brisk pace and was so sensitive that the mere touch of my calf on his side sent him sailing forward.

Terry leaned into the wind whipping in off the sea as she strode energetically across the pasture to where Marshal and I awaited. She paid no heed to the raindrops on her face as she looked up at me with blue eyes gleaming with good humor. My stomach roiled with nervous flutters in her presence.

Once a winning Grand Prix jumper, Terry had become a trainer with her feet firmly on the ground after suffering a spinal injury when her mare crashed into a fence. I tried to ignore the chilly rainsqualls splattering on my shoulders as she began to bark out commands.

"Sit up straight. Don't hold the reins with a death grip. Let him move forward. He knows his job."

I felt overmatched and distracted. Terry's Dalmatian repeatedly darted between Marshal's legs throughout the lesson. As the lesson progressed, I fought back tears of frustration. I could not afford to lose my concentration. Terry talked me over a couple of combination jumps in the confines of the arena and then decided we were ready for the open pasture.

I sent up a prayer, gave Marshal plenty of room with the reins, and concentrated on keeping my heels down to maintain a balanced steady position that didn't interfere with his movement. He easily cleared the four-foot fences separating pastures slick with wet grass. I feared Terry would turn me back if she discerned that my only jumping experience was in the safe confines of a sandy arena. Twice we jumped over a blur of black and white when the Dalmatian bolted in front of the fence just before Marshal's takeoff. Terry, the Dalmatian, and Marshal were all used to such antics, but I was near hysterical titters by the time the lesson ended.

Terry patted me solidly on the thigh. "Riding is 90 percent mental," she said. "You have to have a bit of the 'killer instinct' if you want to jump."

I was devastated when she told me that I would be going on a "cushy" trail ride with the seniors from America that afternoon. I didn't travel 6,000 miles from California to be shunted off on a nose-to-tail walk for the day. I ached to be on the cross-country course stretched out before me. In spite of immense respect for Terry, I couldn't accept her verdict.

After lunch, I approached Paula, the young woman in charge of dispatching the horses. I told her I was to go with the group that would be jumping that afternoon. She went into the office to check her roster, returned, and simply said, "You'll be on Ballymerrigan. Ken will be your guide." Perseverance had paid off.

Ballymerrigan was a fine chestnut hunter who didn't have the presence of Marshal but proved a much more manageable ride. Soon, I was headed for the broad sand beach below the stable with fifteen other students. Within moments, we were pounding down hard-packed sand, posse style, and Ricko, my Italian counterpart, was singing something that sounded like an aria at the top of his lungs. I crashed through low rolling surf in the lead, yelping "Ye-has" and yelling "Charge" along the way. It all felt even more daring, knowing I was a stowaway on the ride.

We made a sharp right turn that took us into the sand dunes, and the trail climbed steadily upward through billowing pampas grass, sprinkled liberally with yellow daisies. Our intrepid caravan moved higher and higher until we reached a bluff overlooking the sea.

The day turned soft, humid, with the sun painting a golden path on the water. A rainbow arced over the tiny town of Bundoran. We had everything but Hosannas from the heavens. I felt quite lighthearted until Ken stopped and pointed over the precipice to indicate that what goes up must come down. Ricko was visibly shaken at the prospect of going over the lip of the bluff and refused to go. For a split second I feared I had gotten myself into something a bit over my head. I could hardly let anyone know my dilemma, so I popped over the seventy-foot drop and sat back as instructed. Ballymerrigan sashayed through the powdery sand, sliding his hindquarters in a

Ginger

masterful mambo step to the bottom of the dune, unbelievably making me appear every bit the master. A trembling Ricko followed my lead, and we proceeded to lower ground where Ken turned abruptly, pointed to the trail, and yelled, "Keep your toes in."

That would be easy, I thought, as we started to gallop single file along a trail that quickly became a narrow four-foot groove cut into the sand. It was gouged with gaping holes made by burrowing bunnies. As the horses barreled through the trench, I realized one trip-up would cause an accident worse than a twenty-car pile-up on the Hollywood Freeway. My toes were glued to the belly of my horse to prevent my lower appendages from being ripped from their sockets. By the time we left the dunes and headed for the cross-country course, my blood was up!

Ken led the group back to the stable, where I was given one last chance to call it off. My common sense told me to turn back, but my heart would not let me go. The group dwindled to Ken, the couple from Dublin, and me.

"I've never jumped a course outside of an arena," I confessed to Ken.

The local couple exchanged a glance that told me they wished the "weeny" American was not along. The Irish are gutsy, accomplished riders and have little patience for the novice. I suspect they are put off by the droves of tourists that tire their horses and clutter their riding schools in August.

"Not to worry—follow the leader, and don't get in the way of your horse," Ken said.

His approach to jumping was simple. Use the stick liberally enough to generate enough steam that your horse has no choice but to go forward. Your job is to stay with that forward motion. He referred to the neck strap as the "Be-Jesus strap." We were advised to just hold on to that strap and yell "Be-Jesus!" in emergencies.

"Well, off you go, then," Ken shouted, pointing his stick towards the jumps. Off I went; sailing over everything in sight.

When I stopped to ask Ken how I was doing, he asked, "Are you still in the saddle?" If I could reply "Yes!" I was doing great! My heart pounded outside my rib cage as I approached a massive set of logs. This four-foot-high jump confirmed what I suspected. The higher the fence, the greater the jumping arc from your horse (creating more air time to settle into your position) and the easier it is!

We slowed for an in-and-out jump that was, in fact, made up of two four-foot fences sandwiching a dirt road. Heather, the more accomplished of our trio, went boldly forth. Her horse took the first jump easily with one great stride between the fences, and another powerful thrust over the second fence that delivered her safely into the next pasture. Sean was next, but his horse stopped short, digging her front hooves into the ground, sucking back and ducking her head, nearly tossing him off of her and into the fence.

"Circle 'round again," came from Ken. "Sit back! Give her plenty of leg and the stick just before takeoff."

Sean circled about in a slow canter and approached again. His face flushed magenta when the horse turned and ran out for a second time. Next time around, Ken stood near the fence and gave Sean's horse a liberal smack on the rump that sent her flying. It was a rough go. The horse lurched over the fence, stumbled on the stride, and nearly plowed into the rail on the way out. They landed with an unseemly thud, but Sean stayed in the saddle by grabbing a hold of the mare's neck with both arms.

"Okay, Bally American. It's your turn," Ken said.

I knew I couldn't be an inert passenger on this one. I circled about and came to the combination with a fierce determination not to die, squeezing Ballymerrigan firmly with my legs, holding his head straight to the gate, and aiming between his ears for the other side. On a single stride out he let fly, and I could feel his powerful haunches bunch and lift us over, then a springing stride through the middle, and a gallant out.

I felt strong, powerful, and high. It was grand!

Ken then led us over five log jumps at a gallop. We pulled up to navigate a coffin ditch that opened to a second solid-log fence. Heather went bravely over the gaping three-foot hole, up the dirt mound in front of it, and over the spread oxer at the end. Sean declined.

My confidence bolstered and my trust in Ballymerrigan confirmed, I approached the combination with a hammering heart and the faith that we would successfully reach the other side. I sailed cleanly over the coffin ditch, smoothly over the oxer, and then went on to fly over those rock walls facing into the fierce west wind. I landed on slick green grass, in a cool mist that magically calms the body while it fires the mind. When Sean asked me if I'd like to share a pint with them at the pub at the end of the day, I said, "Nothing could please me more."

The next day under Terry's firm guidance, I rode Marshal over all the jumps I did the day before on Ballymerrigan. I was settled, calm, and able to slip into sync with Marshal's gigantic stride. We worked for two hours over the entire course. He jumped magnificently for me.

The Irish believe in giving a horse its head, and apparently this philosophy extends to people as well. I discovered that before Paula let me ride, she had informed Terry that I was taking desperate measures. I shall be forever grateful that Terry's response to my misdemeanor was, "Well, she can jump, but put her on Ballymerrigan. He will sort things out for her."

Now, back at my cushy California barn, my sweet gray mare has grown too old to fly, and so have I. On wildflower walks through sage meadows I watch butterflies lift off of orange poppies and dream of Marshal, wet with a gentle Irish mist, and wilder days gone by. My mare is not Ballymerrigan, nor is she able to sail over ditches and touch the sky. She is more like a comfortable pair of slippers that I slip on at the end of the day.

We stop at the bluff that overlooks Happy Valley. She seems to enjoy the view, swinging her head side to side to take it all in. I spread arms to the sun and give thanks that I was able to jump a bold Irish Hunter in the wild west of Ireland before I was done.

Rearranging the Furniture

Emily Alexander Strong

 I fished two pairs of boots out of the cardboard box that I'd labeled "riding stuff" in tell-tale fourteen-year-old handwriting—the *i*'s dotted with hearts. My show boots, with prim Victorian laces still tied in bows, were stuffed with yellowing rolls of newspaper dated August 1982. The elegant custom-stitched black leather was dry but clean. In contrast, my paddock boots were cracked and caked in mud with hints of manure between the heel and toe. Grabbing the paddock boots, I crammed my feet in them like one of Cinderella's ugly stepsisters with the glass slippers. I caught my reflection in the closet-door mirror—an exhausted, anxious, thirty-eight-year-old mother of two in a worn blue robe and dirty paddock boots. Any other time the image would have tickled me, but this January morning, after another night of insomnia, I saw a desperate woman.

I ignored the decades-old dirt sloughing off on my new wool carpet as I slumped down the stairs. I splayed the phonebook on the kitchen table and slid a finger down the list of barns and riding instructors. I couldn't remember the names acquaintances had given me when I'd asked for suggestions. *More evidence of my inadequacy,* I thought. *I could call Sarah again, but she's getting tired of my culls. I can hear it in her voice.* I stopped on a tasteful barn logo and dialed the number.

"Birch Hill Farm," a voice answered. I had expected an answering machine and had planned to hang up. I hadn't made the decision to return to riding—I wasn't making any decisions these days—only considering the idea. Still, I forced a response. "I'm a rider. Well, I used to be. Do you teach lessons?"

Three days later, I navigated my Volvo down country roads, following the directions I had scrawled on a notepad with my daughter's orange crayon. As my tires crunched the gravel drive, a row of blanketed horses—a bay, a chestnut, and a fuzzy black pony—turned their heads in my direction. At the barn of my childhood, January meant horses were adorned in new blankets and halters that had been unwrapped by eager girls on Christmas Day. These blankets were crusted with dirt and manure. Nonetheless, from the moment I cracked the door, the earthy smell of damp straw, steaming manure, and hard-working horses alighted my past. I was bombarded with images of my former self: a girl who sketched horses on the margins of school papers, read the entire *Black Stallion* series (how I had a crush on Alec, the redhead who trained the stallion!), and begged, constantly, for my own horse. By my ninth birthday, my parents conceded, buying me "Alexander's Ragtime," or "Rags." For the next six years, horses consumed my every moment. On long summer days I'd take group lessons before the heat of the day with my closest friends. In winter I'd rush through homework on the school bus, fly into riding attire in our stationwagon, and take a lesson in the frosty arena until dinnertime.

As the years progressed, I spent summers touring the Midwest to compete in shows, but I was only marginally successful. After Rags, I owned a series of stubborn ponies that didn't compare to the ponies of my competitors—girls who were often flown to shows in their father's private jets. Occasionally, all the hours of training paid off, and I'd be called first in the confirmation line. I remember passing the professionally groomed and braided ponies, beaming with hard-earned pride.

Yet my fondest memories weren't of the show ring but of the Illinois countryside, where I'd ride with my friend Kevin. We would gallop Kevin's ponies through the neighboring cornfields until we reached a favorite pond. Now, twenty-six years later, I stood with pinched toes, recalling the bliss of a horse's body swimming under me as I held on to the mane and felt the water glide around us.

Marla, my new instructor, rounded the corner, interrupting my daydream. She wore britches and boots, a barn coat, hip sunglasses, and a trendy corduroy hat over her platinum blond hair. After brief

Levi

introductions she said, "You'll ride Levi. I'll show you where he is." I followed Marla's confident strides to the third stall on the left, home to a large, handsome bay. My chest pulsed with anticipation as I clipped the lead rope onto his halter and cupped his baby-bottom-soft nose. I led him to the crossties where Marla walked me through grooming and tacking him up. I reached for a currycomb.

"No, not that one, the black one," Marla corrected.

I loosened the dirt in even, circular swirls and brushed away the dirt with a bristle brush. I picked his hooves, and placed the saddle pad and saddle on his back.

"Further up and off his withers," Marla barked.

I was getting to that. I sighed. Marla had a protocol for every process, which she shared in condescending detail.

"When you put the reins over his head, don't do it straight on like that; let him see you from the side."

Though I needed the refresher, Marla was bruising my already black-and-blue ego. With unsure hands, I fumbled over the hole in Levi's chinstrap under Marla's critical eye. I hoped Marla would recognize my ability when I got on, but those expectations dissolved immediately. I had agreed to try dressage at Marla's request, but the stirrup length felt way too long. I couldn't even extend weight into my heel—a fundamental element of my hunter/jumper training. Marla's school saddle was stiff, and the girth buckle protruded into my calf. Levi and I were strangers fumbling through an uncomfortable initiation. If it had been a blind date, neither one of us would have wanted to meet a second time.

Driving home I seriously wondered: *Should I start riding again?* My hopes were dashed that returning to something I excelled at would free me from this monthlong episode of anxiety and depression. This wasn't the first time anxiety had hijacked my happy life. Like a dog that collapses with an exhaled "humph" in his corner of the room, my thoughts had settled into a worn bed made with scraps from my I'm-not-good-enough life script. The littlest things ate me up inside. I'd walk around my house, overwhelmed by the imperfection of it all. The photos propped against the wall and still not hung, the chaos of the girls' bookshelf, spilling books out onto the floor. In an optimistic moment, I had organized a charity program for Christmas, but now I felt responsible for a happy December 25 of fifteen impoverished families. I felt myself drowning and I didn't know why.

I was equally stressed about our family's holiday. My husband, Eric, and I feuded over how much was appropriate to buy our girls. At four in the morning, Eric, sensing I was awake, would stagger into the living room to find me curled up in a blanket, my body coursing with adrenaline over whether I had purchased the right American Girl Dolls. Some nights, my body felt so electrified, I'd do yoga in my dark living room just to move the energy through my body. If I could have run in the darkness outside, I would have, racing through rainy streets like a lunatic, in a blue robe and running shoes, just to flee the terrible feeling inside me. I tried so hard to fight it, but my family history of depression, a gray winter, and an undiagnosed condition of hypothyroidism had caught up with me, suffocating my efforts to hold on to a healthy mindset. The light of the day usually reduced the full boil of anxiety to a simmer, but on many days I felt like a gerbil cornered by a cat. I was awed by others' self-assurance, and it seemed everyone but me possessed the secret code to creating a happy life.

Still, that following Thursday, after dropping my kids off at school, I was lured out to the barn by the hope of getting another glimpse of my confident and fun-loving self. Even if I learned nothing about riding from Marla, that feeling was worth the check I'd write her. Marla was busy around the barn, so I tacked Levi up myself. I drank his warm strength like secret swigs from a flask. My heart—deadened lately by the stampede of depressing thoughts—fluttered. Yet my second lesson was as brutal as my first.

"Stop riding like Frankenstein!" Marla hollered. "Your arms are straight at the elbow and you're giving the horse his mouth. You need to round that horse up, ask him to drop his head and collect his stride." What Marla couldn't have known is that my hands were numb from stress—a condition seen in anxiety disorders. She wanted me to feel Levi's mouth and ask him to loosen his jaw, yet I couldn't feel my own arms beyond my elbows. "I'm sorry!" I wanted to tell Levi. "You're looking for my guidance but I can't even guide my own life." Marla instructed me to change my leg position too.

"Stop gripping with your knees!" she blasted.

I had always prided myself on my vice-grip hold on a horse's sides. Once, when my father gave me a piggyback ride up the stairs for bed, he feigned gasping for air as I nearly cracked his ribs. Now, Marla informed me, my goal was to drape my leg and lift the horse from underneath with taps of my heel.

"Riding shouldn't take so much effort," she warned as sweat trickled down the small of my back from the exertion of cantering for less than a minute. It occurred to me that trying too hard to be perfect, whether in equitation or in life in general, wasn't serving me well. In life, the goal of perfection had trapped me in a vicious obsession about what I was missing. While riding, I was stiff and ineffective, trying to hold a pretty position when I should have been in dynamic communication with Levi.

"We need to get rid of your old habits—rearrange the furniture," Marla announced. *If she only knew how much rearranging I have to do*, I thought. I cringed to think of the dust bunnies that would be revealed.

By week three, I came out to the barn early to sit on my car's tailgate and drink in the barn atmosphere. While tying my bootlaces, a memory of asinine twelve-year-old behavior appeared like a genie from a bottle. I once put the tail of Smokey, the dappled gray Thoroughbred I graduated to after ponies, over my hair, and then put my hard hat on. It looked like I wore a wig of long, straight gray hair. My friend Laura and I laughed so hard that we were busted by my strict trainer, Tommy, who stormed over, furious that I would actually attach myself to the rear end of a horse. I smiled, and a satisfying tang of bittersweet recklessness flittered across my tongue. I felt bold and resilient. I wanted that girl back for good.

I hopped off the tailgate and went to get Levi. He was in his stall with his head held high and his ears dancing with danger. "It's all right, boy," I purred, but when I led him out of his stall he spooked like he'd touched a live wire. I held tight as he pulled back from the lead rope, his eyes wild with panic. My stomach cartwheeled and my heart raced. Within a few minutes we'd both regained our composure, but while I tacked Levi up, his ears continued to dance and flicker. Marla waltzed in, eyeing the situation.

"You know, they're all spooked right now—a cougar or bear came pretty close last night. They do that. It happens," she said.

As I rode Levi that morning I thought about how every living thing gets rattled from time to time; it was universal if you had a beating heart. What Levi needed was reassurance. I convinced him to listen to me rather than every rustle of red-winged black birds from the nearby pond. When his body tensed beneath me, I regained his attention with a gentle pulsing from one hand to another, communicating, "Keep your mind on me. Don't let your imagination run away with you." Levi responded, lowering his head and collecting his stride. It was a rewarding experience, like distracting an upset child with a creative diversion. My cursed sensitivity served me as I empathized with Levi's emotions. I realized that Levi and I had a lot in common: We were both strong and capable but often scared of our own damn shadows. I could lure myself back, too, following the same gentle message: "Keep your mind on what is real and present, not on the ghosts lurking in the cattails."

After my lesson, I lingered in Levi's stall. As he slurped from his bucket, I put my ear to his neck and marveled at the sound of water rolling down his throat. I drove home with a dumb grin on my face, singing to an oldie on the radio, like a girl in love. I approached my house with all its imperfections. Weeds sprouted between the stones leading to my front door. Inside, books would still spill from the bookshelf and pictures remained against the wall. And I cared a little less.

Arriving for my next lesson, I entered Levi's stall. "How's my handsome boy this morning?" I asked, fastening the halter strap. I led him to the crossties and groomed him, noticing his coat felt extra silky. When his body glittered in the light, I thought I must have been seeing things. Yet the more I brushed, the more sparkles I saw. Marla rounded the corner and I worked up the courage to ask her, "Am I crazy or is Levi . . . sparkling?" She laughed and said that the fourteen-year-old girl who leased Levi had given him a bath yesterday, finishing him off with a sprinkling of glitter.

"She says he's her enchanted prince."

For all he had taught me about myself, Levi was my enchanted prince too. As I rode that morning, I was amused by the spunky kid who sprinkled her horse with glitter, surprised only that I hadn't done it when I was fourteen. Levi and I hit our stride, sharing roles of teacher and student, listening to and responding to one another. I risked not looking perfect. Marla tossed me a compliment or two.

The following week my mother, visiting from Chicago, came to watch me ride. She had been a loyal fan during the horseshow years, watching every round with a mother's forgiving eye. After the lesson, she said, "Em, for years I could pick you out of a crowd by your style on a horse. Now you look completely different!"

I had lugged armchairs and slid ottomans. I had tested new arrangements—my leg position, my seat, the new bend in my elbows. In my life I tried a new look too—lightness about my house, my kids, myself. In both cases, stepping back, I liked what I saw.

My mom seemed to like what she saw, too. As we drove off, the car tires spewing gravel behind us, she smiled at me—her audacious little girl. It was a knowing smile, the kind mothers and daughters, or horses and trusted riders, exchange. I knew my world was rotating on a different axis now, and I liked the sensation of moving with it.

"We've got an errand to do," I told her. It was time I bought myself some paddock boots in the right size.

Riding Lessons

Janice Newton

 I disappear a lot lately, although never far away from home or for very long. Usually it's just down the road, jogging for the rest of the afternoon, or across town to a Monday-evening yoga class.

I started horseback riding lessons on Thursday nights and even joined a church so I had someplace to be every Sunday morning. The truth is, I go because I can't fix what is happening at home with Henry.

Getting away gives me the distraction and distance I need to forget my problems; it was never intended to solve them.

I signed up for a horseback-riding workshop a few weeks back; their brochure caught my eye: *"We will teach you to communicate in a body language the horse will understand and respond to with trust and respect."* The approach sounded different from my riding lessons at Forest Hill Riding Academy with Stella, an elegant gray Arabian with problems, too.

Recently, I had begun to see there was more to riding than just getting the proper placement of my leg behind the girth or giving a slight slip of my hip to the right to ask for a turn to the left. The workshop was sounding more and more intriguing and hopeful: *"A personal relationship with a horse can help you gain a deeper understanding of yourself, increase your confidence, and demonstrate the value of appropriate assertiveness."*

It is rare to find a school horse that hasn't been turned stubborn or lazy from too many botched commands by beginning riders. Stella, I learned, is different. She moves easily from walk through the canter, has had excellent early training, and clearly wants to please. The problem comes when the lesson is over.

Cooling down at crossties, Stella gets fretful and prances nervously in place whenever I remove her saddle. She tosses her head, eyes darting back, and bolts suddenly for her stall, dragging me along if I don't remember to jump out of her way. This anxiety started when her previous owners rationed feed so she wouldn't gain weight and stress an injured leg even more. It seems she developed the feeling there was never going to be enough to eat.

Forest Hill Riding Academy instructors consider her unsafe, especially to young riders, and they plan to sell her. They are, however, curious about the workshop and promise to give me a chance to work with her if I am willing to spend the time. I am willing to do anything to keep my horse.

Henry is always angry when I leave, but this morning his face is unusually red and his lips have disappeared into a thin, rigid line. He complains spitefully as I gather up my bags.

"You're away enough all week; why do you have to be gone an entire weekend?" He seems more fearful than angry this time, and it looks like he might even reach out and touch me. Instead he pulls back. I do the same and walk out the door.

The two-lane road to the workshop at Springfield Stables has me meandering through small towns and fishing resorts recently deserted, as summer has come to an end. It would take me some 250 miles away to the eastern part of the state. I like this rustic and warmer side of Oregon with sagebrush and winds that blow little circles of red rim dust—horse country. I catch sparkling reflections of a creek swelling from recent fall rains, flowing in and out of view along a roadside forest. I watch for my favorite café where I stop for its trademark Blackberry café latte. I enjoy the solitude.

If Henry were along, he would remind me time and again how the workshop is too expensive, and we would likely disagree on where to stop for lunch. We can't seem to talk about anything for more than a couple of sentences. Our interactions turn defensive, and then we refuse to speak to each other for days. Henry absorbs himself in reading a book or doing projects around the house, passing by me from one room to another without even looking at me. We're like two ghosts unable to touch even if we wanted to. Last night, we argued about whether or not to close the bedroom window. I love the fresh air, but it makes him too cold to sleep. There's no compromise.

I pull up to the stables still thinking about how I had to sleep in the guest room again last night to avoid a fight. I am a little early and stay in the car for a while. The time will do me good to settle down and get focused.

Four or five women drive up and head for the tack room where we are all to meet. They look like they might know a thing or two about riding, taking long, strong strides, bodies erect, wearing jeans and boots that are worn and dusty, and holding riding gloves in one hand and helmets in the other. I follow the last one in and sit near the door in a small circle of chairs.

"Hi, everyone. Thanks for coming. I'm Claudia," the instructor begins.

She is small, almost delicate, with blond spiked hair, wearing light-colored jodhpurs and shiny black boots, professional looking. She looks like she might be an expert at this "horse whispering," and I decide to trust her. I dig in and commit. At least I think I have.

"I know you're eager to start working with the horses, but let's talk about you first. Tell me why you're here."

Not a fan of what sounds "touchy-feely," I slink down hoping to be last to talk or, better yet, ignored as the woman next to me introduces herself.

"I'm Rachel and I ride to relax." Then she adds something about working too much and needing a break from her family.

The next woman is recently divorced and feels that getting back to her love of riding is exactly what she needs. Everyone talks about their family, life's little disappointments, and why they ride horses; some even tell of dreams not yet forgotten. I stop listening. Suddenly, I am not interested in their problems. I have my own to solve.

Henry and I weren't always like this, but somewhere between kids and jobs we lost track of each other. Sometimes I look over at him driving the car or asleep next to me and I can remember what it's like to love him: how he straightens his dark curly hair every morning for work because he thinks it is more professional; how he bounces up and down on the tips of his toes when he gets excited about something—one of the few times he is playful and out of control. His best trait is how he listens to people, better than anyone I know; he understands their point of view and can figure out the real reasons behind why they are so angry or happy. He just doesn't do it with me anymore.

When it is my turn to talk, I want to be quick. "I'm married, kids in college, and happy with my work."

"Tell us why you're here, Janice," Claudia says, catching me off guard.

"I don't know." I hesitate, feeling singled out. "I like horses. Some people like dogs, some people like cats, I like . . . "

"What else?" Claudia interrupts me. "Why else are you here?"

I look up at her, starting to fidget with my hands, searching for an answer beyond what I have already tossed out. I didn't expect to be questioned like this. I hoped to learn, not share.

I thought about shocking them all and telling about when I learned overnight affairs were a routine part of my husband's frequent business trips, the real reason we fight all the time now. That would stop the questions cold.

"I'm not sure what you want from me," I say, distractedly recalling how Henry tried to explain it all away: "We spend endless hours in tedious meetings, go back to the hotel for a celebratory dinner and drinks, and then out to night clubs to decompress. Things just happened, Jenna. It doesn't mean anything." He promised never again and apologized every day, but I was finding the road back to intimacy almost impossible.

I take a deep breath to help me forget and say: "I'm having trouble with my horse. I feel distant. I want to feel closer, more intimate, you know what I mean?"

I see a dozen horses wandering around in the large covered arena adjacent to the tack room, with their heads down; sometimes they nuzzle each other and, at one time or another, gaze longingly toward the pasture outside. The group seems to regard my problems as insignificant compared to theirs, and we make our way to the arena.

The horses look up when we come in and then begin their slow amble toward us.

"I want you to pick a horse to work with," Claudia instructs. "This is very subtle, but trust your intuitions to connect with one; then bring him outside and we'll start the exercises." She points over to the round pen where we will go next.

"And don't be surprised if a horse comes up to you first," she remembers to say. "Horses have great instincts; they know you by how you carry yourself and your gestures, so be deliberate and clear in your movements around them and they'll love you for it. For some of you, this is the hardest part of the class." She seems to have her eyes on me.

I grab one of the halters hanging on the nearby wall and start into the arena. I hold it up and shake it, clanging the buckles together so the horses will look up and come over to me. They dart to the four corners of the arena.

"Why do you think horses bolt like that?" Claudia asks, striding toward me.

"You said to go get a horse. This is how we round up horses at Forest Hill Riding Academy."

"This next time, Jenna, try just standing still and feeling what is going on around you; discover what is unique about each horse when you look at them. *Then* move toward one."

It sounds easy enough, but in the end, I wind up alone with a few horses still sniffing around. One in particular catches my eye. His name, interestingly enough, is Casanova.

Casanova hovers at the gate, preferring to be out with the rest of the herd. He looks like a mix of Morgan and Thoroughbred, which I decide makes him dependable yet energetic enough to be a fun ride. I like his dark brown coloring and black mane, and for a brief moment, I imagine what it's like to ride him. That's when he lifts his head slightly and looks at me. A match is made.

As I leave the arena Claudia motions me into the round pen. I lead Casanova past the others, through the gate, relieved to be out of the arena and on to the next step. I relax as the warm afternoon wind starts to pick up, blowing my hair into my eyes and the dust up around my boots. I take off my jacket and toss it over the fence, then look around for Claudia.

"What do I do now?" I ask.

"Where's your horse, Jenna?"

I realize I've let him wander, distracted again, and see him at the opposite end of the pen nibbling a clump of grass.

I start toward him, reaching out to stroke his neck, something that seemed to work back in the arena. Yet he keeps nibbling the grass.

"Jenna," Claudia shouts. "He is ignoring you. You have to be more interesting to Cass than that patch of grass he's nibbling at." I think she is insulting and far from helpful.

I throw up my hands and shout back, "I don't know what to do. Am I supposed to do a song and dance to get him to notice me? There's not even a rope out here to help me."

I resolve to leave at the break, until Claudia calls me over to one side of the pen, away from others. "Tell me why you ride, Jenna," she asks patiently.

"What's that have to do with anything?" I demand, starting to actually agree with Henry that this is hardly worth my time or money.

"Jenna, relax. These questions just help me to understand you better." She speaks firmly but also kindly and encouragingly now.

Cassanova

"Okay. Okay." I try to explain but feel like I am beginning to whine and repeat myself. I offer up lamely, "I ride because I love horses."

"Think back to when you first started riding. Why did you ride then?"

I remember being twelve years old, riding Shetland ponies with my best friend.

"I rode bareback with my friend Lindy. It was fun, riding without reins through the woods. I fell off when a tree branch would get in the way, but I got right back on. I was fearless." I started laughing as more memories rolled by.

"Why did you start riding again?" Claudia continues.

"Maybe I missed that freedom and fun," I answer spontaneously, saying the first thing that comes to mind.

"What else was going on in your life?"

"I don't know; I was probably overworked or something. It might have been when Henry and I started fighting. I thought our marriage was over and I wanted to do something that made me feel better."

"How do you feel right now?" Claudia asked.

"I don't know," I said. But deep down, I knew I was finally being honest and saying how I felt.

"Where is your horse, Jenna?"

I turn to find Cass standing next to me. It is almost magical.

"Don't lose who you are now," Claudia cautions. "Stay present and let Cass know what you want from him by the strength of your intentions."

"What does that mean?" I almost say aloud. Why would a horse care if my husband and I are fighting, or if I need to relive childhood memories?

I decide it is all too confusing and glance at my watch, hoping the session is almost over. Yet as if hearing my thoughts, Claudia says, "All Cass cares about is that you are fully present for him. It's just heredity, Jenna. Horses used to be prey animals; they still have that fear, so they look for a strong leader, someone to guide and protect them. And right now that's you."

Standing beside Cass, I try to clear out all thoughts that aren't about him and then start walking around the pen. He ignores me, so I go back to scratch him high on his forehead where I noticed other horses have groomed each other. He bumps up against me as though he likes it and I let him lean his body into mine. When I step forward again, I feel responsible for his safety and intend to be clear and focused in guiding him. Cass follows. When I stop, Cass stops. I am overwhelmed by how this is so hard and so simple at the same time.

I cross over through the center of the pen with him close at my side. I walk faster and then break into a run. He keeps the pace. When I stop again and turn to face him, he stops, too, his ears forward, waiting for my next move.

For the rest of the weekend, I guide Cass through turns, circles, and jumps, sometimes running full speed and eventually laughing as I sprint down the center of the arena, like I am twelve again.

Sometimes I hear Claudia shout out, "Where are you now, Jenna?" or "What do you want, Jenna?" And I notice my mind is wandering, sometimes only slightly to watch other students or to think about problems at home that distract me. When I return to Cass 100 percent, he returns to me.

I drive straight to Forest Hill Riding Academy after the workshop, all my newfound wisdom spinning around in my head. The lessons were so subtle, I am actually afraid I will forget them if I don't use them right away.

Before saddling Stella, I walk around the arena with her, clear about when I want to walk or run, jump or stop. I don't remember her looking at me like she does now, interested in what I want. She actually stands quietly while I mount her and even looks back as if to ask me if everything's alright. I realize the more focused I am riding around the arena, the less effort I need. I begin to understand how some people can ride without reins or saddle, just intention and subtle body moves.

When its time for cooling down and removing the saddle, I don't focus on the fact that this is when she usually bolts; instead I want to show Stella when it is time to move quietly forward toward her stall. Even when we step inside with fresh oats in the bin, she waits, ears forward, until I remove her halter and step out.

"Good job, Stella," I say and quietly move away, all the time wanting to throw my arms around her neck and then jump and yell "Yahoo," running up and down the aisles outside her stall. Stella has responded to my new confidence and guidance, and I instantly know Forest Hill Riding Academy will keep her.

At home, I find Henry upstairs in the bedroom changing from work. He doesn't greet me. Instead, he says, "You take the garbage out this time. I worked hard all day and I'm tired." Then he lies down on the bed. Momentarily, I am mystified.

We always fight over whose turn it is to take the garbage can and recycling bins to the curb. Then the next day we fight about who will bring them back in. Sometimes the stand-off lasts so long we hear our neighbors rolling the cans back down the driveway for us.

"I'm tired too," I say in quick response. "Besides, I always take the garbage out. Why can't you do it just this once?"

My body has become rigid and my voice sounds angry and unfamiliar. I know I am heading backward.

Henry covers his face with his hands. "I don't know what you want from me any more. What do you want, Jenna? Just tell me what you want from me."

"I don't want anything from you," I shout, tossing my gym bag on the bed, deciding to escape to my yoga class. I start out the door, until the memory of Claudia shouting across the arena comes to me, "What do you want? What do you want?" And then I turn back toward Henry.

"I know what I want," I whisper, thinking how difficult it will be to risk saying what I want. I take one step toward Henry. It is as if he can feel me move. He drops his hands down to look at me.

"What do you want?" he repeats, softer and uncertain.

"I know what I want," I say again. "I want to feel closer, intimate with you."

Henry looks at me as though he can't understand what I am saying.

"I've been feeling so distant from you. I want to be close again. I want it more than anything," I say.

Henry is up and off the bed moving toward me before I can say another word. He reaches out as if he wants to touch my face, so I step closer, and I lean into his arms. I decide to trust that everything will work out fine.

We sit there, on the edge of our bed, the same way we have a thousand times before. We listen to the sounds of each other's heart beating, and we wait patiently for each other to offer up our wordless intentions. When we do, I think that I have not saved just my horse but myself, and I imagine that Claudia and Casanova would be proud.

Journey of a Champion

Jacklyn Lee Lindstrom

"Mom! Shirlou's not in her stall! She's gone!"

I looked out the window and saw my thirteen-year-old son, Dave, racing up from the barn. Shirlou, my Saddlebred mare, was three weeks overdue with her first foal. Together we ran back to the barn, the open stall door hanging by one hinge.

I had just grabbed a halter to go out and start searching when Dave pointed, "There they are!"

Barely visible in the early morning mist, five horses came trooping in from the pasture, Shirlou among them and, behind her, a wobble-legged baby, so new his sorrel coat was still wet.

We herded mama and baby into the foaling stall and propped the broken door shut. The colt stood trembling, so hard he could barely stand. After treating his navel with iodine, we grabbed towels and gunnysacks and rubbed him vigorously.

"Look at his legs, Mom," Dave said. "What's the matter with him?"

The colt's legs were so crooked they rubbed together at the knees and hocks when he walked. His fetlocks sank down until they touched the ground, forcing his tiny hooves to stick straight out in front of him.

"He's just weak and cold. He'll be okay when he gets some nourishment," I said, hoping Dave couldn't detect the concern in my voice.

The foal perked up and began to bumble around the stall on his ungainly legs. Dave guided him over to Shirlou and encouraged him to suck the life-giving colostrum from her swollen udder.

"I think they'll be okay now," I said as the foal started nursing. "Let's go get some breakfast."

Dave shook his head. "I'm going to stay here a while."

My young son tried to hide his disappointment. I had promised Dave that Shirlou's foal would be his project, a colt he could raise and show. Together we had picked out the sire, Shalimar Ben, a gray Arabian stallion with an impressive performance record. For eleven months we worried and fussed. Was Shirlou too fat or too thin? Was she getting too much exercise or not enough? When Shirlou went three weeks over her due date, I was convinced that all we were pampering was a huge hay belly.

A few years earlier, my husband, Don, and I, with our two sons, had moved out of the city onto a ten-acre ranchette we named Lindonlee Farm—a place where I, born a city girl with a country heart, could at last fulfill my lifelong dream of having a horse of my own. I'd always been a horse-crazy kid. In fact, I was told my first words were not "mama, mama" but "oosie, oosie." The move to the country was my dream come true. But my dream soon became our family dream, something we all shared—a love of horses. It wasn't long before we were hooked on the inevitable—raising foals. The next step, the show ring—a total commitment in time and energy for all of us. Who could have asked for more?

Dave came back from the barn and into the kitchen. "Do you think he'll always be like that?"

"I just called the vet," I said. "He's coming out to take a look at the colt. He also said we should get them out in the sunshine."

After a quick breakfast, we went back to the barn and found the colt standing in the corner, head down, tail switching as he shifted from one hind leg to the other.

"Uh-oh. Looks like he's constipated," I said. "Hold him, and I'll get the enema kit."

Once finished, Dave turned the baby loose, and we watched to make sure he passed some meconium, the hard black marbles that come with a foal's first nursing.

"He'll be okay once the yellow pasty stuff comes out," I said, trying to sound convincing. "Now, let's get them outside."

Dave haltered Shirlou and led her out of the stall. When the colt didn't follow, Shirlou swung around, whinnying and pawing. Hearing his mother's distress call, the colt dashed around the stall. I finally caught him and clamped one arm around his chest and the other around his butt, wrestling him out the door.

"His legs aren't weak now," I hollered to my son.

Shirlou quieted down and Dave led her out into the paddock. I followed, shoving the colt behind her. It was then we discovered the "yellow pasty stuff" had indeed come out and was mashed all over the baby's tail, all over his rear, and all over me.

"Hey, Mom," Dave called out, "Guess *you* don't need an enema."

That evening we trooped down to the barn so Don could see the new foal.

"What about his legs?" Don asked.

I told him the vet had come out, and he wanted us to wait a week or two. If the colt wasn't any better by then, we were to call him.

"I'm trying to think of a name for him," Dave, the ever-optimist, said. "How about Red Charger, or Copper King, or . . ."

"How about Yellow Butt," I offered.

The name finally settled on was Bendito––Little Ben––for no other reason than it seemed to suit him.

By week one, Little Ben no longer sank down at every step. By month one, he exhibited his trademark, an extended trot that looked like he was floating three feet above the ground. So brilliant a mover, he caused drivers along the road to stop and stare.

"Look at him, Mom," Dave exclaimed. "Sahib can't move like that."

Sahib, my pleasure mare's bay colt, had been a thorn in Dave's side ever since he was foaled. Sahib, with his chiseled head and wide-set eyes, always drew the approving looks when the two colts were brought out for inspection. When they shed their baby fuzz, Sahib turned a glossy mahogany bay. Ben ended up with a wooly red mane and a washed-out lavender coat that looked like he'd been left out in the rain. When cold weather came, Sahib turned into a fuzzy teddy bear, but thick winter fur did nothing to improve the appearance of the gangly, odd-colored colt. Dave's Little Ben stood in the shadows while my Sahib drew the oohs and aahs.

In the spring, Ben shed out his heavy winter fur, and a gray horse emerged—a vast improvement over the faded lavender. His registered name was Lindonlee Bendito, his barn name was Ben, but I soon called him "that blasted horse" because of his maddening ability to get out of anything we put him in. Ben could untie ropes, open any gate not securely latched, and somehow find the loose fence boards that would give with a good push. More than once I would get the phone call, "Is that your gray horse out on the road?"

In the autumn of Ben's yearling year, I watched the lanky gray colt take a well-aimed hoof in the chest trying to prove to a disinterested mare that he was "king stud."

"Looks like it's time for an attitude adjustment," the vet told me.

"I know," I replied, "but Dave has this thing about keeping Ben a stallion. I've tried to talk him out of it, but he won't listen."

The next time the vet came out to check on one of the mares, he asked about Ben. Dave proudly brought the gray horse out for inspection.

Ben

"You've got a nice horse there," Dr. Roberts said. "What do you plan to do with him?"

I watched my son's face light up as he told of his dreams for his gray stallion, how he would train and show him, breed him to good mares and raise champion babies.

"Too bad there's no registry for colts by a cross-bred stallion," Dr. Roberts said. "You can register Ben as a Half-Arab, but you can't register his colts because he's not a pure-bred. Breeders aren't going to send you their good mares knowing they'll end up with foals they can't register, and you don't want to breed to inferior mares and have a bunch of culls bearing Ben's name. I don't think you want to shut him up in a stall and a twenty-foot pen for the rest of his life for the few mares he might breed. But he's your horse, Dave, your decision."

I nodded my head emphatically. Dave said nothing.

Every morning I'd watch Dave turn Ben out in the pasture with the bred mares, then stand at the fence as the gray colt swung into his floating trot. I knew I would say nothing. This was my son's horse. It would be his decision.

A couple of weeks later, Dave came into the kitchen. "I've decided to have Ben gelded. I don't want to keep him shut up any longer." Sending a quick "thank you" heavenward, I watched him pick up the phone, make the appointment with the veterinarian, then walk out without a word. My young son had taken a major step from a happy-go-lucky kid with a new toy toward becoming a responsible young adult making a difficult decision.

When Ben rejoined the herd as a gelding, he had lost none of his presence and style. As he grew into his two-year-old frame, his high-stepping in the pasture showed us a preview of what he was to become. He also let us know he could still be a mischievous troublemaker.

In the spring, Dave started Ben's ground training. I watched from the rail, nodding with approval as the two-year-old learned to walk, trot, and canter on the longe line. However, Ben also learned if he angled his body just so, stiffened his neck, and turned his head out, he could bolt off with Dave hanging on at the end of the line yelling, *"Whoa! Whoa!"*

I found these sessions amusing until the day Dave stomped into the house, his clothes streaked with dirt and grass stains. "He did it again, Mom. That blasted horse did it again!" He held out his hands, swollen and red from painful rope burns. "Just when I think he's doing well, he bulls his neck out and takes off, and I can't hold him."

"Why don't you call Bob Nelson?" I suggested. "That's what I do when I have a problem."

Bob Nelson was the head trainer at Rolling Hills Stables just two miles down the road from our place. When we first moved in, he had stopped by to welcome us to the area. After cups of coffee and plenty of horse talk, Bob had said, "Give me a call if you ever need a hand here."

We had taken Bob up on his offer more times than we cared to count.

Dave shot me his familiar stubborn look. "I'm *not* calling and telling Bob Nelson I can't even longe my own horse."

I'd had enough of this back and forth. "Either you call him or I will! I won't have you getting hurt because of stupid pride!"

A stubborn mother and an equally stubborn son stared each other down. Dave finally turned and picked up the phone. "Hello, Mr. Nelson? I guess I need help with my horse. He keeps busting loose when I try to longe him." Pause. "Okay, we'll bring him over."

I had just seen my young son take another difficult step along the road to manhood––the painful acknowledgement that he didn't have all the answers, and the humbling experience of having to admit it and ask for help. Things were moving along.

The next day, we loaded Ben in the trailer and drove the two miles down to Rolling Hills Stables. Ben, obviously feeling his oats, snorted and danced the whole way to the arena.

Bob turned toward me. "Remember that chain you used over Ben's nose when he was a stud?"

I nodded.

"We're going to put it on him again and attach it to the longe line." He turned toward Dave. "You have to have good hands when you work Ben with the chain, Dave, because you've got something on him that will 'bite' if you jerk him, and you only want it to bite when you want to make a point."

I stood at the rail, thanking the powers above for giving us our ranch, our horses, and Bob Nelson as our neighbor.

I watched Dave attach the chain and send Ben around in a circle.

"Now, if he tries to bolt, holler 'whoa' like you mean it, and give the line a jerk," Bob called out. "If he stops, send him around at a trot again like nothing happened. If he tries it again—and he probably will—'whoa,' then jerk. The bottom line is, if he doesn't stop when you say 'whoa,' he's going to feel it across his nose."

Dave worked Ben, and after a few whoa's and jerks, Ben stopped, looked at his young master, shook his head, then calmly trotted both ways around the circle with his long, easy stride. I felt so proud one might have thought it was *my* horse and *I* was doing the training.

That night at the supper table, Dave told me Bob Nelson made him feel like he wasn't so stupid after all and that this thing with

Ben was no big deal. My son was growing up. I thought again of the conversations Don and I had had with each other, wondering if we'd done the right thing by moving the boys out to the country just so "Mom" could have horses.

Months rolled by. Ben turned three and we sent him to Rolling Hills for six weeks of basic saddle training. When the gray horse came home, I stood at the rail, mentally riding every stride as Dave moved Ben out in a collected trot, then canter with the balance and form of a mature show horse. It had been a long time coming, but well worth the wait.

Summer flew by. I worked Sahib and Dave worked Ben, sometimes in the ring together. The lanky gray horse was muscling out and losing his gangly, not-quite-put-together look. Sahib put his head down and began to look like a proper western pleasure horse.

Then came the day we decided to take Ben and Sahib to a local fun show to get some ring experience. I rounded up an English outfit for Dave to wear, a borrowed saddle-suit coat that was too large and pants that were too short. Don didn't know it, but he "donated" a felt hat to the cause.

On show day, I rode Sahib and Dave rode Ben around the grounds, getting the green horses used to the announcer's stand, the crowds of people, and the mud puddles from the recent rain. Ben walked out like a flop-eared milk-wagon horse, showing just a casual interest in the strange new sights around him. Sahib danced and jumped at every sound. It would take a while before he would make it as a western pleasure horse for me to show.

When Dave's class was called, I gasped as Ben came through the gate in his extended trot like a locomotive in full throttle. I couldn't believe this was the same horse we had raised from a crooked-legged baby. And my son looked every bit like a seasoned saddle-seat rider.

After the rounds of walk, trot, and reverse, the announcer called, "Canter your horses." At the rail I mentally set myself up for the right lead canter: weight to the right, left leg back, left rein tight, squeeze and go. Dave gave the cue. Ben trotted—his beautiful floating trot. Dave stopped and tried again. I held my breath. Ben trotted. When the announcer finally called for the lineup, Ben pranced into the middle of the ring, neck arched, the look in his eyes saying, *Boy, this is fun.* Cantering was not in his cards this day. But there would be other days.

During the next few years, the backyard horse became a show horse, and the teenage boy who had waited so impatiently for his birth was now about to enter his first year of college. I had watched both horse and rider mature together, Ben learning to step into his gaits with balance and form, and Dave realizing that even though he had a horse that loved to perform, it was the hours of practice at home that led to trophies in the ring.

In early September, we headed to the last show of a long season—up since dawn, hauling over one hundred miles. As I had done for the past month, I refigured our points in my head. We had never been out of the ribbons, but we'd missed some of the out-of-state shows. If we could win this one, I thought we might have it made.

We pulled into the show grounds late, arriving just as the class before ours went into the ring. I hurriedly backed Ben out of the trailer and threw the saddle and bridle on him while Dave changed into his saddle suit in the trailer.

Dave's class was large; the judge, fussy. In the line-up, the judge walked down the line, stopped at each horse, and asked for the back. One by one, the horses backed the required four steps, then moved forward to stand at attention. The judge stopped in front of Ben and nodded. Dave gave the cue to back. Ben refused. Dave tried again. Ben stood as if riveted to the ground. The judge shook his head and walked away.

"Stubborn horse!" I exploded to Don as another rider came out with the trophy. "We haul over a hundred miles and Ben decides he's not going to back. He's never done that before. *We needed those points!"*

The class filed out of the ring and as soon as Ben hit the long grass, he stopped, stretched out his hind legs, and emptied his bladder. It was not "stubborn horse" that day, I realized to my chagrin. Because "the people" were late getting to the show, "the horse" had been hauled for over three hours in a cramped trailer and had not even been given time to relax.

"I knew he wasn't right," Dave said during the long ride home, "but I was so gung-ho for those points, I kept pushing him even when I could feel he was off." He stared out the window. "It won't happen again, though. When a ribbon becomes more important than the horse, I'll quit showing."

I said nothing, just sat in the truck, heavy with the realization that my son and his horse had just taught Mom a thing or two about getting her priorities straight. I learned the hard way just how easy it was to get too caught up in the chase for the ribbons.

At the Annual Awards Banquet that fall, I sat like a Nervous Nellie as one by one the winners walked up to receive their awards. At last, the call we had been waiting for: "Tri-State Champion English Pleasure Horse." An agonizing pause, then: "Lindonlee Bendito, owned and shown by David Lindstrom, Prior Lake, Minnesota."

Through suddenly blurred eyes, I watched a tall young man walk up to receive his trophy. I thought again about the journey a young boy and his odd-colored colt had taken to the championship and how much that boy, now grown up, had taught his mother.

Dave left for his first year of college soon after, and the Tri-State trophy sat in its special place on our mantel. Ben, no longer the pampered show horse, returned to the pasture, grew heavy winter fur, and once again looked like an oversized billy goat.

The following spring with Dave gone, I rode Ben at some of the local shows. I was not that good at showing park horses, but Ben knew what he was doing and we fared pretty well. I was also campaigning my western pleasure horse, Sahib, and getting two horses bathed and ready at five o'clock in the morning took more dedication than I had. I decided to concentrate on Sahib and leave Ben home in the pasture. Soon I was reminded that when Ben was idle, everybody suffered.

The phone began to ring again. "Is that your gray horse out on the road?"

As the season progressed, people asked me, "Why aren't you showing your park horse? It's a shame to let a horse like that stand in the pasture."

I'd been wrestling with those same thoughts myself. The dream of every show-horse owner is to have a horse good enough to campaign on the national circuit. We had the horse, but, alas, I knew the dream was far more expensive than we could afford. The wise thing would be to sell Ben to someone who could promote him. The next time Dave came home from college, we had a serious discussion about the gray horse's future. Dave agreed, reluctantly, if the right person were found, we should sell Ben.

When word got out that Lindonlee Bendito was for sale, we received many calls, but it was the young voice of Martha Shaw that gained our attention. I knew Martha vaguely. She followed the Arab circuit and we had seen her at the local shows. Martha said she wanted to compete in the National Arabian Association shows, and if she bought Ben she would be putting him in training with Bob Nelson at Rolling Hills Stables.

I felt good about this one. Ben couldn't be in better hands. Plus, he would be nearby so we could go see him. After checking with Dave, we settled on a price and Ben was sold.

Martha came by about a week later and announced she wanted to ride Ben cross-country over to Rolling Hills. We saddled Ben, and Martha mounted up and headed down the drive. Fifteen minutes later, I heard a knock on the door.

Martha was standing on the front porch, holding Ben by the reins. "Uh—I'm so sorry," she stammered. "He keeps wheeling around and heading back here. Do you suppose you could haul him over there for me?" *Ah Ben, you never change.*

"He's in good hands," I told myself as we made our two-mile drive down the winding road to Rolling Hills Stables. Yet it took a while to reconcile myself that when the phone rang, it wouldn't be somebody asking, "Is that your gray horse out on the road?"

At the end of the show season, I learned that Lindonlee Bendito completed his first year of national competition on the Arabian Show Circuit, winning High Point Driving Horse and High Point Park Horse under Saddle, and finished the season just four points away from his Legion of Merit.

Secretly I beamed. "You're on your way now, Ben," I said, remembering the odd-colored colt with crooked legs and my thirteen-year-old boy saying, "Just you wait, Mom; Ben's going to be a champion some day."

And I thought again of that day so many years ago when Don and I decided to move to the country where a horse-crazy mom could live out her dream—the love of horses.

Kiss and Tell?

Lynda Fenneman

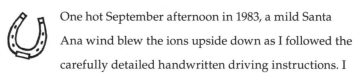 One hot September afternoon in 1983, a mild Santa
Ana wind blew the ions upside down as I followed the
carefully detailed handwritten driving instructions. I
traveled on circuitous freeways destined for a horse boarding facility,
inconveniently located in the northeastern-most part of the San
Fernando Valley, snuggled cozily in a narrow canyon gorge of the San
Gabriel foothills at the edge of the Angeles National Forest. My friend,
Denise, had recently commissioned me to paint a group portrait of
her horses for her newly wood-paneled dining-room wall. I planned
to spend the afternoon taking photographs of her seven beautiful
Arabian horses for the ambitious project.

We enjoyed a pleasant, lazy afternoon among the lush green
pastures, perfect white wooden fences, climbing roses, and the
many tall fragrant eucalyptus trees, which spread a cool blue shade.

While we fed the horses from buckets of carrots and caressed their inquisitive faces, Denise told long, elaborate genealogical histories about each horse—its name, what it meant, how Arabians came from the desert, how that one bucked her off and flipped over backward and is now considered "intractable" (but she loves it, it's sooo cute), and all about the other one. The one that bites. The one Bob gave her for her birthday, a racy little bay no one can catch without carrots and doesn't like saddles anywhere near it.

As she talked, a truck pulled up next to us, and out stepped a cute cowboy in tight, perfectly faded jeans emphasizing a cute ass and a breezy attitude. An open pack of Marlboros poked out of his spiffy new Wrangler denim shirt pocket. I didn't mind his interest in chatting and enjoyed listening to his slow Texas drawl. After awhile, he got around to the object of his visit.

"You gals wanna see my new colt? He's just up the road a piece. Pile on in my truck; there's plenty of room."

He apparently knew Denise to be the rich, skinny sucker for Arabian horses that she was, but what else did he have in mind, out here in the middle of nowhere, yet still within spitting distance of the Hollywood sign?

Throwing caution to the wind, we all three piled onto the bench seat of his truck. I slid over to the middle, next to him, with the long-handled gear shift on the floor between my legs as he swept empty beer cans and other junk right off the seat and onto the floor, on top of my feet. Squished in the middle, I jiggled back and forth happily as we took off down a dusty, bumpy dirt road while he expertly maneuvered the truck and gearshift.

He told funny stories in his thick, manly Texas drawl, making me a little reminiscent about the time when I thought I was going to marry a true Texas cowboy, though I had never met one who could actually carry on a conversation before. We wound our way up one winding canyon to yet another, until we finally came to a remote ranch, where supposedly the prize colt resided. By the time we got there, I halfway expected to see Charles Manson.

We arrived at an off-the-beaten-path, chichi rustic ranch, a relic of Old Hollywood and Cecil B. De Mille. He parked the truck in a dirt parking lot surrounded by oak trees at least a hundred years old. The brightness of the sunshine made the inside of the sparkling, new red barn appear dark and mysterious, and my nose filled with the smells of musky earth, hay, and horses. The quiet was ultra-luxurious.

My new cowboy best friend hollered out as he walked away, "He's way on down to the other end. You gals take a look around while I get me a saddle and some stuff. Be raaaight back."

I whispered to Denise, "Is this okay? Where are we? I didn't bring bread crumbs. No one knows where we are. I don't know where we are."

She gave me one of those "Don't be silly" glares. "Oh, I'm sure it's fine," she said.

But I know from experience that Denise is a little—how can I say this nicely—whimsical? She doesn't always have good sense; a girl with seven horses who can ride only one can't be said to have superior judgment abilities. I, for one, was not comforted.

Looking around at the horses improved my comfort level slightly as we wandered through their darkened stalls, smooching their velvety noses. My Cowboy came back carrying a big, old western saddle, leading a jittery little chestnut Arabian with three white socks and a wide white blaze down his nose. I could see the whites of his eyes as he skittered about, all fired up, spirited and a little out of control. His arched tail flowed and he whipped his long mane back and forth . . . eyeing the cowboy suspiciously. My Cowboy played it cool, didn't even blink over the horse's frightened antics. But he did flash us a big toothy smile and, with balletic maneuvers anyone would admire, shifted the animal so we could better observe his confirmation.

They danced, pirouetted and spun, stirred up the dust, scattered the flies, and conjured up fantasies of what it must have been like during the great wagon-trail riding days when cowboys were gods and horses were their souls. All the while my heart raced curiously. I couldn't catch my breath. My Cowboy suddenly swung the big flopping saddle in a graceful arc over the little horse's back. I was surprised to hear an audible gasp escape from my mouth, which was wide open in a kind of fan-girl awe.

Denise thought the horse was very cute, lots of spit and vinegar. A very "typey" Arabian dished face, she said. But I don't know an Arabian from a quarter horse or any other kind of horse. And yet, I was increasingly enchanted, mesmerized, in fact, by the unpredictable scene unfolding before me. I only had eyes for one, and it wasn't necessarily the Cowboy.

He talked to Denise like she might be a prospective buyer of this apparently unmanageable creature. He flashed his best Hollywood charismatic smile, showing off most of his glinting pearly whites.

"So, y'all want to ride him?"

I was surprised at the offer. I thought he would demonstrate his cowboy prowess for us and I'd be in for a show. I was even more surprised at my response considering I donned a little designer sundress, spiffy strappy sandals, and most importantly . . . I didn't really remember how to ride. It had been thirty-plus years since I'd been on the back of a horse—back when ole one-eyed Blinky was over the hill and I was barely a decade old.

"I do," I replied, apparently caught up in the moment.

In my haste, I pushed Denise aside to be first to stand at the colt's head, melting in his velvety-soft brown gaze. I kissed his soft whiskery nose. My heart pounded with curious, unexpected anticipation.

"Come on, I'll give you a leg up," my Cowboy, Andy, said in a husky voice, grabbing me with two strong hands clasped firmly around my waist. He lifted me effortlessly up off the ground and situated me for mounting the somewhat skittery horse. He aimed me toward the moving saddle. That I wasn't dressed appropriately for the occasion only added to the romanticism of the moment. I don't remember considering how much of my leg or other what-not might have been showing at the time.

I do remember that my sandaled bare feet with red freshly painted toenails didn't quite reach the long, flapping western stirrups, and I had to shift to the side for stability. It wasn't exactly a comfortable fit, but the overall sensation was pure rapture.

I had a lump in my throat the size of a giant Texas bullfrog that hurt so bad, I was afraid I was going to have to cry to let it out. And just as I expected, that little horse took off as soon as I got the one leg over the saddle, and that lump dropped straight down to my feet. I hung on to the horn, but I somehow lost track about the fact my dress was bunched up around my waist, and the long split reins dangled helplessly by my side. As we dashed around the huge sandy arena, cantering and trotting, doing whatever the horse wanted to do, I realized I was in heaven.

I barely noticed the world over the roar of my internal emotions, the ringing bells and whirlagigs, the wind in my hair, the sun on my face. I was astride an incredible creature, and it felt like a fantasy. Was it a desert mirage? Fate? Destiny? A dream?

Our cowboy in his big white Stetson and Denise with her pretty pink rhinestone visor sat perched on the fence, watching me and yet not seeing the inside of me, backlit by the golden California sun casually setting, drawing long purple shadows in the sand, creating a quintessential romantic vision of that fateful September afternoon. An image frozen in my mind when an epiphany began forming and I heard someone singing. . . .

Tevis

That's it! It all added up now; all the curious sensations could only mean one thing: I was in love! And then I felt the tears welling beneath my wide eyes and I began to cry in earnest, tears streaming down my face, barely able to breathe in the dusty, electric sunset air.

What on earth was I going to do?

How would I tell my wonderful husband I'd fallen in love? He was going to be furious, but I thought, yes, I have to do this! I was beyond redemption, beyond logic or reason. I realized I must do this. It was fated, and I, powerless to resist. Looking down at my beautiful Arabian, I realized the attraction was obviously mutual.

Denise, who had no earthly idea what was really going on inside my heart, said from the fence, "You guys look good together! You already look like an 'item.'"

I heard my own voice and couldn't believe it. "Can't you see what a pickle I'm in? I'm sunk. Done for. I'm in deep trouble with this one, in over my head for sure. My husband could leave me. . . . "

She tittered some nonsense reply, not seeming to realize the gravity of my situation. "Oh, go for it, girl. You deserve it. You only live once," and she reminded me of what I always say: "Nothing ventured, nothing gained."

Somehow I made it home, agog with my thoughts, confused and bewildered and absolutely possessed with my latest obsession. My poor unsuspecting husband noticed right away that something was up, and with his hands on his hips, legs wide apart, he ever so innocently inquired.

"So, how was your day? Your clothes are a mess. You're . . . dirty? What's going on here?"

"Arrrrrrrrrg . . . " was all the meaning I could form on my tongue and pass over my lips. I ran out the back door in agony, slamming the door behind me, just like I've always done when things get too tough.

I pulled at my hair. Oh, my god, what am I going to say? How am I supposed to do this? I can't lie. I yelled out for all the neighbors to hear: "I kissed a horse and now I have to buy him!"

My irate husband came crashing through the screen door. "Arrrrrrrrrrrg . . . blankety blank blank!" he said, which was expected, and then he ranted and raved about logic and reason, finances, time, careers, emotional stability, and my apparent neurotic, suicidal tendencies.

I told him; I had no reasonable defense. Nothing to do with logic, just something that I thought I was destined to do, and did do. And now, twenty years later, I still have the same beautiful horse and the same wonderful husband. But my whole life was changed irrevocably that day by a fateful kiss, on the nose of an innocent creature, so full of consequence.

Outsiders in Navajo Land

Therese Zink

Spring sidled into summer, and daytime temperatures transitioned from cool to sweltering, but in the high desert of the Navajo reservation, evenings remained pleasant. It was the season of ceremonies, and I hoped to participate in at least one during my three-month stint at the clinic. My opportunity came from the clinic janitor who invited me to ride my horse in the *Enemy Way Ceremony*, a healing ceremony for his in-laws. I was touched that Ernest and his wife thought to include me.

"Of course, I'd be honored," I told him.

Ernest had been friendly from the start. In the evenings I worked out in the clinic gym and he'd look in; we'd chat about this and that. He would share stories about his grandchildren and I talked about my horse, Indy, whom I'd trailered to "the rez."

"About this ceremony," Ernest leaned on his mop like a cane, adjusted his balance on his bum leg, and explained, "It's called *NaDaa*. You'll ride with the group who carry the sacred staff from one hogan to another."

"I'd be allowed?" I asked, acutely aware of being an outsider.

Ernest nodded and said, "Ask Marti. She rode with us a few years ago."

Marti, another *belleguna*, or white person, taught at the Navajo Community College for more than twenty years. She also boarded her horses near the rodeo stable, a short distance from the clinic. I met her one morning when Indy defiantly laid down, rolled over, and bolted. I almost heard him snort, "Enough of you!" as he pulled the reins from my grasp. I bird-dogged his hoof-prints for nearly a mile, each step fueled by his determination. I found him munching hay under the care of Marti, her face wrinkled by sun and age. I was pleasantly surprised that she met my embarrassment and anger with compassion.

"I could tell by your walk that he belonged to you," she said. After that, Marti became my trail guide and cultural ambassador.

"When is *NaDaa*?" I asked Ernest.

"Emphasize the daaaa. Otherwise you're saying 'Sit down,'" he said. We laughed. It would be in a few weeks; they were negotiating with the medicine man. "You wearing your helmet? It can be your drum after the ride."

My cheeks flushed as I recognized the gentle prodding, Navajo humor, a hint that I was accepted. I didn't bother to explain that I practiced what I preached. Well padded and coated with shiny green plastic, the helmet had saved my head from several dents during the defiant years of Indy's youth. Of course, no one else on the rez wore a helmet, not even Marti.

The following day I asked Marti about *NaDaa*. She explained it was one of the few ceremonies whites could attend. *NaDaa* means war. Originally, *NaDaa* was a healing ceremony for soldiers who participated in foreign wars, but now they also honored ill community members. The main patient was a male, and his wife, or a substitute female, played a supportive role. In the past, the ceremony lasted for several weeks, but now it was shortened to a week. Many families participated, and mid-week the ceremony moved from one camp to another. A sacred staff, constructed by the medicine man, was carried on horseback from the host camp to the camp where the ceremony concluded. Horses, of course, were as sacred in this ceremonial traditional as the healing objectives. I was smitten with the spiritual meaning and lore of what I was about to experience.

"Don't pass the horse with the stick. Otherwise, you'll do fine." Marti advised. "And get someone to drive your trailer to the endpoint." The ride was cross-country and I'd have trouble finding my way back.

I asked Barb, the *bellegana* optometrist, to help me. She'd never attended the *NaDaa* ceremony but had participated in other ceremonies and was accepted by the locals. Despite her fear of horses, she was excited at the opportunity and agreed to drive

Indy

my horse trailer. I was thrilled to have an accepted wing man, or woman, as the case turned out, for the adventure.

Over the next few weeks, I periodically asked Ernest when the ceremony was scheduled. The answer was always the same, "We're negotiating."

"*NaDaa*" remained scribbled on my "to-do list" for a while. Navajo time. Here things happened when they happened. I dealt with my impatience and need for precise planning by working, and riding, of course.

One day, Ernest pulled up to the barn in his battered red pickup truck. I was grooming Indy, who loves being brushed, especially under his head and along his neck. Indy is a cross between quarter horse and paint, creating a chocolate brown coat, four white socks, and a coal black mane and tail. Depending on your generation, he has either a lightening bolt or a Nike "swish" on his left shoulder.

Ernest called out his window. "You weren't at the clinic or home. Thought I might find you here. The ride's tomorrow."

"Thanks," I said and walked over to his truck, tugging Indy behind me. I loved that about living on the rez. No cell phone towers. No calling ahead to make an appointment. People observed your routine, then showed up and waited. At the end of the day, it wasn't unusual to find a sedan parked in my driveway, a Navajo sitting in the driver's seat, sometimes with kids, hoping to sell rugs or jewelry for gas money.

Ernest gestured toward my red SUV. "You drive. I'll show you where to go." I secured Indy in his stall and unlocked my SUV.

"You lock your truck up here?" Ernest asked.

"Still a city kid at heart," I explained. What I didn't say was that as much as I adored the cultural ways of their communication patterns and many other beautiful aspects of living with the Navajo, I was afraid that somebody might steal something, CDs, the player, who knows what. As a belleguna and a doctor, I was wealthier than most people on the rez. It also didn't help that others fueled my own paranoid concerns. I had my vet implant a microchip into Indy's neck after one of the nurses warned me, "Your horse is better fed than most around here. Some Navajo could stash him in a canyon and you'd never find him." It seemed a little mistrustful to be wary of my hosts, but it was better to be safe than sorry.

Ernest gave me an accepting nod, as if he knew how things were, and directed me to head south on Highway 12. The two-lane asphalt road wound past the lake and through the mesas of the high desert on to Window Rock, the capital of the Navajo nation. We traveled about five miles until we came to a hand-lettered, cardboard sign that was nailed to a two-foot-high stake at the side of the road that read NaDaa. I made a left on to a gravel road that zigzagged between two hogans. Sheep grazed at the perimeter of the road and I waited for a ewe and her twins to saunter across. About a fourth of a mile in, the wider path veered to the right, but Ernest instructed me to continue straight, down a dirt trail and through a stand of scrub oaks. He recommended that I remember this detail when I returned; he understood the limits of my *bellegana* sense of direction. Once while trying to find the home of one of the Navajo nurses, she had told me to "go a ways, then turn at the brown barn with the rock." Only on my return home did I find that barn and rock. I'm still learning to look for other "signs."

After traveling only a short distance, Ernest announced that we had arrived. A shed constructed from small tree trunks and roofed with leafy branches stood near a wooden shack. A few cars were scattered around.

"When you come, you'll park somewhere in here. There'll be lots of vehicles." He explained that Roger, his wife's nephew, would take care of me.

"Roger," I repeated and asked when I should arrive.

"'Bout five," Ernest said. "We can head back now. I just wanted you to know where to come."

For the umpteenth time I thanked him for letting me ride and asked again for the reassurance that it was okay.

"We talked with the medicine man about you riding," Ernest explained. "He approved." They also asked Marti to join me, thinking I'd be more comfortable with another white, but she had other commitments. She'd told me herself.

As we retraced our path to the barn, Ernest said, "We thought the ride would be an experience for you." He smiled, the creases next to his eyes curled upward, his white teeth a stark contrast to his tanned Navajo face. Despite the warm air, goose bumps prickled on my arms signaling my excitement as well as uncertainty.

The next day, the nursing staff shooed me out of the clinic early so I could get ready. A little before five, Barb and I pulled the trailer into the grassy area. Dusty trucks and cars filled the space between the shed and shack. A dozen horses were roped to the sides of trailers or trees. I brushed and saddled Indy and watched a young Navajo saddle a misbehaving stud. Barb and I cringed as he struck the horse with a tree branch to make him obey. The horse wiggled free and galloped off. Indy stomped and pawed and looked at me for reassurance. I soothed him with strokes and whispers then led him in circles to calm him. The air was electric with anticipation.

As usual, it was Navajo time. It was after 5:30 when Ernest walked over and introduced his young, muscular nephew, Roger, who gave me the Navajo handshake, open palm and fingers touching. We talked horse pleasantries—name, age, breed, and how long we'd owned our horses until it was time for us to gather. Taking slow, deep breaths, I swallowed my anxiety and mounted Indy, feeling the sides of his belly with my calves, as much for reassurance *from* him as it was *fo*r him. We both waited pensively.

Suddenly, we were off, and I was in a western movie, the only female and the lone *bellegana* cantering with ten whooping Indians, real Indians dressed in blue jeans, T-shirts and cowboy hats. I was at least a decade or two older than my companions, and my helmet crowned my "otherness."

A warm and spicy fragrance filled the evening air as we trotted up the piñon and juniper hillside. The jagged black and rust peaks of Black Pinnacles sliced the sky; low sunrays lit them on fire. The silent forest I'd walked in only last weekend was now invaded with the yells of Indians lassoing steel-gray boulders. Distrustful of my companions (and not keen on being lassoed myself), I struggled to hold Indy back, blending into the perimeter. Indy danced on the edge of his reins, yanking against my grip, testing to see who was in charge. His muscles twitched under me, tense with adrenaline; I could feel his excitement and his yearning to run full speed with the other horses. Borrowing this uninhibited power is the sheer joy of owning and riding a horse, and for minutes I become one thousand pounds of muscled speed. But for now, I struggled to keep my control. We couldn't move ahead of the lead Indian.

As our cross-country path merged with the gravel road into Black Pinnacles, a ribbon of cars and trucks filled the asphalt road below. Marti had prepared me for this.

In the old days only horses processed, but today cars joined the cavalcade and now outnumbered the horses. I was dismayed at being faced with what this reality meant now that it was here. Horses and cars rarely saw eye to eye, and the whole thing ran against my romantic vision of the experience. Setting my concerns aside, however, I focused on thrusting my weight into my legs and the stirrups. Back to Indy was where my attention needed to be. He snorted; his awareness also on high alert, he acknowledged what was ahead. We descended the hill and merged with the parade. Car horns honked and passengers yelled in Dine, the Navajo language, at our cavalry. And though the vehicles added a new dimension to the challenge, we soon clomped alongside the cars and eased into a slow trot.

My self-talk intensified—you can do this . . . be calm . . . give Indy courage. An elderly gentleman sat in the passenger side of a truck, prying open his droopy eyelid to see. I recognized him as a patient I've treated at the clinic, ninety-five years old and one of the few traditional medicine men, trained and mentored in the art of healing by his father and grandfather. I guessed that Ernest had talked with him about me.

Several cars behind him, a heavy-set woman in a black Infinity handed out yarn. Again Marti's coaching was accurate. "The lead

Indian boy ties yarn on the sacred staff and you drape yourselves and your saddles. Make sure you don't tie yourself to your saddle," she'd laughed.

Streamers of red and yellow yarn dangled from antennas and fluttered in the light breeze. Windshield wipers sported green fringe, the Walmart version—no homespun wool carded from the local sheep. I held out my hand toward the yarn woman, but she ignored me. Again, I directed Indy close to the Infinity and stretched out my hand asking for yarn. This time she glared at me and snapped in Dine.

Roger rode up alongside me, spoke with the yarn woman, then turned to me. "They don't want you riding."

"But your uncle and aunt talked to the medicine man," I replied. "He said it was okay."

Roger, his burly arms now wrapped with bright green yarn, explained, "This lady thinks it's bad for the ceremony, bad for the patient."

I wanted to say, who is this yarn woman! But I held my tongue and repeated, "The medicine man said it was okay." I could feel my frustration rising to a boiling point. All this effort and now this!

Roger shrugged as he draped his horse and saddle with purple yarn. He began to move on. It was clear he had no intention of defending me. I felt like the kid who wasn't chosen to join a team when the other kids were picking sides. I felt like a little girl told to sit down and be quiet. "Rejection" flashed in neon.

Crushed and disappointed, I wanted to cry. Truthfully, I wanted to scream. How unfair, I thought; how could this woman's opinion versus the medicine man's approval possibly matter! I wondered: Could I talk with him now, and remind him that I was his doctor, ask him to intervene? Marti had participated several times through the years and once last season. Why not me?

All I knew for certain was that I couldn't turn back, for all the emotional reasons, but also practical ones—I didn't know the way back. I could feel Indy's muscles tightening, sensing my frustration. I had to shove back my tears. This was neither the time nor place to lose it, so I inhaled, breathed slowly, and let my anger subside. Yet with this rebuff the excitement crumbled. I was suddenly exhausted.

And then it hit me. This was Navajo land. I was a *bellegana*, a white woman, who was a guest, yes, but still very much an outsider. Somewhere in the back of my mind it registered that this was a feeling my hosts encountered daily, were used to, perhaps even desensitized toward. I was now grasping the sting of outsider rejection, being different, for the first time in my life, or an "ism" that was unnamed but hurt nonetheless. I felt ashamed. And yet I'd been rejected by male colleagues and silly girlfriends. But to be spurned as a human being for being different from another, at the very, most basic heart of it, was new and entirely unexpected. It hurt like a hoof pick slicing into my palm.

Roger's voice came hurtling through my wall of self-wallowing. "You can cut off on the road to the right after we cross the next field. Best you don't ride into camp." He spun his horse and whooped as he bolted off. The other Indians followed as if I didn't exist. I nodded at their dust. Unadorned and cast out, Indy and I trotted at the rear, a goose among the swans.

The vehicle-horse procession continued along the pine-lined gravel road, and I wanted to quit, but I hung in there. My attention flip-flopped between disappointment and contrition as I tried to focus on keeping Indy composed. I crooned to calm him. I needed to be there for him; somehow as long as I zeroed in on him, it seemed bearable.

We reached an open field, cantering up a knoll. From the peak, a huge bonfire blazed about a mile away. Parked cars and trucks circled the fire, like the old wagon trains. Nearby, the hogan and branch-constructed shelters marked the final destination, the camp where the ceremony concluded.

Suddenly, my companions bellowed and galloped off, leaving Indy and me behind, once again abandoned. Indy stomped in dismay, snorting and struggling to join the others. I knew how he felt. His instinct was to follow the pack, as was my own, and he was confused as to why I was restraining him. We rode in small circles, like a kite that had lost its breeze.

Eventually, I edged toward the road and my horse trailer. With the repetition and my whispers, Indy's muscles rippled and began to relax. Mine did, too. Barb saw us and waved. Reluctantly, Indy trotted toward her. I felt defeated.

"How was it?" she asked, keeping her distance, her horse fear evident. "Why aren't you with the others?'

"They cut our part," I said.

"What?"

"You know the old movies, Indians and cowboys. They dumped the cowgirl." My tears were just beneath the surface and overwhelmed in my attempt to explain what happened. Sobs shook from every corner of my body and erupted as I climbed down from Indy.

I unsaddled and loaded him into the trailer, tears streaming down my face the entire time. Indy kept looking at me with his sweet, sorrowful eyes, yet I found no comfort there.

Now it was I who wanted to bolt. I sat in the cab of my truck exhausted, wanting to call it quits. As we drove back to the barn, a fine rain misted the windshield, but my inner storm raged, less like the gentle rain and more like the windshield wipers that flipped back and forth.

Barb watched, keeping her distances, as I unloaded, fed, and brushed Indy. He had calmed, but I still stroked my wounded spirit. Barb empathized with me and gently suggested, "I think we should go back to the gathering. Just for a little while. I have some food we can leave."

Barb was right, but I was reluctant to admit it. "You know, it's not their fault," she said. "Ernest and his wife did all they could to assure your participation. I've learned to bend over backwards here. Despite the rejection, keep extending your hand."

There would be food and dancing until morning, I thought. A party might be fun. We'd find Ernest and his wife and pay our respects; if the mood was right, we'd stay.

We parked at the camp, just as a threatening bank of gray-black clouds broke at the horizon, revealing a narrow golden band, then a blazing orange ball of the sun's fire. It slipped quickly behind the purple mesa. Had you not been looking, you might have missed it.

We approached the central bonfire, Barb with gusto, me with something slightly less than that. Intense heat radiated from the fire as it crackled and snapped, launching sparks like rockets into the chilly night air. Hot chips landed in the damp grass with a sizzle. I dodged to avoid one, zipping the collar of my fleece jacket high around my neck, digging my hands deep into my pockets. I guess I was trying to be present but invisible at the same time.

We wandered among the succession of parked cars, trucks, horses, and smaller campfires looking for Ernest and his wife. Adults and children stood or sat in lawn chairs around the fires. Many were in traditional dress, women with flowing cotton skirts, velvet tops, and thick silver necklaces and belts, wrapped in Navajo rugs. And stories and gossip were traded throughout. Men sported clean jeans and fresh shirts adorned with silver clasped bolero ties or belts, and both men and women wore denim jackets with cowboy boots. Some topped off their attire with a baseball cap or cowboy hat. The Indians from the ride had melted into the crowd, their horses munching hay off to the side.

A relative told us that Ernest and his wife were in the hogan with the medicine man, not a time to interrupt. So we left our gifts and wishes with the relative and traipsed back to my truck. Our breath was frosty; they'd need to keep dancing and eating to stay warm, stay close to their fires or burn lots of gasoline running their truck heaters.

Someone yelled at us through the rolled-down window of a muddy pickup. "Where's your horse? You didn't ride in with the others."

It was Barb's Navajo optometry assistant. She and her husband and kids had the heater blasting to stay warm.

Barb took over. I was relieved because tears were brewing beneath the surface. "Someone got uncomfortable with her riding so she stayed back."

"Too bad—we could see the sun reflecting off your helmet on the hill. You would have been a beacon of light for the others." Her broad Navajo face bubbled with amusement. In the driver's seat her husband chuckled.

My mood lightened. "So you like my helmet?"

"You should have brought it. Could use it as a drum now," the husband said.

"Or a bowl for the food later," the assistant chortled.

"Multi-purpose," I replied.

"Maybe we Indians should reconsider the value of helmets," the assistant said and shoved an open bag of potato chips toward us.

"It'll go on till tomorrow morning," the assistant informed us, "even if it rains." We chatted for a while, about what the night would hold, talked of food, dancing, and more food.

Weary from the busy day at the clinic, Barb and I eventually made our way home. I dropped her off at the housing compound where the chorus of her seven rescued dogs erupted as she unlocked her front door. Barb had been here long enough to earn the respect of the Navajos.

I drove on to the barn to check on Indy. We would commiserate together. As I tugged open the barn door, he greeted me with a nicker. He was good for that. Taking the brush from his trunk, I stroked his muscular body and took in the sweet fragrance of his alfalfa hay. His warm body heated the air. One firm, sinewy shoulder flowed into a taut abdomen and firm buttock, and he stretched his neck, begging me to scratch underneath. A quiver and he snorted his contentment. Currying him soothed me—the smell, musty and earthy, the quiet of the barn, the other horses munching hay. I began to settle down. In a hypnotic state, I played with a whorl of hair clustered where his back met his hip.

I complimented Indy on his fine job and talked about my disappointment, his too. What can you do when you are confronted with being "other"? When you are excluded because you are different? When the rules you understand don't apply? The experience was not foreign to me as a woman in a man's world. I wondered if a horse ever had that same experience.

Life is not fair. Society's rules are not fair, especially when you are on the wrong side of them. Powerlessness hurts. But here on the rez, I have inherited the sins of my ancestors, and a certain amount of humility and grace were demanded. "Bend over backward, extend a hand," Barb reminded me.

And as we did what we do, Indy and I, me brushing, him loving it, and me growing centered and grounded, I was reminded that his equine nature was as different as my *bellegana* nature here among the Navajo, both outsiders. I could come to terms with these differences in the same way Indy had come to understand mine. But it takes time and patience and deep grace to accept that which is so different, to heal the sins of our mutual pasts. My Navajo hosts were here long before my ancestors, but it occurred to me that Indy's relatives had a history on this land as well.

And Indy had been my partner in figuring this all out. We were a team. I was not alone, and his ability to be in the present was a reservoir of strength. The past was the past, the future had not yet arrived, but here in the present we had greeted what emerged with all the grace we could muster.

Hoofbeats

Jane Ayres

Three months, four days, and six hours. That's how long I'd been waiting, writing letters to my mother in my diary, keeping time. I closed the book with a sigh just before the door opened and my father came in, his coat dripping wet from the heavy rain.

"I'm a bit later than usual, love," he said, his voice tired and strained. "The nurses thought that there might be a change . . . but we were wrong."

"I'll make us some coffee," I offered.

I'd grown up quickly since Mum's accident, and sometimes I felt more like thirty than sixteen. There were moments when I blamed myself for what had happened, although I knew no one could have prevented it. Dad tried to avoid talking about it. The pain for him was too great. Mum was the love of his life.

They were childhood sweethearts, married at eighteen, and ironically, given Dad's general indifference toward horses, they met through one or, more specifically, around one. They were just fourteen at the time.

My mum was passionate about horses, and her mischievous first pony, Jingle, had escaped from his field for the umpteenth time and ended up relieving a nearby garden of its grass. It happened that Dad, then just a boy, had recently moved to the area with his family. He'd been playing outside when Jingle made his beeline for their garden, but Dad managed to catch him before he started eating the flowerbed. When Mum turned up to claim her pony, they joked and laughed about it and instantly became best of friends. Everyone knows humor has been the glue of their relationship and that my mum brings the laughter into his life.

There was no laughter in our lives at the moment.

I handed him his coffee. "I'd better go and see to Splinter, give him some fresh hay. . . ." My voice trailed off as the words stuck in my throat. Dad looked away. This was a very sore subject for him.

Although Dad accepted Mum's love of horses, he worried about her riding on the roads alone, especially this past year when the traffic seemed to get heavier and the roads busier as more houses sprang up and more people populated the once-quiet area. Maybe he thought when she got older she might give up the saddle. Maybe "hoped" is more accurate.

Given Dad's lack of empathy for horses, I suppose I wasn't

entirely surprised that he blamed Splinter for the accident. If he knew horses, and Splinter in particular, he would know this was no more his fault than it was Mum's. It was an accident, a fluke that neither Mum nor Splinter could have predicted or prevented.

But arguing this point further seemed futile. Sensing his dark mood, I headed out the door to find refuge in the warm stable and Splinter's welcoming whinny. Every morning I fed and watered him, before turning him out in the paddock for exercise. After school, I'd bring him back to the stable, groom and clean out his feet. It seemed this was the least I could do to care for him now, when Mum couldn't. This was her baby as much as I was.

She'd raised him from a foal. He was found abandoned in a snow-covered field, crying and bewildered beside his mother, an abused and neglected mare who tragically died shortly after giving birth. Thankfully, he'd been rescued and taken in by the animal welfare center, where my mum worked in the finance office. It was love at first sight for her. He was equally smitten.

Splinter initially needed round-the-clock care, and since we'd recently lost our dear elderly mare, Smokey, there was a space in our stable—and our hearts. Mum bottle-fed him, staying up all night in the stable, and I would sneak out of the house in my pajamas in the early morning, peer over the half door, and watch them together. She never knew I did it. I was only seven at the time. Mum would brush his soft, bay baby coat, cradle his head, and talk to him as if he understood every word. And he listened intently to her words, hanging on her every syllable. He would nuzzle her dark hair, as if she were another horse. At times I envied their special bond. I was an only child, and I sometimes wondered if caring for this vulnerable foal filled the void she had because she couldn't have another child. Deep down, though, I knew my mum loved me with all her heart.

And because of her loving devotion, Splinter grew and thrived. We grew up together. She trained him with patience and kindness, taught him to hold up a foot for his daily feet inspections, and prepared him for visits from the farrier. She soothed him with her smiling words of encouragement, as she had done with me, and got him used to a tiny foal head collar from an early age, taking him for walks around the garden and down the lane. I often tagged along, and I recall feeling a kind of kinship with him as he peered curiously at everything he saw, poking his nose at whatever caught his fancy.

When it was a sunny day, we would all lie down together in the meadows and doze, and Splinter would playfully nibble Mum's long hair and blow on her face. She used to breathe into his nostrils, which he loved, a horse whisperer's trick. She said it was how horses communicated with each other. It seemed to work pretty well for horse-to-human communications, too.

Every morning, Mum would get up early, whistling cheerfully, and Splinter would whicker a friendly greeting in response. She would make a fuss over him, talking constantly and calmly, refill his hay net, and check his water bucket. She would clip a lead rope onto

Splinter

his head collar and take him into the yard, where she would brush his coat and pick out his hooves.

And the years went by, flew by actually, and when he was old enough, she backed him and schooled him to be the perfect riding horse. Most weekends she would tack him up and they would go for a quiet hack by the river and over the hills. Sometimes I would join her on old Hector, a sweet-natured cob that I learned to ride at the local stables. And between the age of seven and twelve, I shared Mum's passion for horses, until I discovered I had a talent for singing and dancing and joined the local Stage School and found a new focus. I still loved horses, and I still enjoyed riding now and again, but they came to mean different things to me than they did to Mum.

Since the accident, I became Splinter's caretaker, although Dad refused to allow me to ride him. I looked deep into the horse's dark eyes. "It wasn't your fault," I told him. He stared back at me with genuine sadness, and I know that he missed her painfully.

It had been a wet and windy afternoon on the day of their last ride. I'd followed on my bicycle. We had to cross a busy main road to reach the woods, and the traffic was worse than usual. Splinter had crossed this road a hundred times before and was used to the barreling cars and their constant buzz, even the occasional truck blaring by with its low-growling diesel engine and formidable eighteen-wheel frame. On occasion Splinter had been scared by a truck that sped by too fast; its load had not been fastened properly, or the tarpaulin that covered it flapped violently in the wind, making a noise like thunder. This time, a truck roared past without warning, and Splinter reared up, knocking Mum off backward, her head hitting the concrete. She wasn't wearing her crash cap. I thought at the time: she'll get up, dust herself off, and that will be that. But she didn't.

Dad was mad with grief, declaring it was Splinter's fault, demanding the horse be destroyed. Somehow I managed to convince him that when Mum got better she would never forgive him if anything happened to her beloved horse. But the days melted into weeks and then the weeks faded into months. My mum didn't recover.

We tried everything we could think of to bring her out of her coma: talking to her constantly, holding her hands, playing music—I even sang to her, hoping she would respond. She always loved to listen to my voice. But she just lay in the hospital bed, still and silent, with tubes coming in and out every which way.

Every day that Splinter remained with us, Dad's resentment of the horse grew. I was grieving as well, but it was almost like Dad felt that every breath Splinter took was stealing the life from my mum. I knew we couldn't all go on like this for much longer without something breaking. Then I had an idea.

When Dad was at work, I took my mp3 player and led Splinter up and down the yard, pointing the microphone at his feet as they clip-clopped on the concrete. It felt a bit crazy, but I was convinced the key to Mum's recovery lay with Splinter.

The next time we were at the hospital, I told Dad I wanted some time alone with Mum. I daren't tell him what I was planning. I waited until we were alone, held my breath, and placed the mini-speakers on the bedside table as close to her head as I could. I played the recording, praying for a miracle. The hoofbeats sounded unreal, and I watched Mum for any sign of change. Did her finger twitch? Maybe her eyelid moved? I was willing it to be. I felt certain something would happen. But nothing did. I was out of options, and Mum was out of time.

Later that night I told Splinter, "It didn't work." My heart ached and I wondered if I had imagined that the dark bay horse took this information into his soul. He seemed more subdued than ever.

Days passed by, and it was the end of the month when Dad decided to try to stimulate Mum with music again. He downloaded tracks of the theme music from her favorite television shows. We sat next to her hospital bed, hoping for a reaction. Nothing. We waited some more. Nothing still. Dad broke down, trembling in grief and frustration. Blinded by tears, he jabbed at the controls on the mp3 as if it were the machine's fault. I don't know if he meant to press the "Off" button, but he must have hit "Shuffle" because a familiar voice (mine) declared in self-conscious tones, "One, two, three, testing." I must have passed through three shades of pale until I felt all of the color drain from my cheeks. Before I had a chance to react, the sound of Splinter's hoofbeats rang out loudly.

"What the hell is that?" Dad demanded. "Jane, how could you?"

I was suddenly angry. "It was worth a try," I retorted, poised to launch into him even more ferociously, when a voice from the bed forced both our jaws to drop to our chests.

"Where's Splinter?" Mum asked. "Did someone catch him? The roads are so busy."

Dad and I exchanged astonished glances and then turned to her, dumbstruck. "Where's my horse?" she repeated. "Oh, I hope he's alright."

Suddenly we were all hugging each other, dissolving into tears of joy and relief. Had our nightmare really ended at last?

Later on, as we drove home exhausted, Dad said quietly, "Thank you, Jane. That recording was a stroke of genius." I knew how hard that was for him to say. I smiled, too emotional to speak.

It had taken the sound of Mum's beloved horse to bring her back to us. I'd had to fight Dad tooth and nail, even sneak around, but my faith in the strength of her bond with that horse was affirmed. As soon as we got home, I rushed to the stable.

I gushed into Splinter's ear. "You did it, Splinter! You woke up our princess! Mum is coming home!"

He gave a low whicker and rested his head on my shoulder, as if to say "Good work." He did this with Mum, too, his breath gentle and reassuring. I couldn't wait for him to lay his head on her shoulder and watch them together again, as it was meant to be.

In his eyes, I saw all the love he had reflected back. Yet I also felt the strength in the link of this three-way chain that he, my mum, and I shared. It came from our connection with each other. Mum was a direct connection to Splinter's happiness; she was the fuel to mine, and he was her muse, her door to freedom and joy. My father laughed because Mum brought the laughter. I felt loved and learned how to love because Mum and Splinter taught me how. I knew, in that moment, whatever the future had in store for us, we would always share this bond—me, Mum, and the horses we loved, together.

The Pros and Cons of Bombproofing

Andrea Richards

 "Don't worry," Karin says as she leads me over to Rusty's stall. "You could shoot a gun next to his head and he won't spook."

This is good news—though I don't expect firearms. If we were to be shot at today, I understand Rusty's lineage would serve me well. Rusty is what is known as a bombproof horse. After extensive police training, he was used in high-density areas such as downtown Los Angeles. He worked protests and riots, so you can blow horns and throw water bottles at him and he won't move. My friend Karin is Swedish and wears Merimekko clogs around the stables, clomping down the aisle as if she, too, is equine. She is patient and good at cracking jokes that cut through my terror. So far, so good.

The horses have until now been nothing more than long, slender heads poking curiously from their stalls. Since they're mostly muzzles,

I have learned to approach them from the side, so they can see me coming. I've also been told not to go straight for the neck, the place where a predator would attack, and not to touch the sensitive face until it is offered to me. In the stall, I stand at Rusty's shoulder. He kindly lowers his head so I can get the halter on. I fumble with the clasp; my hands are shaky. To calm myself, I stroke along his withers with a firm grip, pressure in the palm so Rusty knows it's me and not a fly.

Karin explains to me that horses register your heartbeat as a way of sensing fear. There are many other unique equine capabilities; they are attune to body language in a way humans aren't—gestures indecipherable to us read like neon signs to them. I know every sign Rusty receives right now tells him I'm up for grabs; my entire body bleeds beginner. I take deep breaths and feel humbled at the fear of simply walking, and then I remind myself that I walk all the time; now I just happen to have a horse on a leash (okay, lead rope).

I open the stall door and off we go, until he suddenly stops before crossing the threshold. I make a mistake: I look back at him.

"Keep moving forward," Karin corrects me. "Your body has told him to stop. Don't look him in the eye; that's a sign of aggression," she adds.

It seems there's so much to remember and we haven't even made it out of the stall. But I move on deliberately, and on cue, Rusty follows behind. I am grateful for his acquiescence; I need him to follow my lead.

He does and I take him to the next phase. Tied up for tack, Rusty suddenly appears enormous. Outside the stall, there is a massive perspective shift; instead of just a head or a soft nose peeking over a stall door, a full, powerful creature stands before me with a bulking body and long, muscular legs—each one positioned perfectly to kick me in the face.

"Think of him as an eighty-year-old man," Karin says, handing me the grooming bucket. "Kicking you would be too much work."

I am glad to be dealing with a senior citizen. He offers only a few protests during grooming, kicking once at the wall as I brush him and stomping down his feet hard when I try to clean his hooves. I suppose I would stomp my feet too if a stranger came along, picked one up, and started brushing.

Here's how picking the hooves should proceed: Run one hand down the leg, feeling all those fragile, knobby bones. This signals the horse to shift its weight to the other legs and raise the foot. Then, bending at the knees, hold the foot in one hand, and use the other hand to pick it. In theory, this works; it's the way horses are trained. Rusty, however, is old and arthritic and so not inclined to enjoy standing on three legs. To get his foot up, I have to lean into his shoulder with all my weight, using my body to off-center his. It's like pushing against a linebacker, but finally he gives in. While the foot is up, I act fast. Still, before I finish, he slams his hoof down on the pavement, just missing my feet.

"Quit!" Karin calls in a low voice. She explains to me that this behavior is bad manners. "Make him do it again." Karin, it seems, is trying to kill me.

Rusty

    I make Rusty raise his foot again and take comfort knowing that I'm not the only beginner intimidated by Rusty. Of course, they are twelve-year-old girls, and I am a thirty-five-year-old woman, but despite the difference, I feel better.

    Karin works for an organization that teaches life skills to underserved girls through an equine-based program where they learn how to care for and ride horses. Along with the horseback riding, participants take creative arts courses; I've taught the creative writing classes for nearly a year without knowing much about horses. I do know I like petting them when they are in the stalls, all velvet noses and black-bottom pool eyes, but it's the idea of riding that causes trepidation. During my time here, I've heard many of these teenage girls who come through the program complain about Rusty in particular because of this nasty habit of slamming down his feet. They bicker over who has to groom him, and every once in a while there is a foot fatality. Usually the injured girl is waiting in my classroom when I arrive to teach, sniffing her runny nose and holding an ice pack to a fat, swollen foot while the rest of the girls are untacking the horses. Sometimes the girl will cry; other times she will just sit there, stunned and offended. I see now what hurts perhaps more than being stepped on is that Rusty's action feels so unjustified: We girls are just doing what we're told.

But a bombproof horse, even one with a nasty habit of slamming down his feet, should be an ideal horse for a beginner. And for the most part, he is. Rusty is quick to respond to commands and won't spook when another horse breaks loose or when a helicopter flies overhead. He may occasionally get grumpy, but in the arena he's as steady and solid as can be. Above all, he can be trusted. A swollen foot is not too bad when you consider the alternative. I know all this, but still the fear comes from an unknown place inside me. I hoist up his saddle, surprised by its weight—how do such little girls do this?—and by my anxiety. It isn't until halfway through the lesson with Karin that this nervousness subsides. It's not that I ever really relax while riding Rusty, but it dawns on me that this ride isn't going to be a disaster. In fact, it is fun in those moments where the pleasure outweighs the fear and I am so focused on what I'm doing that I forget to be afraid. When I concentrate on giving Rusty the commands the way Karin tells me to, using my leg to send him on, and breathing so that I go back into my seat, not just a new perspective, but a new space opens up. Karin is guiding us both, but it's Rusty that is teaching me.

The "classroom" where I teach writing classes is a converted horse stall, and as I work with the girls, the horses that surround us in their stalls go about their business, neighing, nickering, and nodding their heads in anticipation of a meal. There is always something going on in the background, events that inevitably are far more interesting than my lesson plans. Occasionally, the distractions are so great that I take the class down to the nearby Los Angeles River to write.

The girls know that while working around horses, they have to stay calm and relatively quiet. As we walk the dirt path to the concrete banks of the river, I witness an increasing wildness develop; in the shade of the pepper trees, they perk up: eyes wide open, talking louder, moving quicker. Some begin to skip. Like excited horses, they want to run. For the most part, these aren't girls who spend much time outside; they mostly live in neighborhoods where it isn't safe, and so even our sad trickle of a river is a green paradise to them. "It reminds me of Disneyland," one girl tells me, and often on hot days, despite the garbage and the sour smell, they want to swim in it. They are confused about the algae, which grows thick in the water this time of year. They think it is pollution, something poured in like antifreeze.

"It's alive," I tell them. "It breathes. But don't step on it; it's slick." Using sticks, they pull strands of algae out of the water, touch it, and squeal.

Before we can settle in to writing, there is always some minor battle of wills. They need to assert their agenda against mine.

"Miss, instead of writing, can we throw rocks in the river today?" Marisa asks innocently. I know how good it feels to press a piece of the broken concrete in hand and toss it as far out as you can, listening and watching for the plop in the water. There is satisfaction in throwing a rock somewhere you can't go. Rocks make perfect tools of complaint and sometimes even rage.

"Everyone, find a rock," I say. Throw first, learn later. Even though my adolescence was long ago and, no doubt, different from theirs, I remember all the stupid secrets someone made you listen to and all the rules you had to blindly follow. I watch my students throwing bits of broken concrete into the water and think about how they all deserve so much more than a river that smells like sewage.

After some impressive hurls, we write, and then, as usual, I ask the girls to read their work out loud. They must stand and project so that they can be heard over the rumble of the I-5 freeway. Juliana reads her poem confidently, taking her time instead of rushing to the end of the page, owning her words. Others act as if they are surprised to find words on the page, like the pen marks are hieroglyphics they can't understand. This is not unlike how I feel sitting astride Rusty, feeling my way, surprised to find I can.

Marisa and Veronica are passing a note, and because they haven't done the assignment, I ask if one of them would like to read it aloud. They can both be bullies, and so I'm not surprised that Veronica rises, unafraid to share private sentiments. Hilariously, the note consists of a story about a stolen note. It recounts how a girl took a note from Veronica and read it on the bus. Since this stolen document described, in detail, how Veronica planned to break up with her boyfriend, who, yes, was on the bus, there were serious repercussions. As Veronica reads, she adds details not included on the page for our benefit. She performs this work with fury, and as a final flourish, she crumples the sheet of notebook paper into a ball and throws it into the water, its shredded spiral edges falling like snow.

"Veronica," I say, watching as the blue lines on the page blur, "you've got to pull that out of there." She does without any argument, because for all her show, I am still in charge. That is all it takes to be a leader, the willingness to say you are and then to accept responsibility for what happens. I try to remember this for my next ride with Rusty. But then, I am reminded just how tenuous control can be: On the way back to the stables, Eliana heeds neither the admonishment not to run nor the warning about how slick algae is. Racing through puddles, she slips and falls down flat on her back. I'm relieved she hasn't split open her head. She isn't hurt, but from her ponytail to her tennis shoes she's covered in smelly, green slime. Horses are scrubbed down after they walk in the river, so I know this girl needs a bath. At the stables, there is a bathroom with a shower; Karin culls together some clean clothes. I walk Eliana to the bathroom, and we find someone has left some soap and shampoo.

"Use it," I tell her.

"But it's not mine," she replies.

"You need it more than they do." Covered in goop, she looks smaller and more timid than I've ever seen her before. She doesn't cower like this in the arena. The embarrassment of needing a shower is worse than the possibility of falling off a horse. "It's okay," I say. "Don't worry about the shampoo." I wait outside.

Suddenly she calls out, "Miss, Miss!"

I run inside the bathroom. "What is it?" I ask.

"There's acid in the shampoo!" she says frantically. "The label says there's acid in it!" She is dripping wet and wrapped in a towel and holds out the bottle suspiciously. It is an expensive shampoo from Kiehl's, and amino acid is printed large on the label.

"It's okay—that kind of acid is good for your hair. Use a lot." I hope amino acids fight bacterial infections, but I'm not sure science works like that. I have seen Eliana ride Rusty; she is so much better than I. She sits tall in the saddle, her commands clear and confident. She lopes him with a smile on her face and picks his feet without fear. Yet here she is, afraid of shampoo. The simplest of life's tasks can become daunting when communication is confusing or signals are misread. With horses, she's fine, but when faced with unfamiliar word usage, Eliana enters that place where fear and lack of trust collide. But because she trusts me, Eliana washes her hair.

One of the activities we do in class is an assignment where the girls map the route from where they live to the stables on a piece of canvas that they paint with bright colors. The idea is not only to refine their observational and descriptive skills but also to help integrate this experience into their lives. If we can get the stables on their psychic maps, maybe the girls will continue to come back. Helen, one of my star pupils, likes to write and produces a number of beautiful poems. With a little encouragement, she reads them to the other girls, and when they respond positively, her cheeks flush with pride. She is fifteen and has been in Los Angeles for only a year. Right now her family lives in a shelter, and last week she brought in the yearbook from her previous school. She and a group of three other girls went through the book page by page. When I ask to see her map, she shows me the landmarks she's drawn: the stables, a McDonald's, the freeway, the river. Somewhere near her snow-capped San Gabriel Mountains, there is a group of stick people—one colored red is flat on the ground beside the freeway. It's labeled in print: "dead body."

"Did you pass an accident on the freeway today?" I inquire.

"Nope, that's some guy who got shot—we saw his body from the van." She relays this information in the same tone she used to point out the McDonald's on her map or her friends in the yearbook. There is no shift in intonation between the living and the dead. It hits me that these girls are bombproof, too.

There are five different horses that are used in the riding program, and it's interesting to see which horse particular girls gravitate to, especially since the girls stake claims quickly. Usually, after the first lesson, they've picked a favorite to whom they are fiercely loyal. Just try to put them on another horse and they complain.

Should another girl express affection for the same horse, the first will exclaim, "He's *my* horse." In reality, they own and control so little of their lives, so perhaps this sense of territorial ownership is some sort of odd compensation for how little else they have been given.

The riding instructors try to nip this tendency since it thwarts teamwork, but everyone agrees that the exertion of ownership is the awkward start of a real relationship between girl and horse. Certain patterns emerge in the pairings: Shy and timid girls tend to go for our oldest gelding, Oakie, a patient old man with a sweet, quiet nature. Rowdy girls like Nelson, a slightly younger gelding who boasts a boisterous curiosity and the remains of a Thoroughbred physique. Some of these girls grow frustrated when they find Nelson won't do their bidding unless they learn the proper commands. He's a stickler, and the girls who stay with him have both moxie and the patience to learn technique. Buddy, a middle-aged palomino, is a more difficult horse—a former cutting horse who appears to have been mistreated by his cowboy handlers. He can't be tied and has a host of neuroses. Anytime he's the least bit stressed, his golden coat breaks out in hives. When the girls approach his stall, he pins back his ears and bares his teeth. But it's all an act—beneath the fear and anxiety, he is tenderhearted and true.

It is a wonder to me that it is always our most damaged girls— the ones who have been neglected or abused—who fall for Buddy, as if they know what he's going through. Empathy is a bridge between the species, and these horses communicate to the girls in ways that I catch only in isolated moments, such as when one of my longtime students,

Isabel, stood outside Buddy's stall and read him a sonnet she wrote him. Of course, he had his ears back, but she did it anyway. This, I believe, is what it takes for both of them to heal.

For me, it was a big discovery to learn that each horse has a different personality and that, like people, they come with odd quirks and mood swings. Now that I know the characters, I sit back at the barn and watch the equivalent of an equine telenovela unfold. The older students, who have come for years, detail the minutia of these goings-on—they know all the horse gossip: who is feeling high-spirited, who is in a funk, who ate his or her supplements, who ate somebody else's supplements by sneaking in the bin, who bit whom, and who needs what. They love the way Oakie pines for Tara when she's taken to the sun pen without him, and they adore mouthy Nelson and laugh at his acrobatic tongue tricks to untie his lead rope. They patiently court Buddy like lovesick suitors. Each of these girls has her own story, and as they claim "their" horse, they make the horse a part of their story. It is my job to convey that these stories are important, even if I don't succeed in getting anyone to actually write. Each of them, I hope, will carry this experience with her: the first time she found her horse and what that means.

I take it all in objectively and then think about the horse that's in my story—the little police horse who has me wafting poetically and rushing to work. Just as he's done for some of the girls, Rusty has ignited my inner poet and hope peddler. It can't be because I ride Rusty well: I am terrified to do more than a trot. Is it because, like my students, he is an ongoing challenge, a force equally adorable and obstinate? Do I sense his power, sitting in the saddle, and know that if I lead him correctly, he will trust me? Will that power—the unexpected lope of an old bombproof horse—unleash from within him and come into me? I believe that with time, this will happen—as Rusty and I learn to trust each other, we can let more of ourselves go. The story will eventually stop being about my fears or his history and we will start with a blank page together. That's the sense of freedom I'm starting to feel in the saddle, one similar to writing the first sentence: possibility.

In my class of nine, each girl does have a story; some are light and funny, and some are heartbreakingly sad, about shootings and homicides, neglect and disappointment. We share so much with the experience of the horses now, but still my own reality is far away from their truths. In their short lives—most of the girls are eleven or twelve—the corpses have piled up. Like Rusty, they have been desensitized through repeated exposure to situations and stimuli that would scare most people. Like Rusty, they have learned not to react and come across as stubborn, tough, and unshakable. Like Rusty, they often want to stomp the ground in sheer frustration. And, like Rusty, they will reciprocate fiercely once you win their trust. But I don't kid myself; it's not me or the writing exercises that find the tender spaces that remain in these bombproof kids—it's the horses, who seem to unknowingly sniff out the sweet spots in their worn souls as if they are concealed carrots.

Thrown

Chansonette Buck

I rode to safety through a catastrophic childhood on the broad and sturdy backs of imaginary horses. Then, the summer I turned eight, I started riding lessons. I remember that first day, being led to a small black horse with a broad white blaze down his nose, his mane cut short so it stood up. I remember being helped up so I could get my foot in the stirrup and then swing my other leg over the saddle and land there, my thighs screamingly wide. I remember that first heady feel of smooth worked leather under my hands, the saddle horn, the reins, the warm body of the horse beneath me, so solid, and the mane right there so I could reach out and grasp it, feel the coarseness of the strands of hair running through my fingers.

I had never felt so perilously high off the ground. I was surprised at how high it felt, yet how secure, how right-where-I-belonged it felt, and how dangerous.

On the last day of the lesson program we all brought sack lunches and

rode out into the countryside for a half-day trail ride. It was glorious. I felt
so proud that I could ride. So proud that as hard as he tried to brush me off
against every passing piñon, my horse couldn't dislodge me. Dismounting all
by myself without help and sitting against a tree trunk eating sandwiches, I
felt at home in my own skin in a way that felt like a first. Felt like fire.

I was fifty-two the first time I rode at Five Brooks Stables in Olema.
They put me on Mia, a twenty-six-year-old buckskin Paso Fino/
Mustang mare who had spent her entire life as a rental string
horse. I fell instantly in love. The next time I rode, I requested her.
The wrangler looked at my paperwork, on which I had checked
"Beginner" because I hadn't been on horseback much since my teens.
She looked me up and down.

"Mia is not an easy ride," she said.

"I know," I said. The wrangler shrugged as if to say, *Suit yourself,*
greenhorn.

I had been riding Mia ever since, graduating quickly from
public rides to half-day private rides with a guide who had become
my friend. There had been times, running along the trail, when Mia
and I had merged so fluidly I felt one with her, one body, one being.
I wanted what she wanted, she wanted what I wanted; we were so
perfectly tuned it didn't make sense to divide us—rider separate from
horse, horse separate from rider.

We would glide—fly, really—along the wide, soft trail under
eucalyptus and tall pine, a sharp drop of valley on our left, a sheer

cliff of wooded rise to the next level of the ridge on our right, our bodies in utter agreement. At the slightest cue from me, Mia would slow or speed up, her ears pricking forward, me looking straight ahead through them to guide us, my body slightly forward and loose, hands over her neck, reins loose, my hips liquid in the saddle, rolling to the rolling rhythm of her gait. We were one strong, sure body. One willing heart. That kind of magic between a horse and a human—an experience of absolute trust—it happens sometimes, if you are very, very lucky.

On the other hand, Mia had some bad habits. She shied. She tried to bolt. She turned sideways on the trail to stop the horse behind her from encroaching on her space. She backed up with such recalcitrance that sometimes we had to abandon our ride and go back to the barn. She even jumped laterally from one side of the trail to the other at a flat run because the guide's horse did that. There were moments in every ride when I found myself up against the limits of my own growing skill as a rider, and, inevitably, I felt a surge of fear.

I was coming back to riding late in life. I had fallen in love with a horse who would always test me. I knew she had issues, and I knew I was an inexperienced rider who was not always a match for her. I knew, because she had shown me, that things could go wrong between us. But it never occurred to me that she might buck. And that was my big mistake.

One day we were heading back to the barn after what I thought would be my last ride for a while; I was about to sign papers to buy my house, and all my discretionary money would soon be swallowed up in mortgage payments. Mia tried to bolt. She tried to go off the narrow trail that winds through the tall golden grasses of the meadow we canter through at the end of our half-day ride. I was expecting this, because she always tried to bolt in that meadow. I kept her on the trail. She shook her head against the bit, peevish. We started to slow to a trot. We were coming up the rise toward the bushes we pass through to emerge out onto the trailhead directly across from the stable.

She bucked.

I wasn't expecting it. I thought I knew all her tricks. It baffled me at first. I felt hurt. Rejected. Betrayed. But in retrospect, after the physical pain lessened a bit and I came out of shock, I realized Mia was probably just feeling frisky. I certainly was. We had gone off into new territory, and she is a rental string horse. She's not used to new territory. She likes it. I bet she was feeling powerful. Free. Young.

She kicked up her heels just as I was posting, above the saddle, slightly off balance because I wasn't concentrating. I was blissed out, as I always am at the end of a trail ride. We had passed through the place where Mia acts up and I had managed her. I was expecting a nice, normal, placid return to the barn. As usual.

I remember feeling her hindquarters lift. I remember posting, off balance, reaching for my center and not finding it. I remember the choppiness of her descent from canter to trot, not sitting it well. I remember saying "Oops" as I sailed over the side and out of the saddle. And I remember thinking *relax* and consciously relaxing my body, going

Shadow and friends

limp so the fall would not damage me as badly as it would if I tried to stay in control. I hit the ground, as if I were liquid. Or light.

It's funny how the mind takes over in a moment like that to protect the body but not to resist what is happening. To resist would be to ensure maximum injury. I was clear-headed enough in the moment of falling to know that. Or maybe a better way to put it: I was inspired *not to resist.*

Even so, my fall would have a lasting impact.

My guide Theresa told me later she had heard me say "Oops" and turned back to look, to make sure I was all right. She saw me lying curled on my side on the trail. Mia took off back to the barn. Theresa said she asked me if I was okay and I answered her as if I were lucid.

I said, "Yeah, I just need to catch my breath." I don't remember saying that. I don't remember lying curled on the ground. I don't remember Theresa dismounting, and I don't remember her asking me questions.

Theresa said she only realized I was in trouble when she had dismounted and dropped the reins, and her horse, a hot Arab gelding, started prancing and pacing and circling me, his hooves landing less than a foot from my head. I didn't react. I just stared out in front of me, blankly. As if I didn't see him. And that was when she got scared. Rightly so. The only reason I know that happened is that she says it did. I didn't see him. I have no idea where I was, but I was not in the body looking out and registering a 2,000-pound animal within inches of crushing my skull.

She used her walkie-talkie to call the ranch for help. Luckily the ranch was only a three-minute walk away. Halfway through the ride we had been an hour and a half out, deep in the forest, on narrow trails crowded by towering evergreens, high up on a ridge. I can't imagine what it would have been like if Mia had bucked there and I hadn't been ready for it. How would they have gotten to us? How would they have gotten me to the Trauma Unit at Marin General?

I don't remember Mark arriving. According to Theresa, I said I was okay and I wanted to get up, so they helped me to my feet. I don't remember that. I vaguely remember standing between them. I vaguely remember darkness descending and my body crumpling from the inside while Mark said calmly and calmingly, "You're just fainting now. You're okay, but you're fainting. I am going to help you lie down on the ground."

I don't remember being laid out on the ground.

I remember waking up, coming into the light out of darkness and feeling the ground under me. I remember feeling the pain begin in my hip, a girdle of pain. I remember Theresa's voice and Mark's voice like a call and response floating above me as I woke, as I noticed the sky, and Andy's voice on the walkie-talkie as they decided whether to call an ambulance. I don't remember caring whether they called an ambulance.

I remember mostly watching the sky. Feeling pain and watching the sky. Feeling the sky as part of me, the earth part of me, my body somehow irrelevant, except for the searing pain like a band around my center. I felt the solid earth beneath me, all along the length of me, and the sky above me. And between me and the sky I saw faces, concerned faces, loving, kind, calm. I remember watching the clouds. Noticing how they moved. Watching them break apart. Seeing the blue appearing. I remember seeing birds soaring high and black against the backdrop of blue and cloud. They were probably turkey vultures, but to me at that moment they were simply dark shapes in motion.

What a beautiful place to be felled. To go down. To give in. To give way. To give up. I felt myself spreading out. I was the faces. I was the clouds, drifting, pulling apart, clustering, rejoining, being pulled apart again. I was the shape-shifting patches of deep blue autumn sky between them. I was the birds. I couldn't move. I was in excruciating pain, worse and worse every moment. But I didn't care. It really didn't matter.

I felt . . . I don't know . . . *lucky.*

I had only been riding regularly for a few years. I had had some close calls but had never been thrown. I had only ever fallen off a horse once, when I was eleven and living on a ranch in Idaho. I rode a lot then, often with a friend from a neighboring ranch. One time we were on our way back from an all-day ride. We were galloping, nearing the ranch. My horse got the scent of home in his nostrils.

Suddenly he put on an extra burst of speed and took the bit between his teeth. He was pelting along at a dead run and I had nothing to control him with. Then the stirrups popped. My legs were flapping loose with no anchor, and I found myself holding on to the saddle horn for dear life. He kept twisting, barrel-racing the sage. I was bouncing in the saddle now, bouncing up and down and sideways. I knew I was in trouble. I knew I could either choose a place to fall or fall where he threw me. So I calmly waited, riding this out-of-control horse going at a flat run, to pass a likely-looking sage, a sage big enough to be a good, softish place to land.

When I saw a good one, I simply dropped off the side. I let go and fell into the middle of the sagebrush. I was barely hurt. Scratched up. A little bit bruised. But only scuffed. I rode again the very next weekend. I rode every chance I got. I don't remember feeling pain, and I don't remember feeling fear.

This time, in my fifties, it was different. This time I was lying on the trail and I couldn't move. I didn't remember what it meant to be able to move. This time the rangers came. The rangers asked me questions. They touched me. And then the EMT guys came, and they did all the same stuff the rangers did, with the same care and the same careful explanations. And now more of my back was starting to hurt, all along the base of my spine, and my hips were aching. When they moved me ever so gently to assess the damage, the pain felt like knives ripping into me.

They were saying things to reassure me, but I didn't really understand, because now I was starting to feel cold, so cold, and I was starting to shake, and my teeth were chattering even though it was an unseasonably warm day and only about noon or so. I was still watching the sky. It was the sky that got my attention. The voices were just background noise. The faces above me were indistinct, except for their warm, caring eyes. I saw their mouths opening and closing. I heard the word "okay" punctuating sentences I wasn't really following.

The second before Mia bucked, I knew precisely where I was. We were heading onto the little path between the bushes, and in three horse lengths we would burst out onto the Five Brooks Trailhead—the wide dirt road that cuts between the ranch and the meadow we had just cantered through, in which I was now lying motionless and part of the sky. We were just about to walk our sweaty, exhilarated horses across the road and along the trail between the stable and the pond. We were just about to take a sharp left onto the soft, dusty road that leads from the corral out to where the Olema/Bolema Trail converges with the Randall Trail. Where you can go left and end up where we had been, out at Dog Town, climbing the Texeira Trail up through the woods, or where you can go right, to Greenpicker, or to the Rift Zone Trail, through the Stewart Horse Camp—across the stream where the horses are likely to spook because the campers sometimes put tents there—and out through the meadows beyond, toward the Vedanta Retreat.

Before Mia bucked and I hit the ground, I knew all this. But now, now I was lost.

The EMT guys gently slid me onto the body board and strapped me down tight so I couldn't move. They lifted the body board and walked me up the slope and out onto the road where the ambulance was waiting. Every slight jostle was screaming pain. During the forty-minute ambulance ride to Marin General, every second felt like hours. Every bump in the road was a torment. They asked me questions I didn't know the answers to. I heard them making sounds into the walkie-talkie. I heard the walkie-talkie squawk back at them. It meant nothing to me. I was waiting for the pain to stop.

At Marin General the trauma team efficiently and expertly cut away my favorite riding jeans, my favorite riding top, and my favorite fleece pullover. They were afraid I might have broken my back or my neck and didn't want me to move. They carted me off to x-ray and then carted me back.

Through all of it, the pain was just inexpressible—every slight jostle, every movement, everything they needed me to do so they could make sure I was okay was searing pain. They tried to help me up so I could go to the bathroom, but once I was on my feet the pain was so disabling I begged the young man to put me back on the gurney. I hadn't peed since early morning, but I was in so much pain I had to lie about it. I told him, "I don't have to go that bad, really." After that the doctor came in, took one look at me, and told the nurse to increase my morphine.

My, but life in the body is glorious! *What* an experience!

That feeling sang in me all through that first week, when I was drugged, lying on my bed, moving only when absolutely necessary. I learned then that to move is pain, to stand up is pain, to take a step is pain, to sit is pain, to shift positions in even the most minimal way, pain, pain, pain. Yet in some broader part of my being, I also felt it as just another turn in the narrative: "and then this happens, and then this, and this, and this. . . . " As an experience. Pure. *Glorious*.

And that feeling was for me a kind of epiphany.

Although I have always been a risk-taker, I have also always craved safety. The former quality is inherent to who I am. I love life. I take chances. I want to soar. I do soar. The latter is a result of family happenstance, having been a stepchild in the house of a man with a brutal, explosive temper. From before I could talk, I felt an unaccountable passion for horses, and as my childhood progressed, this passion became my refuge. I rode at intervals, but most of my experience with horses was inside my own head. In there, horses were my Safe Place.

It never dawned on me, until after Mia grounded me, that my

Safe Place was also a Dangerous Place. In the six months it took me to heal, friends would try to convince me to quit riding. "It's dangerous," they'd say. "You could have been killed," they'd say. "You're not getting any younger," they'd say. "I know," I'd say, "but I'm not quitting." They'd say, "Why not?"

All I could ever answer was "I don't know. I know I could be killed riding. But . . . " And then I'd tell them the story of the time I rode a different horse, not Mia, a much bigger horse and one I didn't have a relationship with and was less confident riding. I'd tell them how Theresa decided to go off on a trail she hadn't been on for a while. We were running fast down an unfamiliar section. We rounded a sharp bend. A hundred feet in front of us a thick branch protruded across the trail—about a foot higher than my horse's head. We were going at a flat run. I had only seconds to react. I ducked down so my torso was against my horse's neck. We flew beneath the branch with inches to spare. If I had not looked up in time, if I had not had the reflexes to change my position, the branch would have taken my head off.

I told my friends this story every time they pushed me to quit. I said, "Yeah, I could have died right there. But you know what? We all die. We are all going to die. I'd much rather die that way, doing something I love, than get hit by a bus crossing the street, or have a heart attack, or waste away from cancer. When I'm riding . . . when I'm out there . . . in that landscape, on horseback . . . on Mia . . . I feel . . . whole. I can't give that up. Why would I give that up?"

Mia gave me a huge gift that day when she friskily kicked up her heels and sent me tumbling over the side. She gave me the answer to that question. It is so easy to live a fear-driven life. It is so easy to say, "No, I'd better not . . ." when possibility comes knocking. Or to imagine that the best possibility for me is the one that comes risk-free. But the truth is that Possibility always contains Danger. Always. There are no absolutes. Or, better said, that is the only absolute: *Danger is the essence and the beauty of possibility.*

If I had not taken the risk of riding the horse I loved, a horse I knew was trouble, if I had not been thrown and lain there on that trail, there is so much I would not have experienced. I would not have experienced the beautiful care of Theresa and Mark and Andy. I would not have experienced the beautiful care of the rangers and the EMT guys and the emergency medical staff at Marin General. I would not have experienced the beautiful care of my family, of my loving friends who tried to convince me to quit riding. I would not have experienced the extraordinary merging with the landscape I love so much, and I would not have experienced merging with the sky.

If Mia had not thrown me, I would not have had that miraculous experience of knowing myself in that new and expanded way.

But most of all, if Mia had not thrown me, I would not have experienced meeting my own fear head-on and surviving it. In all those months when I rode Mia, every single time I rode her I came up against my own limitations as a rider. Every time I rode her I came up against the possibility of losing control and the possibility of getting hurt. When she threw me, she threw me directly into the thing that, as a rider coming back to horses in middle age, I feared.

Mia taught me the measure of who I am. That experience shifted my view of what life is. And because of that shift, I have found myself, more and more, year after year, saying "yes" to possibility. Saying *yes* and *yes* and *yes* and *yes* and *yes*.

And in teaching me that, Mia also taught me this: I am not a "no" kind of girl.

Two Loves

Samantha Ducloux Waltz

I've begged Ray more times than there are hairs in my horse's forelock to please go riding with me. Ray is the love of my life, and I can't stop dreaming about gallops on the beach and horse camping together. But Ray has been afraid of horses since seventh grade, when he rode one named Little Buck at a birthday party. Little Buck never even crow-hopped, yet his fear of the equine experience settled deep into his psyche.

Miracle of miracles, as a birthday present, today he finally agreed to go. For him, I have my eye on Czar, a gentle, well-aged Appaloosa that belongs to the owner of the small barn where I board my beloved Arab mare, Vida. My friend Jeanne, a riding instructor, will give Ray some pointers and then ride with us on her tall palomino, Daydream Believer—Buddy for short.

The weather is late-spring balmy, the sky a cloudless azure;

the deliciously green grass along the pasture fencing dances in this perfect day as Jeanne and I bring the horses in from the pasture.

Ray tentatively pats Czar's white, muscled shoulder. "He seems pretty calm," he says.

"He's a grand old soldier," I assure him and tie Czar to a ring on the arena wall. Ray reaches for the grooming brush I offer and Jeanne and I tack up Buddy and Vida.

Vida looks beautiful, her daily meals of spring grass swelling her chestnut belly. I scratch the white spot on her nose and blow in her nostrils before smoothing on the saddle pad and loosely buckling the girth.

When I bought Vida, she had a weak back and a high-anxious attitude. She reminded me of me. Seven years later, with several hundred hours of bodywork for her, several series of weekly yoga classes for me, and a lot of riding lessons together, we're both stronger and more relaxed. Sometimes, when I'm brushing her, I lean into her, and she leans back. We've held each other up on many occasions when one of us is discouraged or doesn't feel well.

I look over and see that Jeanne is ready with Buddy. She ground ties him and offers Ray a leg up on Czar. He puts his left foot in the stirrup and swings on like he's ridden a horse a thousand times. I smile. Why not? He's an athletic sort. He runs, golfs, plays basketball and racquetball; I expect he'll be a natural horseman.

Ray smiles his terrific, crooked smile as he gathers up the reins and nudges Czar into a walk. It's a smile I have come to trust, but I still always wonder what hidden concerns lurk behind it. My husband is the consummate man's man.

"Shorter reins," Jeanne coaches. "Hold them like an ice cream cone right over the horn." He's holding the reins somewhere close to his own ears but does his best to grip them closer to Czar's neck. He looks like he's working hard to seem in control. I want to tell him he is in control, but I know he needs to discover this on his own, the way we all do.

After ten minutes of instruction, mostly about shortening the reins, Ray can walk and trot confidently around the arena and we decide we're ready to hit the trails. Jeanne takes the lead, then Ray, and I just think the words *Let's go,* and Vida moves out. We're all heading down the long, gravel driveway, Vida's coat gleaming in the sun like new copper. Her ears prick forward and she jigs in anticipation. "Having fun?" I ask Ray. He gives me a look that tells me it is not a simple question.

I was born yearning for horses, not just in my heart but in the core of my being. When I was five years old, a salesman came to our door in Altadena, California, with a camera and a spotted pony. He snapped a picture of me on that pony, complete with bandana, cowboy hat, and spotted chaps, grinning ear to ear. I have the photo framed on my desk today. About the time I started school, I began walking to Ralph's grocery store two blocks from our house whenever I had a dime. I'd plug my money in the gray-and-white mechanical horse at the store's entrance, put my foot in the left stirrup, and swing on. As the horse swayed and bumped, I imagined I galloped along a dusty trail, my hair whipping in the wind, my smile a thousand watts. At home I pretended to ride a magnificent stallion as I galloped around and around our big, white, turn-of-the-century house. Sometimes I pretended to be the horse, snorting and prancing. I read every book in the library about horses and watched every episode of *Roy Rogers* and *The Lone Ranger*, inhaling glimpses of Trigger and Buttermilk, Silver and Scout, acknowledging the superhero status Roy and Dale, and the Lone Ranger and Tonto deserved but coveting their mounts more.

I'm remembering the gallant Trigger as Ray turns his head and smiles at me. "So far, so good." There's that smile that always quickens my heart. He looks like a horse guy to me. I've waited for this moment since we first fell in love.

We walk along, single file, beside the edge of a filbert orchard. We amble across a gravel road and through an open gate to a grassy trail about as wide as a narrow driveway. Alongside the right, a barbed-wire fence encloses a pasture where half a dozen cows graze. "Does Czar like cows?" Ray asks, sounding worried.

"Czar loves cows," I promise.

Within ten minutes the path ends in a small meadow where someone has thoughtlessly left signs of a campsite: charcoal and a few charred logs, several beer cans, an overturned white plastic chair. Buddy plods past, Czar right behind him.

Vida is curious about the white chair and we spend a few minutes getting acquainted with it, then trot left along a hillside trail to join the others.

Vida

"We're going down there?" Ray asks, looking at a gentle drop-off on his left where downed logs mix with tangles of blackberry vines and thistle.

I shake my head. Ray looks marginally relieved. The sharp descent would be difficult for Czar with his arthritic hips, and I don't want to expose Ray to a stumbling horse.

This is a perfect time to admit that, ironically, I have my ex-husband, Hal, to thank for owning a horse. Our children were three, five, and nine when Hal bought ten acres on a hillside near Portland and moved them and me into the original homestead. He had long wanted to create a self-sustaining lifestyle for the family. I lauded the values but dreaded the bone-wearying lifestyle. I gritted my teeth as we moved in a chemical porta-potty and a fifty-gallon barrel of water. But when a friend asked me to keep their Arab/Welsh pony Scooter, my heart did a somersault. I could put up with a lot to have a horse.

Until then, at age thirty-five, my actual riding experience had been limited to a few outings on Shetland ponies during childhood summer vacations. I read every used book I could find about training and riding horses; still, learning to ride Scooter was something like learning to swim by being thrown in a lake. I would wrap my hands in his mane and swing on bareback. Before I could even settle onto him he'd twist and kick like I was a giant horsefly he had no intention of tolerating. When he didn't lose me that way, he would take off galloping down the nearest hill, and I would hang on for dear life.

My daughter Tami, then in fifth grade, joined horse 4-H with Scooter. This seemed like a reasonable adventure. And they seemed to be getting along reasonably well until I got a phone call from the 4-H leader one Saturday afternoon.

The group had been trotting their horses in a filbert orchard, and Scooter took a quick detour under some low branches. When I got to the leader's house, Tami lay stretched out on the couch, her scraped chin and neck cleaned and medicated. I returned Scooter to his owner and bought Magic, a beautiful bay running quarter horse, and Tami let me have some fun for a while.

Magic shied at everything from mailboxes to dandelions and bucked at the slightest provocation, or no provocation at all. Hal liked her for a few days because she nuzzled his neck when he fed her ice cream but soon came to believe I had a death wish when I chose to ride her every day. I loved her madly and figured we'd eventually learn together to move nicely down the road.

A friend offered to sell me her stalwart old gelding, Lucky, for just a few hundred dollars, and I bought him for the kids to ride, though I kept Magic, too. Tami, my boys, Ben and Joel—we all enjoyed Lucky, a gentle sorrel quarter horse. I would take one child at a time to ride with me and Magic to the end of our country road where a stand of tall cedars bordered a rock-strewn stream. On those rides they would tell me their secrets. It was our private time, and the warm presence of the horses opened their souls to me in a way that to this day I am grateful for. I believe those rides were part of the foundation of my children's self-confidence in the world.

As I look over at Ray, that self-confidence is something he seems to be stretching toward.

"We're going up the hill," I tell him. "There's a great trail here somewhere."

Grasses and shrubs covering the hillside have grown knee-deep since we've ridden here. Horses remember trails when I don't.

"I found it," Jeanne sings out and turns up the hill through dense foliage.

Czar and Vida follow, but when we come to a big patch of blackberries, Ray yelps as they snag his arm and face.

Jeanne looks back. She and I are holding our horses to the right of the brambles, but Czar seems to be blundering through them.

"Press hard with your left leg and he'll move to the right," Jeanne tells Ray.

Ray moves Czar successfully away from the blackberries, but the path is getting harder to follow.

"Are we still on the trail?" Jeanne sounds concerned. Ray looks somewhere north of concerned.

"Give Buddy his head and he'll find the way. We're right behind you." I have immeasurable confidence in the ability of horses to find passable trails. I try to convey this confidence to Ray, locking eyes with him and hoping he at least trusts me.

The moment Jeanne loosens her reins, Buddy turns onto a deer trail heading steeply up the hill. He considers it passable, lunging through underbrush, over downed logs, and under branches, Czar and Vida scrambling behind him. I hadn't planned on a deer trail. It's clear Ray didn't either. The horses are crashing through the woods, veering around trees, stumbling on roots, and Ray holds on, but barely. Vines are lashing at our legs and faces, and it's a wild ride for me; I can't imagine how Ray is faring.

I remember Hal rode Lucky once. The minute he got on, he dug his heels into Lucky's sides, and my usually gentle horse burst into a frantic gallop. Hal managed to stay on and eventually pull Lucky to a stop, but he was as white as the blaze that ran the length of Lucky's nose.

Hal grew to resent, more and more, all things equine. I trimmed fence, dug drain fields, and stacked hay bales alone. Truthfully, the fact that Hal didn't like horses didn't end our marriage. While sharing an interest in horses would have made the hard edges of our relationship easier to trod, it was the daily arguments about everything in our lives from the right way to kill a slug in an organic garden to the height and width of windows for our new house. By the time I filed for divorce, I was swimming upstream in a muddy river of depression, lost in the whys and why-mes.

I found that horses were my Prozac.

As I watched them graze in our pasture, my heart would rise in my chest with pleasure. Brushing them, I would pour out my troubles and they would turn their heads to nuzzle me. Riding them, I forgot, for a moment, that I was desperately unhappy. With my arms around a horse, I could feel, if only for an instant, that I was the luckiest woman in the world, and I could imagine life lived happily after Hal.

When I left my marriage, I gave Magic to a friend. She agreed to keep Lucky, as well, so I could ride him whenever I had the time. Lucky was the bright spot in my day as I worked my way out of depression. I'd been divorced three years when he died quietly, one night, in the pasture, probably of a heart attack. I got the call at school where I taught. I had to request a substitute, then spent the day in the pasture with my loyal equine friend, sobbing good-byes. I cried for Lucky, but I eventually let the tears flow for me and the kids, too, for what we'd lost and had to let go.

That day seems like eons ago.

Today we struggle not to let go, and the steep incline Ray, Jeanne, and I traverse to reach the ridge—the three of us breathing as hard as the horses—reminds me that life is more a series of switchbacks than an even, straight line.

So far, I've snagged my riding pants in two places, and Jeanne has a trickle of blood on her arm where a thorn caught hold and wouldn't let go. I notice, however, Ray's face is glowing. His eyes are dancing, his grin beaming. "My god! That was exhilarating! I just hung on to the horn."

Inside, my heart sings.

"Ready for more?" I ask.

Jeanne says nothing about using reins versus gripping the saddle horn, although it might make Ray's journey a little less tenuous. But she is a wise woman and knows when to tamp down enthusiasm and when not to. Ray's is off the charts and sure to carry him through the day.

We thread our way down the hill at an angle, the horses sure-footed, while birds seem to call out to us from branches overhead. Trillium blooms litter the hillside to my right and I feel a kind of contentment that I have never known. I am with my horse, my good friend, and my honey; the day is beautiful and the ride is one of the best I've ever taken. I'm beginning to see that a romantic gallop on the beach and horse camping may be right around the corner.

Several hundred yards down a heavily wooded path, we turn and follow a switchback to a stream. The stream is too deep to ford, and someone has spread sheets of plywood across it for a makeshift bridge.

"Are you okay with crossing the bridge?" Jeanne asks Ray.

He says sure, but I look over to check his confidence temperature. He's solid.

"We need to go one at a time," I insist, concerned about the bridge's strength.

I tell Ray he should go first; if Jeanne or I start across, Czar might hurry after us. I don't want the weight of two horses on that plywood.

"Sure, I can go first." Ray nudges Czar with his heels.

Nothing happens.

"Kick him hard," Jeanne says.

Ray does and he and Czar go right across the bridge, Ray grinning proudly. Where is my video camera? He *is* a natural horseman.

When we're all on the other side, Jeanne asks us if we want to canter.

"Of course," Ray says, his confidence now riding somewhere south of expert horseman.

The canter turns into a gallop as the horses vie for the lead before we can rein them in, and Ray sits superbly in the saddle through it all. I laugh inside; barrel racing might even be in our future.

We stop and rest for a while, then continue up the trail, but it soon dead-ends. Jeanne demonstrates a haunch turn for Ray, and Czar does a stiff approximation of it. Bravo to horse and rider. Vida and I turn and we all head down. We haven't gone very far when Jeanne notices a narrow path branching off to our right. It tempts us all. We take it and are leisurely walking along, visiting back and forth, when abruptly we're on the edge of a patch of thistles up to the horses' shoulders, the plants bursting with purple flowers as big as our fists. Immediately I pull evenly on Vida's reins and keep a steady pressure on her sides as I back her away. Jeanne gets Buddy to safety too. Czar is dancing nervously, nostrils flaring. He tosses his head as if his sides have been scraped by thistles. I'm worried that he'll buck, dumping Ray in the stickers, or spin and bolt for home. I broke my back once riding a horse, and it sticks with you. For Ray, it could spell the end of his horse adventures.

The accident was my fault, not the horse's. It was a few years after my divorce, and I was playing Dale Evans to show off for a new beau. With no saddle, no bridle, not even a halter, just stupidity mixed with a pinch of arrogance, I twined my fingers into Lucky's mane and swung on. Sitting on him might have satisfied me, but I was out to impress. I gently squeezed my legs against Lucky's sides to move him forward, assessed he was fine, and we walked along the pasture easily. I squeezed, urging him into a trot.

About that time Lucky realized he had a fool on his back. He broke into a canter, then a dead gallop, frisking around the pasture. I don't know why I decided to bale right in front of this guy. I might have stayed on and ridden out Lucky's playfulness, and I guess I thought I could land on my feet like some equestrian acrobat. But when I baled, I landed flat on my back, fracturing a left lower lumbar. That feeling is something I can recall with vivid clarity to this day.

The expression in Ray's eyes as he faces this next obstacle tells me an injury like that is his greatest fear. "What do I do?" Ray's smile has morphed into a grim frown. His lesson in the arena didn't include backing up. He holds the reins with one hand and the saddle horn with the other.

Jeanne coaches him step by step. "Hold on to both reins." They're even with his ears again. "Shorten them more. Pull evenly. That's it. Keep even pressure on Czar's sides."

Czar takes a careful step back, then another, then scoots backward onto the trail where we're waiting. Ray lets go of one rein and runs a hand across his forehead. "Whew."

"Had enough for today?" Jeanne asks.

"Yeah. I don't want to push my luck."

"You never seemed scared," I say.

"I wasn't. This was actually really pretty great."

My heart leaps with joy. Ray has braved brambles, overgrown paths on steep hillsides, a bridge, a race, and a thistle patch. A few more rides on Czar, another lesson or two, and we'll be husband-horse shopping.

Back at the barn, Ray dismounts, stiff legged. "There's a lot more to riding a horse than climbing on his back," he says to Jeanne.

Then he turns to me. The serious look in his eyes and straight set of his mouth rein me in to reality. "Honey, I'm glad I came today. I'm not scared anymore." The way he says it, slow with a hint of sadness, I know what's coming. "Riding takes a lot of time and skill. I know you want me to feel the way you do about horses, but I have enough going on in my life already. I'd rather golf."

Just like that. I was dumbfounded.

In seconds he littered the driveway with fragments of my shattered hope. I know I shouldn't be surprised. Ray didn't spend his dimes on mechanical horses as a child. Still, my heart is somewhere in the toe of my left riding boot when Vida nickers softly. We're approaching the barn and maybe she's greeting one of the other horses. Or maybe she's reminding me that I needn't be disappointed. After all, I still have her.

Back in the arena, Ray says he thinks he can get Czar's saddle and bridle off himself, and I turn my attention to my mare, blinking back tears of disappointment. She nickers again, and I'm sure this time it's for me. As I fumble with the girth, she turns her head and looks at me with liquid brown eyes, then stretches her neck a bit farther and catches my shirtsleeve in her teeth.

My tears turn into laughter. I swear she reads my mind. Of all the men, kids, and creatures, she's always there for me, a solid presence in my busy life. She's an eager mount when I'm up and want to ride, a comforter when I'm down and need to talk, and I simply can't be sad for very long around her.

Unbuckling the throatlatch on her bridle, I feel a hand on my shoulder. I turn and see Ray smiling that crooked smile. Only this time, I know exactly what lurks behind it. He isn't afraid of the horse. He's afraid if he doesn't love the horse, I may not love him as much.

But I can see his love for me as clearly as I can feel Vida's loyal affection. "You okay, babe?" He kisses me and I smell the musk of horses on his skin. Fleetingly, I can't help but wonder how my short game will be. Golf can't be that hard, can it?

It may take me awhile, but I'll come around. We can still horse-camp; we'll just golf-camp, too. I have Ray, and I have Vida. I have everything I need.

The Billy Dal Gang

Michele Scott

We called ourselves "The Billy Dal Gang." Four ten-year-old girls, their horses, and my dad.

My dad, Dal, was, of course, Billy Dal. There was Billy Stace, Billy Renee, Billy Laura, and me, Billy Shell. While grooming and saddling up our horses, we'd get into character. Billy Dal would set up the scenario. "Okay, girls, we got three bad guys, and I mean *bad guys,* on the run. They stole a lot of money from that there bank." He'd point to our house. "Now we gotta go find them and arrest them, and bring 'em back."

"Yes we do, Billy Dal!"

"We gotta be real careful and sneak up on 'em. They're armed and dangerous."

We would giggle at my dad's silly antics, but once we were up on our horses it was a different deal. We were playing the roles. Dad had a sure-footed quarter horse named Smokey that led the gang. He was a horse with sharp instincts. Several times we would wind down single file from the mountain, the thick chaparral smelling sweet and earthy, surrounding us on the rocky trail, and occasionally, Smokey would stop on a dime. Billy Dal would turn around, bringing a finger to his lips, his blue eyes tinged with a stern warning for us not to move. Our adrenaline pumped as we'd come to know before we ever heard the zing and rattle of the snake that Smokey had spotted a rattler.

We would wait for the snake to back away before clucking the horses forward, as Billy Dal's constant rule was to leave nature alone. He didn't believe in killing the snakes out on the trail as many others did. "They were here first," he'd say.

Making it down off the mountain, we would ride through what we learned was former Indian grounds in San Diego County. As we descended into the foothills, we passed a crumbling stone wall built hundreds of years ago, ancient remains at the bottom of the mountain. Danger lurked around every corner, on every trail. It always seemed as if a slight breeze was blowing through that passage, even on days when there was no wind. It was the kind of breeze that carried a whistle on it and would make the hair on the back of the neck stand on end. It was easy to let our young imaginations get the best of us, wondering if someone was watching us as that feeling of an otherworldly presence remained strong until we got down onto the flats. We would all grow quiet passing through the open crevice in the stone wall. In a word, it was spooky. And Billy Dal loved to add to the mystery of it all.

Once we passed the cobblestone wall and entered the flats, Billy Dal would again bring a finger to his lips and shake his head. We all understood that this time it wasn't a snake. He'd point straight ahead and mouth, "Bad guys." In retrospect I think my dad was just trying to get all of us little girls to stop yapping our mouths because we could make a lot of noise, particularly my friend Billy Stace and me.

Billy Stace and I had a kind of competition between us. It was called "My horse is faster than your horse." This debate could take up the entire three-hour trail ride if we didn't have the distraction of the Billy Dal Gang. Stace had a petite gray Arabian mare named Zelle. Zelle was a little loose in the brain. Okay, she was nuts much of the time, but, yeah, she could run. My horse was definitely faster, though—definitely. I'd had the good fortune to raise this mare from a yearling when my dad had her delivered for my sixth birthday. He bought her for a hundred dollars without ever seeing her. He coined her "ugly duckling" when she stepped off the trailer. But to me she was the most beautiful horse in the world, and she was by far one of the most patient animals I've ever had. This mare as a two-year-old would let me lie on her back while in her corral. I'd climb all over her. I have no clue what my parents were thinking, but thank goodness the horse was as sweet-natured as she was.

Full grown, Dandy stood over sixteen hands. She had only two spots on her rear, but apparently that was enough to be a registered Appaloosa, and this horse could haul butt! Stace and I liked to get down to the flats and race each other. I can still hear the argument

Krissy

now. "I won, Shelly. I did. You started before me, so technically I won and you cheated."

"No way. I started when you started and I won fair and square. My horse is faster than yours," I'd say.

"No, she isn't."

"Wanna make a bet?" And this was how it went. We started bringing stopwatches with us, but the argument to this day (thirty years later) still has not been decided. Both Stace and I (we are still great friends) have agreed to disagree on this count. Dad wouldn't let us race each other when he was with us, but on those days when he couldn't go, we were all about getting down onto the flats and moving out.

Dad also liked speed, and as Billy Dal, he added a bit more tension to our game besides only seeking out the bad guys. My father, as you've guessed by now, is quite a storyteller. We'd be riding along down on the flats with cottonwood trees on either side of us. Many times cotton would blow in the wind and we might suggest it was snow falling, even in eighty-degree weather. Each of us with long hair hanging down our backs, our faces turned up to soak in the sun, and all of a sudden Billy Dal would say, "Oh, no. Oh, no. We gotta get outta here!"

"What? Why?" the Billy Dal Gang would squeal.

"It's the hoop snake!"

"The hoop snake?"

"Oh, yes. The hoop snake. You don't know about the hoop snake?"

"No."

Billy Dal would point up. "Look up there at the top of the ridge. Don't you see it? He's the color of coral with black rings every few inches on his diamondback skin. He's related to the diamondback rattler, but he's much deadlier. And he's after us."

"What do you mean?" one of us would ask.

"I mean he's spotted us, and in a minute if we don't get out of here, he'll be down off that mountain so fast and bite your horses and have us all for dinner."

"He's a snake, Billy Dal. He can't eat us all for dinner."

"He's not just a snake. He's the hoop snake. He rounds himself up like a circle, takes his tail in his mouth, and rolls down the hill. His prey are horses and their riders, and believe me, he could eat us all up. We gotta go. Now!"

Billy Dal would put Smokey into a gallop and we'd all follow suit, laughing and squealing and carrying on about how we'd better hurry so we didn't become snake food. I don't know how many times we played out this scenario. It could have been a hundred or more. It didn't matter. It was so much fun and we'd add to it, change it up a bit, but it always came down to pure ecstasy and freedom on the backs of our horses.

After a good gallop and getting away from the hoop snake, there were all sorts of other "enemies" we had to keep an eye out for. There was a pack of hostile Indians we had to watch out for, who, if we weren't careful, could track us and we'd wind up scalped. We had to watch out for all sorts of wild animals and, of course, those bad guys. Any chance we had to "get away" from anything considered an enemy, we did, and we did quickly.

Our trail rides typically wound up at "the saloon." We'd ride along a trail that would take us through a golf course. We'd only go onto the course if it was later in the day and Billy Dal scoped it out to make sure there weren't too many golfers on the course. I still have no clue how we never got kicked off that golf course. We'd ride through on the cart trails and on up to the bar, where Billy Dal would order us all Shirley Temples and he'd have a beer. I think part of the reason we didn't get kicked off is we were sort of entertainment. I'd learned how to stand up on Dandy in the saddle and I was even able to do a headstand on her. We were like a regular circus show. Looking back, I have to wonder how I made it out of childhood.

"Okay, gang, we've had our refreshments and now we gotta get back out there and track those bad guys."

"Yes, sir, Billy Dal!" And we'd be off again and back out onto the trail. If the day was a hot one and the river bottom had water in it, we'd many times head over to the river, untack the horses, slide off their backs as they went into the water, and hang on to their tails and swim with them. Of course there were always "dangers" in the river bottom, too.

"Watch out for that crocodile, Billy Shell," one of the other gang members would yell.

"Yeah, he's gonna eat you."

Fits of laughter would break out among us as we truly were having the best times of our lives.

We also had names for our trails. Our favorite was the jumping trail. My mother would never allow me to jump as a kid (guess what I do now?), so I'm pretty sure if she knew about this trail she'd have come totally unglued.

The jumping trail was covered with brush and cottonwoods. Talk about a cross-country course! Jumping the trail was always precluded with another story, like almost everything we did as the gang. The best part is that with all of the trees and brush, there were shadows that filled the area. Imaginations ran wild, and even on days my friends couldn't join us, I could come up with all sorts of fantastical story ideas. As far as I was concerned, fairies hid underneath the rocks that lined the trail, elves played in the shadows, and trolls hid underneath the logs we jumped, waiting to surprise us with their snaggly teeth and green, grotesque faces. They never did, but it was great to imagine that they might.

And, of course, there were the horses who were characters in their own right. They tolerated our fantasies. Dandy was never one to spook or do anything flighty. She was calm, strong, and patient for a young horse. Smokey was the leader, like Dad—both wise. Billy Stace had Zelle, who ironically enough was a lot like my friend—both a bit hyper and strong-willed. Billy Renee had an older Thoroughbred who tolerated whatever was tossed his way without much ado, and Billy Laura had a Buckskin gelding who wasn't the best-mannered animal of the group (loved to nip others' rear ends), but all the same he followed the pack, and no matter what, we knew when we set out on those horses with my dad that we weren't going to be disappointed.

The only disappointment came when we heard those words, "Well, gang, we better head home. The mother folk will have dinner ready and it's getting dark."

A collective sigh would ring out and we would head back up the hill and into our neighborhood.

There are days now, as I learn more about the horse than I ever learned as a kid, that I wish I'd participated in Pony Club or horse shows, other than the little backyard shows I'd occasionally do. At times I feel ignorant about these amazing animals. But as I reflect back on my childhood and how horses were such a huge part of it, I realize I wouldn't change it for the world. I may not have understood the mechanics of the animal, the right feed to give them (we were known for feeding them coffee cans filled with grain daily with their hay— the horses loved it), what the right lead was, or the right diagonal, or any of that. That all came as I grew into an adult. But what I did learn, what I do understand, is that to me the horse represents far more than an animal who tolerates me up on his or her back. To me, the horse represents family, friendship, imagination, and total fantasy. The soul of the horse has driven me to explore who I am as a creative person, and that comes from the animals I enjoyed as a kid and the father who was never too old to be a kid himself but always wise enough to be safe, loving, nurturing, and fun.

Bear

Dobie Houson

Like a demon possessed but with the grace of Pegasus stripped of his wings, he commanded attention. He reared, jumped, and spun, stirring up thick clouds of dust. And his size made him even more imposing; a stunning dapple gray coat and dramatic black mane and tail streaked with flowing white tresses. But it wasn't his beauty that caught my eye; it was his anger. It was only later, a few months after meeting him, that I understood the cause.

My daughter took lessons at the ranch where Bear lived. She rode a chubby red Shetland named Pony Baloney; I played around on a sweet quarter horse named Maggie. My friend Meg owned the ranch, and while she schooled my daughter, she'd watch my progress with Maggie. Apparently I'd impressed her, because one day Meg began rattling off a list of things she wanted me to do—with Bear. I stared at her in disbelief. I was a good rider but not *that* good.

"Meg," I said, stopping her stream of consciousness. "I'm afraid of him."

"Oh, honey." She laughed. "We're *all* afraid of him. I don't want you to put ninety days' dressage training on him; I want you to get into his head and figure out what's going on with him."

Oh, I thought; *that* I might be able to do.

All I knew about Bear was that his sire was a Grand Prix jumper, famous for throwing talented gray offspring who went on to compete successfully in the disciplines of jumping and dressage. I also knew that he rebelled during his training, going over backward on his trainer repeatedly, until his owners decided that there were only two options—either he would be given away, without his papers so that no one could trace him back to his sire, or be put down. Meg, who had a way with difficult, problem horses, was one of several people they called about taking him. She opted to take him and see what she could do but made no promises. Two years later and one very unsuccessful ride, Meg looked to me.

So began the game. An hour here and there, just watching from outside his pen, since I wouldn't dare consider getting that close. It wasn't safe. Besides the fact that he rarely had all four feet on the ground, Bear also had a habit of biting. As the days passed, he began to watch me back. And as the weeks passed, he allowed me safe passage into his corral, where I would sit on the soft dirt while he munched his hay. From time to time he would wander over to me, lower his head, and nibble gently at my shoes, his nose nuzzling the laces back and forth. As time went on, I taught him to play tag. Initially, I stayed outside his pen, but eventually I ventured closer for that too.

Soon the pieces of his story fell into place. Bear's issues were all about *timing*. His timing had never been honored. He'd been weaned too soon, shipped away from his mother too soon, and put into training too soon. In fact, every important event in his life had been thrust upon him before he was ready. When his training became more accelerated than he could handle, he rebelled. It was to be expected.

At Meg's request I began doing groundwork with him on a longe line. At first he tested me, stopping and facing me on the circle instead of changing direction or responding to my signals. It was almost comical the way he made me earn every success. But after a few weeks he was walking, trotting, and cantering on cue. Six months passed before I considered riding him. Meg worried about how he would handle a bit and bridle, so we agreed I would ride him in a halter with two lead lines attached. Looking back, I'm surprised I didn't see the risk associated with the lack of control, but sometimes innocence is our best protection. I swung my leg over his back and settled gently into the saddle. Instantly, I knew I belonged on this horse. I was home. I squeezed my legs and he walked on quietly. I felt elated.

Months passed and I continued to ride Bear and work on refining his manners. But he was a challenge unlike any horse I'd ever met. I'd previously trained with a Grand Prix level trainer, but I learned quickly that this horse was going to make me learn everything from scratch, on his terms, and in his own sweet time. I was both humbled and conflicted. On one hand, I knew if I stuck with it, Bear would make me become the kind of rider I'd always dreamed of becoming; on the other, I wasn't sure I wanted to work that hard. But Meg kept encouraging me to return.

Bear didn't understand the meaning of surrender. His main goal was speed. No matter what gait we were in, he wanted to go faster. When I first began to canter him, I'd have to run him into the fence to stop him. If I was too heavy with my hands, he'd rear, shaking his head from side to side. If I was too heavy with my legs he'd swing away from the pressure and buck. His gaits were big and bold. Often I'd feel inept as I fought to stay balanced simply at a posting trot. And at a canter, I usually had to ride balanced slightly out of the saddle in two-point to float with, rather than try to sit, his movement. People often commented that we were such a harmonious team. I didn't share their vision. We didn't feel harmonious at all.

I'm not sure what I was thinking the day I took him on his first trail ride. After all, I didn't really have him under control in the arena. But we struck out and meandered between two long rows of orange trees. His back was long, supple and fluid, and his head bobbed in a relaxed rhythm. Since he was behaving so well, I took up the slack in the reins, rose out of the saddle slightly, and pressed my legs, slightly cueing a canter. Bear dropped his haunches and sprung like a cat into a full gallop. I tightened the reins slightly using a half halt to signal that I wanted him to slow down. Nothing happened. I half halted him again. He kept galloping. We sped, flat out toward a paved road, and I knew if I didn't stop him, we'd hit the road—and at this speed, we'd slip and go down.

I should have panicked, but anyone who rides will tell you that when things go wrong, they happen in slow motion. I remember being confused about what to do next. Suddenly, I heard my trainer's voice, her thick Austrian accent pounding in my head. *Your seat is your brakes. You cannot influence the horse just with your hands and your legs. Sit down!*

I sat down hard in the saddle and hauled back on the reins. In mid-stride I felt Bear hesitate as if to ask, did she mean it? His feet continued to strike the ground with no sign of slowing. I hauled back again; the rhythm of his feet slowed, and I hauled back again. He began to downshift into a light, submissive canter. He finally slowed to a walk and, uneventfully, we turned back toward the barn. I walked him slowly and, once back at the barn, slithered off of him like a wet rag. It was awhile before I ever let him canter on the trail again.

It is said that timing is everything—that it has the power to heal wounds and allows opportunities to unfold in the appropriate moment. All along Meg had told Bear to manifest an owner for himself, to choose who and when the time was right. "Bring me your owner," she'd say. When I first learned of this, I was surprised—surprised because I thought she'd intended to keep Bear for herself. And the question of his ownership escalated when a trainer from a local jumping stable came to see Bear and assessed his worth at about $25,000. Again I was surprised she would consider selling him as a hunter/jumper, knowing he wanted to do far more than jump.

As Bear's fate became uncertain, I wondered how things would shake out, but Bear *had* manifested his new owner. I realized that new owner was *me*. All along he wanted me to buy him. I had some soul searching to do since I wasn't in the market for a horse. And even if I had been, Bear was the opposite of everything I thought I wanted. He was difficult, hot, untrained, and expensive. Because of his energy level, he wasn't an easy keeper and required expensive supplements. And he couldn't stand still, so it took twice as long to shoe him. I would have preferred an obedient, push-button dressage horse.

As I pondered the decision to buy him, I thought I was just being compassionate—that I didn't want to see him relinquished to a situation that might have crushed his beautiful spirit. But in truth, the only thing that mattered was that I had grown to love him. So I made the commitment, and he became mine. I was on a cloud for twenty-four hours telling everyone I knew. Then panic set in at the daunting responsibility of owning a horse like Bear.

Bear's first love wasn't dressage; it required too much discipline and control. It required surrender, and he was in resistance, because he is—as his name implied—wild at heart. He strained against the bit, hollowed his back, and stiffened his neck in defiance as he pranced sideways around the arena. Some days I was frustrated with him. Some days I was frustrated with myself. I couldn't understand why he wouldn't surrender. I was confused about why *nothing* was working. But I knew deep down that if I was doing everything right, Bear would, too. I knew he was telling me that I was over-riding with

Bear

my hands, and under-riding with my seat. I just couldn't make the transition with him. I could with other horses, but they were already in surrender. My trainer had told me that if things weren't going right it was never the horse's fault. But on the rare occasions when she rode Bear, it was reassuring to see that she had some of the same struggles with him.

I threw other things into the mix to break the routine of dressage. We jumped, hacked on the trails, toyed with liberty training, and even experimented with some obstacle courses. But I continued to return to dressage, partially because of the deep joy I found in the briefly harmonic moments when everything came together, light and utterly perfect, and because I knew what it felt like to ride at the Grand Prix level.

Now, while we work hard, what I cherish most is our time together hanging out. I dodge his playful attempts to bite my shoelaces and clothes. Or when we stroll down the lane drifting in the moment while he munches lush grass. I know this is his favorite time, too, and I wonder what my life would be like had I not met him. Or his, had he not met me.

And I wonder sometimes what we're thinking when we dictate a horse's future based on his or her parents' past or only what we want. If the sire is a Grand Prix jumper, then is the son or daughter's only destiny to become a mirror image? What becomes of the horse's goals if the humans don't ask or pay attention?

After eleven years, Bear finally surrendered to dressage. And I finally learned how to ride him. The rise and fall of my seat are in harmony with his back. My hands create an elastic connection from my elbow to his mouth. My legs drape gracefully at his sides. I hear nothing but his hoofbeats pounding in rhythm to my heart as they echo in my ears. We surrender to a moment where time and space stand still and we float as one.

Plenty of people might wonder how a mediocre rider and a rebel like Bear meshed. Quite simply, I took the time to understand his needs and desires. I listened to him. I honored his timing, his intelligence, and his spirited complexity and asked him to honor the same in me. I balanced his needs with my own and I worked on myself. Ours is a relationship of love, balance, and trust. It's the basis for all great relationships.

Whenever I climb up on any horse's back and settle into the saddle, I always feel that I am where I'm supposed to be. But when I settle onto Bear's back, I know I am home. It was that way from the very beginning, and years later it has only deepened. He is my knight in shining armor.

No matter what my week or day is like, no matter what list of untended tasks, or stack of unpaid bills, or troubling situations loom large, being with him eclipses life's rough spots. His eyes speak a language I have come to know as well as my own; I can feel the weight of the world lift off my shoulders, and Bear's love makes my heart swell.

It is a simple fact that Bear has taught me many things. Most important—that horses experience the same complex emotions as humans. They hate schedules and being forced to do what is not in their nature as much as we do, as much as I do. They hurt, become depressed, feel joy, have their hearts broken, and love deeply. They are as wise and as spiritually complex as humans. Maybe more so. And if we can put our agenda aside and attempt to understand theirs, we will be rewarded with a partnership beyond our wildest dreams. Even if it takes more time than we thought it would.

Quite often, our animal companions are a mirror for us and we for them. We walk parallel paths—facing obstacles, overcoming challenges, and celebrating triumphs all while holding up the looking glass of reflection for one another.

I told Bear one day that there was such irony in the fact that it took him so long to surrender to dressage. Especially since like all of us, he wanted to be admired. "There is such beauty and grace in surrender," I said. "You're far more beautiful in surrender than you ever were in resistance." As soon as I'd uttered the words I knew they were more for my ears than for his. A simple reminder that we are all more beautiful in surrender—a state in which we open ourselves to the infinite well of abundance, we flow, and we allow the true light of our inner being to shine, to be revealed to the world, and to be admired.

I have often thought that I was here to be Bear's teacher. In truth, he is here to teach me.

Akualele

Jill Widner

He moves recklessly beneath me down the face of the crag, his hooves clattering over the scree in the last of the light.

By the time I see the kinks of barbed wire, he's walking straight through it, shaking his head, taking me with him, my knees slashing through molasses grass, high as his withers, taking us to the trail that leads to the road. And I let him. Or I don't know how not to let him. Or I don't want not to let him. Because it's what he wants. And I love that he knows what he wants.

Green horse, green rider, is what people say. In general, I disregard the things people say. I wanted a horse. Now I have one. But when he nips at the branches of haole koa in his way, as if to prove to myself that I'm not as green as they think, I yank his bit to the side, knowing that I've pinched his tongue. Cold and impatient to get back, I shift the torn stems of the wild orchids I picked in the pasture to my hand holding the reins, and lean to the side, reaching beneath the belly band, losing myself in the damp, warm feel of his coat. I sniff at the animal smell on my fingers. *This* is what I wanted. I love the way being with him makes me understand what I want.

I keep him staked out at Kōʻele, the small, unfenced paddock on the other side of the road. His grain waits in a bucket in the back of my station wagon, and his barrel of water stands half-hidden in the pampas grass beneath a guava tree. He knows this, and I know he wants to run, but I hold him back and return my hand to the soft rope of the reins, glancing as I do at my fingers clamped around the flowers—bunched in my fist like a rifle—so blackened and oily with leather and sweat they look as if they belong to someone else.

Just ahead, a track of tire treads smears out of a puddle and across the grass. It's been nearly a year, and still, when I see the tracks of his tires, I'm a little surprised that he's come. I don't think, *Marlon has come to exercise the roan.* I think, *the game warden* has come to exercise the roan, as though I don't know him. And maybe I don't.

His truck is parked beside a bulldozer that faces an area he has cleared into a kind of arena. Behind it is a stand of eucalyptus trees.

"In case the roan bucks loose," he tells me.

The windows of his truck are rolled down and his two small dogs are inside, looking out, waiting, I like to think, for the smell of me, for the sound of my horse's hooves, as if they know when I return they can go home. I tighten my thighs, urging him forward to the back of my car where I dismount, tie him to the trailer hitch, and drop the torn-stemmed field orchids through the open window onto the seat. Already he is rubbing his forehead against the bumper, scratching the paint with the bridle. I move to his side to unbuckle the throat latch, and the bit clanks against his teeth as it falls into my hand.

I like the yellow-grass smell of his mouth. The warm feel of his saliva in the palm of my hand. From the beginning he let me touch him. I like the way he lets me brush his legs and haunches. I like to quieten his back, hot and damp with sweat beneath the blanket before I loosen the cinch.

When he smells his grain, his nostrils flare and he paws the ground. *It's too soon,* I tell him. *You need to cool down first.*

Marlon is walking the roan on the end of a longe rope inside the invisible lines of the makeshift arena, tall and dark in jeans and an army jacket. My eyes go to the black ball cap on his head, the words LAW ENFORCEMENT OFFICER embroidered in yellow thread across the front, and then to the roan's coat, which is the dry red color of the foam that scuds up the beach after a hard rain. Though I know he has heard me and has seen me, he doesn't speak.

As the roan reaches the top of the arc in the circle she has trampled in the grass, the rope grows taut in Marlon's hands. He raises his arm, swings it over his head, and turns on his heels so that he remains facing her as she continues to circle the ring, watching her as I watch him. When she slows down or breaks her gait, the frayed end of another rope he holds coiled beneath his jacket shoots out toward her hind quarters. Each time he does this, the roan balks in surprise and shakes her head, the whites of her eyes large and wild, her body heavy and squat, short in the neck and the legs.

I crouch beneath a eucalyptus tree and pull my jacket close. As Marlon turns the roan on the rope, I listen to the even beat of her hooves striking the ground through the grass, and to the sounds Marlon makes with his mouth that are also like grass somehow—like wind in the hoof-beaten grass.

When it is nearly dark, I carry two cold bottles, dripping because the ice in the cooler has melted, toward him. Marlon pulls the longe rope short and calls out to the roan. She stops and turns to face him. He strokes her throat as he unties the knot in the rope looped round her neck, glancing at the bottle of beer I hold out for him. He takes them both from my hands, twists off the caps, and hands one back to me.

I am always caught off guard a little when he speaks to me directly. "Have you thought of a name for your horse?"

"Not yet," I say.

"It will come." He stalls a little, blowing over the lip of his bottle of beer. "What are you having for dinner?"

"I don't know. Toast. Nothing."

"My brother gave me a side of deer," he offers. "It's hanging in my garage. If I invite you over for deer meat, it would give me the incentive to butcher it."

"Are there ribs in the side he gave you?" I ask.

"Why? You like ribs?"

Sanoe

I nod.

"Go home, then. Take a shower. Come when you're ready. We'll make a barbecue."

Marlon loops the rope into a make-shift halter around the roan's head and leads her to the swivel at the end of her stake rope. I carry the empty beer bottles back to the station wagon where my horse is stamping and snorting, gnawing at the paint again where crystals of salt from the ocean air have dried on the finish.

Instead of reprimanding him, I slide my hand along his flank and down his haunch to the place where his hip meets his belly. It is one of the softest sensations I know, to touch him there where his hair spirals like the head of a comet into a smooth pale circle. He strains his neck against the rope to nuzzle my shoulder, his teeth so close to my face that I can see the grass particles between them. Marlon has told me not to let him do this. *A horse is not a dog*, he says. But I am not afraid.

Later, driving in the rain under the low-hanging ironwoods toward the subdivision where he lives, I think of him pacing the roan. I think of the backs of his legs. The way the backs of his legs look through his jeans; the way his hands look holding the rope.

By a quarter of nine I am standing on the concrete floor of Marlon's garage, my hands in my pockets. A plywood board covered in butcher paper is set upon two sawhorses. The blood-brown side of venison swings from a beam on a silver hook between the coils of rope, the saddles, the halters, the bridles. Marlon holds it steady and pulls a blade through the flesh. From their rugs in the corner, the dogs watch as he lays the hip and the leg on the makeshift table. He points to his workbench and asks me to hand him his hacksaw. Before he begins to saw through the bone, he pulls a Polaroid snapshot from his shirt pocket and hands it to me.

"This is for me?"

"If you like."

The photograph is a faded grainy green. The body of the horned-axis lies beside him in the back of his truck, its muzzle resting so gently in his lap that I think it is alive, until I notice the unnatural twist of the neck, the limp folds of the throat, the dull glaze of the eyes. I study his hair in the photo, black and cropped short, his silver sunglasses, his bare narrow torso, his rifle beside the animal's head. I set the snapshot on the workbench behind me, unimpressed all of a sudden with the way he is cutting the meat so close to the bone. I don't want to take my hands out of my pockets when he asks me to tear the pieces of masking tape he needs to seal the portions he has wrapped. But I do, and I follow the rest of his instructions, sorting the small white packages into piles, writing the names of the cuts of meat he calls out to me on each one.

"I thought you said your brother shot it."

"He did." He wipes his bloody hands on his jeans. "These go in the freezer. The ribs need to soak a little while before we barbecue them. I have to get a fire started, and then I want to take a shower."

There is something different about the tone of his voice. I have the feeling he has forgotten who he is speaking to, and then, as though he heard it too, the formality returns to his voice. "Do you know how to make a marinade?"

I nod and carry the raw rack of ribs standing upright on a plate into the house, knowing as I do that I won't eat them.

I am standing at the sink, slicing rings of green onion on a cutting board when the telephone rings. Marlon is reading a magazine in the living room. There is only one person who could be calling this late. I know it, and Marlon knows it. I see his reflection in the window above the sink and, in it, I see him looking at me. The red telephone on the wall beside the sink rings again. The brown telephone rings upstairs in the bedroom. I don't answer Marlon's telephone. It isn't mine.

He leans out of his chair, rushes his toes into the rubber slippers he keeps outside the sliding screen door, and slaps across the deck toward the black telephone on the wall in the garage.

The ringing stops. I hear him laughing. I rinse the knife blade in a stream of water from the tap. She hasn't always made him laugh. He hadn't laughed much when she decided she wanted to come home for Christmas when the polo player she'd run away with to Honolulu hadn't included her in his holiday plans. He wasn't laughing the night he called to tell me that he had left her drinking at a party. It was the evening something that looked like a spotlight had followed me at a distance as I rode my horse down from the mountain.

"Sounds like an akualele," Marlon said when I told him what I had seen.

"A what?"

"Did it look like a burst of light before it disappeared? Something like a meteor, but closer?"

"How did you know?"

"There's more than one kind. People have reported different types of sightings. Some say it looks like a floating fireball. Sometimes it's fast moving; other times it's slow; sometimes it's quiet; sometimes it makes a swooshing sound. Some say they've seen a row of lights, like night walkers, each carrying a lantern, sometimes down a mountain track; sometimes along a shoreline trail."

"Do you mean like a spirit?"

"Something like that. But also physical. Like a meteor. The difference is that meteors disintegrate and disappear. Akualele follow."

"Then it is a spirit."

Marlon didn't answer.

"What, then?" I asked impatiently.

"Some people think to see akualele is a bad omen. I like to think they can also have positive connotations. My general understanding of akualele is that it appears for a reason. To certain people."

"Why?"

"Maybe to give assurance. Maybe to give guidance."

I could not articulate the thrill that I felt. "What are you doing right now?"

"I'm reading a report I wrote this afternoon. It looks like it needs to be proofread by a schoolteacher. What are you doing?"

"I was getting ready to take a shower."

"I'm going to go chase poachers and look for your akualele."

"What makes you think it would show itself to you? I'm the one it followed."

"Then I better take you with me. How long will it take you to be ready?"

"I'm ready now."

I reach for the dishtowel when I hear the slap of Marlon's rubber slippers on the back steps again. As I dry the knife, a saying comes to me. I can't remember it exactly, only that it has something to do with the way the sharpness of the knives in a kitchen reveals how committed a man is to his home. I drag the blade across the surface of my thumbnail. It cuts like a razor.

Marlon slides the screen door open. He bends down to examine a squeak it makes and slides the frame back and forth on the track. *Committed.*

I open the refrigerator for the bottle of shoyu and pour it over the sugar and green onions I've measured into the pan. I shake the jar of sesame seeds recklessly over the marinade, spilling them across the counter and onto the floor.

"Where do you keep your broom?"

"I don't have one."

"What do you mean you don't have one?"

"My wife took it with her when she moved to Honolulu."

"It's bad luck to move a broom out of a house."

"I'm not superstitious," he tells me, scraping the seeds into a pile with the side of his bare foot.

"How do you sweep the floor?"

"I try not to spill things."

"She's coming back, isn't she?"

He doesn't answer right away.

"For a visit," he says.

"For another visit," I say. "And then what?"

"I don't know."

"Were you going to tell me?"

"The house is hers. She can come back whenever she wants."

"Give her the house. Move out. You don't have to live here."

"What am I supposed to do? Move into the teachers' cottages with you?"

I can't meet his eyes. I can't think of anything to say. And neither can he. I lift my jacket from the back of the chair and scan the kitchen before I leave.

My house is dark when I pull in the driveway. I leave my boots on the front step and turn the doorknob. When I switch on the light, thick rolls of dust blow across the paint-ruined hardwood floor. I don't know how long the woody branches of lantana and wilting orchids have been standing in the jar on the table. Their purple tops are shed like dried thyme across the oilcloth, and what is left of the water is brown and infected-smelling at the bottom of the jar.

I reach beneath the kitchen sink for a can of cleanser and begin to scrub the top of the stove. I wash the dishes that are piled on the counter. I scour the sink. I sweep the floor. Then I move to the bathroom and start on the shower, all the time thinking, *I have to do something about the horse and I have to do it now. If I keep him staked out at Kō'ele, I'll see Marlon. If I see him, we'll begin again. I know we will.*

The Norfolk pines look eerie, silhouetted in the headlights as I turn the corner and follow the highway out of town. When I reach the dirt track that leads to the paddock, I turn off the headlights. Through the lowered window, I hear the whipping sound the grass makes against the tires. My horse is chewing grass, his head down, his ears turned suspiciously toward the hood of my station wagon.

I open the back and climb inside, leaning against the saddle to watch him. In a little while he lifts his head and drags the rope through the grass toward me. He leans his head inside, reaching for the empty bucket lodged behind the saddle.

I begin to realize that everything is Marlon's: the bucket, the saddle, the bridle, the ropes, the stake, the mallet, the water containers, the hoof pick, the brush, the comb. And then I remember that he is wearing shoes. I can't put him out to pasture wearing shoes. I don't know what to do. And then, as if to help, he noses the bucket and lifts his head several times.

I want to climb on his back and wrap my legs around his belly. I want to wrap my arms around him and inhale the animal smell of his coat. I pull the neck rope short. Maybe my reach is too sudden. Maybe it is the smell of the detergent on my hands. He lifts his head hard. It feels as if I've been struck in the face with a steel bar. I reach for my nose, expecting blood, and jump out of the way before he turns. His hooves lash out, and he runs with all of his might, kicking the air, snorting, dragging the rope through the grass, until he is forced to turn around when the end of the rope pivots on the swivel attached to the stake. He flicks his tail and paws the ground, head lowered, ears held back. A cuttering sound comes from his nostrils.

There is only one thing to do. That he hurt me makes it easier. I take the rope and pull back against his weight, yanking hard, using the trailer hitch for leverage. But he won't come. I push my way through the knee-high grass, following the rope in the dark. When I reach him, I loop the end of the neck rope around his head and lead him back to the car, where I tie the other end of the rope around the bumper, savagely close to the tailgate.

I gun the engine and trace a circle through the grass. I pause at the edge of the road, then accelerate up the hill toward the pasture, listening as I shift to second and then to third to the clank of his shoes striking the blacktop. All I can think of is black and silver, hooves and steel. His hair and his sunglasses. His watch on his wrist. His knife and his gun. The clank of his shoes on the road.

A small herd of horses is grazing along the fence line when I reach the pasture. I stop to open the gate. Move the car forward. Turn off the engine and walk to the back of the car. I can hear him heaving. I can smell him, and though it's dark, I can see that he has lathered through his coat, that his legs are caked with mud. I untie the knot under his throat and hold the rope, wrapped around his neck, while I untie the knot at the hitch. He watches me, blinking in the night.

I don't want to love him. I don't even want to like him. I lift the rope, and when I make as if to throw it at his rump, he takes off, head free, tail extended in a straight line behind his rear, his hind legs kicking out at all of the space of the sky.

Later in bed, a draft blows into my room through the screen. I turn on my side to look through the window at a pair of stars. I don't know their names, but they always seem to be there just before I fall asleep. They look like landing lights blinking on the wings of a small plane. They always have. But I've never been able to determine whether the plane was approaching or departing. I've always been able to think of it both ways.

I close my eyes and think, *In the morning I'll leave the saddle and bridle and the rest of Marlon's things in his garage with a note, asking him to remove the shoes.* I try to visualize my horse running with the herd along the edge of the canyon, but all I can see is the bed of Marlon's truck.

It wasn't the night we went searching for akualele. It was another night. The night Marlon called to ask if I wanted to go with him to watch the meteor shower.

"What meteor shower?"

"You didn't read about the Leonid meteor shower?"

"No."

"There's a comet called the Tempel-Tuttle that orbits the sun every thirty-three years. As it passes through the solar system, it leaves trails of meteor showers behind. For about three hours tonight, the earth is going to be gliding right through the trail of debris."

"Debris?"

"That's what meteors are. Dusty, disintegrating debris. If the trail is dense, the meteor showers can be intense."

"How intense?"

"Like a storm of shooting stars. We may see as many as forty meteors per hour. If we pass through the center of the storm, we might see a thousand.

"A thousand meteors?"

I am lying beside Marlon in the back of his truck, holding his binoculars against my face, glassing the horizon for meteors. At first, all I see is the dark expanse of needle-pricked space. It looks as if someone has ground abalone shells into a fine, iridescent powder and flung a fistful of it against the black dome of the night. Then long green tracks of light streak down across the sky, and the stars begin to fall like rain.

Marlon is lying beside me, quiet and fixed as the stars appear to be on an ordinary night. Historically, he reminds me, meteors have been considered bad omens.

"Some people think akualele are bad omens."

"It isn't the same."

"I know. Meteors disintegrate. Akualele follow."

Marlon exhales.

"Do you want to know what I think?" I say. "The purpose of meteors is to make us believe we're unloved. The purpose of akualele is to make us believe that we are."

Marlon looks at me. "Do you know why history repeats itself?"

I won't look back. I press the eyepiece of the binoculars against my face. "I don't care," I say, pressing harder, as if the pain will help me to see more clearly. "I don't care."

Trevor

Sonia Saruba

"You sure you want this horse?" I asked my husband for
the hundredth time. I was appalled by the vision before me.
I saw mountains of veterinary bills piling up around a
scrawny sorrel-and-white Paint horse, looking like a cardboard cutout
that would topple over at the slightest breath of wind. I glanced over the
raw, itchy belly, hairless tail, weeping eyes, and the sore on his nose that
looked like it had been bleeding for years. My husband's pick for our
equine acquisition—Trevor, they called him, as if he were a fancy interior
designer—was not exactly what I had hoped for in our first horse.

Trevor had been working as a school horse at a riding stable,
submitted to endless hour-long lessons with adults and children
in sleeting rain, hundred-degree heat, and anything in between. I
couldn't imagine his potential for us. But Bill definitely did.

So we bought Trevor and moved him to a place that seemed

like heaven to me: twenty-five square miles of unimproved Stanford University land, gently undulating hills dotted with ancient oak trees, laced with miles of trails, and crowned by a sapphire jewel of a lake set amid the golden grasses. The ranch was immaculate, the paddocks large and roomy, the people friendly. It was equine paradise.

Trevor became Bill's favorite horse to ride. It seemed Trevor would do anything for him, even things the instructor never thought Trevor could. Bill had faith that Trevor would rise to the occasion and challenged him with walking over a wooden bridge or stepping through an old tire. Trevor responded like a pro. He transported Bill to his boyhood dream of someday riding a painted pony, just like the Indians in the movies did. Bill was in love.

Unfortunately, Bill's work demands began to eat into Trevor time, so I took over Trevor's care. This wasn't easy. Trevor was stubborn, withdrawn, and less than cooperative. On a lead rope he acted like a quarter-ton boat anchor. He bit mercilessly without provocation, nipped at everything, and soon I was at my wits' end.

The breakthrough came in the form of a small orange cone and a clicker. I can't remember where I got the idea, but I figured since we weren't making any progress anyway, I would try to teach Trevor some tricks. It was exhilarating to see the initial light bulb go on in his head as he quickly associated the click of the metal square I held in my hand with a job well done and subsequent reward of a handful of grain. It seemed you really could teach an old horse new tricks.

Trevor's learning escalated, my frustration subsided, and soon he knew an extensive number of tricks that he loved to run through. The cranky, stubborn shell of a horse melted away, revealing a budding, quirky character with quick intelligence. Bill was amazed.

"Say yes," I'd ask, and Trevor's head would solemnly bob up and down.

"Pick it up," I'd command, tossing a well-worn leather hat on the ground. Trevor would walk to the hat, pick it up carefully by the brim, and hand it to me, a proud look in his eye. He loved the treat rewards, but even more he loved the hugs and praise.

People often stopped to watch our performances under the shaggy eucalyptus tree in the arena. We became a bit of a legend at the barn. "We're going to Hollywood," I'd announce proudly, rubbing Trevor's now-fuzzy belly.

As Trevor and I bonded, Bill's health suddenly declined. By Thanksgiving, a year after we bought Trevor, Bill was rapidly losing weight and could hardly swallow. He was diagnosed with esophageal cancer. We were both in shock, unable to bring our minds to grip this new reality we were facing. Surely this wasn't happening.

In early January, two days after Bill's surgery, he passed away. He developed a blood clot while in intensive care. There was nothing the doctors could do.

Until then I had honestly believed we would, we could get through this; we had done it before when either of us had a crisis or steep mountain to climb. But now my world came to a grinding, earth-shattering halt. Bill's death seemed more than I could stand.

Trevor

Bill had been everything, my soul mate, my mentor, my supporter, and my biggest fan. He brought an unshakable love into my life, and without him I was lost. Shell-shocked, I went straight for Trevor's mane, which I clung to and wept into until my sobs ran dry. Trevor stood patiently, letting my tears soak into his fur, as if he understood that he was all I had I left. Gently he'd nip at me, bring me back into reality, as if to say, "I'm still here. Take care of me."

And so, I did.

Trevor, himself a survivor, gave me the courage to keep moving. He became the reason I got out of bed in the morning, went through the motions of feeding and clothing myself. Carefully, slowly, as if made of eggshells, I began to move forward in a hazy world where all familiar ways had been destroyed, leaving only the quiet sanctuary of the barn and my horse.

My barn friends rallied around and supported me, bringing me food, including me in their lives as much as they could. We rode, we talked, and we tried to laugh. But something was still wrong. I wasn't recovering emotionally like I should have been. In a few months I developed a stubborn cough and every day I felt myself losing more strength. Even walking up stairs became nearly impossible.

Rule number one when working with horses is to never let your guard down, or get too cozy with the status quo. This applies to life as well, which can sometimes seem terribly unfair. Just because you've been through something hard doesn't mean you're off the hook when the impossible comes calling. Life throws unexpected lessons your way just at the time you feel least able to handle them. Yet that's exactly when you can end up finding courage and resources you never thought you had.

Five months after Bill's passing, I was diagnosed with a tumor in my heart. I came to believe my disease was a physical manifestation of a heart that had broken when Bill died.

"You're only alive by a miracle," the doctors told me.

I found myself using Trevor's mane again for all my tears and pain, and this time fear as well. I'd survived the death of my closest love, only to confront the very real possibility of my own. Yet somehow the fear morphed into a deep-rooted knowledge that I would survive. Surgery came and went, and when I awoke, my ribs ached, clamped together by steel staples. I felt like Trevor had galloped over me a million times in my sleep. But I knew I was cured and on the mend, and that somehow I would turn the next corner and be able to handle whatever I might find. I felt alive and hopeful for the first time in a long, long time.

By then it was high summer, time to return to life and live as I was meant to—a time to ride, to run, to feel the wind of possibility blowing again through my hair and Trevor's flowing mane.

"Life is short, but it is wide," the Spanish say. How right they are.

After months of sorrow and pain, the world seemed brilliant, its colors vibrant, almost blinding, and its surprises as wide and deep as my imagination could take me. I felt I was really seeing the meaning of life for the first time. I spent my days recovering at the barn, drinking in the best medicine in the world: that of horse and nature. Trevor kept me grounded and in the moment and demanded every last ounce of concentration from me. It seemed our communication evolved to a deeper level of understanding as we wove a language all our own.

"He's more like a dog than a horse," my friends commented, shaking their heads and smiling. "You're breaking all the rules of horsemanship treating him that way."

"I know I am, but it's working for us," I replied, smiling inside at what I knew they didn't yet seem to understand.

In the days and weeks that followed my recovery, Trevor followed me around without a lead rope. The incessant nipping had turned into part of the language we shared. I loved the way he nipped at me when he wanted something. He liked to grab my backpack and shake me around to cheer me up, as if having a private equine laugh at my expense. We had conversations. "Are you thirsty?" I'd ask. The big head would nod solemnly, and off we'd go in search of water. He'd try to "converse" with my friends and return to me disappointed and frustrated. Only Trevor and I spoke our language.

I liked to think that somewhere Bill was smiling at us, at me for finally admitting Trevor had been the best horse trade Bill ever made, and at Trevor also for standing in for him when Bill couldn't be there himself. I had to admit, Trevor had proved to be quite a return on investment.

Slowly, life started to return to normal. The vibrant colors muted somewhat, but still each day I remembered to enjoy each moment as best I could, and be thankful for what I had. I missed Bill every day, but being with Trevor reassured me that everything was as it should be. My new barn friends became some of the closets friends I'd ever had, and on days when we were riding, walking, or just plain hanging around the barn, talking up a storm, I saw how unconditional their love was, how much I valued each and every moment. I look back on those halcyon days, the days of growth and understanding, weaving a bond between animal and human, the days that Walt Whitman called "the teeming quietest, happiest days of all." The most difficult year of my life was drawing to a close, and I couldn't have done it without my friends, either four- or two-legged. It seemed the rainy days were finally behind me.

Only they weren't. The open sore on Trevor's nose, which had always been a source of concern, had begun to steadily grow larger. Early on we had determined it was squamous cell carcinoma, which the vet reassured me was extremely slow-growing in horses. We did a number of procedures to try to remove the cancer: excision, laser burning, and chemotherapy. The wound would shrink to the size of a pinhead, stay dormant for a few months, and then slowly enlarge again.

Time turned toward winter, and as the days shortened and the temperatures plummeted, Trevor began to lose weight. His gums turned pale. A previously dormant lump under his chin suddenly began to balloon. I had to cut part of his halter away to make it fit. Desperately I tried every remedy I could find, but nothing worked. The cancer had made its way into his system.

April soon arrived. The grasses were at their greenest and most lush, irresistible to any horse, yet one day Trevor stopped eating. I knew it was time, and yet I wanted it *not* to be more than anything. I didn't think I could manage one more loss. Trevor was the last remaining connection I had to Bill, his gift of life to me.

On that last day, amid a tangled group of tearful heads and aching arms, Trevor got one last hug goodbye from all his human friends. We turned away, lifting our faces to the green hills as the vet ended Trevor's suffering. Crying unashamedly, we watched the spirit of Trevor bound away over the grasses, free at last.

It's remarkable how you learn to cope with the absence of what you've loved the most. Time brings a kind of dull acceptance that softens until you remember mostly the sweet details of the love you had. I frequently remind myself that our loved ones come and go throughout life. Nothing remains constant. And this is as it should be. As Bill used to say, "Enjoy what you have while you have it." To which I'd add, "And even after the physical parts of us have vanished, the memories and love remain."

I can accept the past and wrap my memories in cottony peace, knowing Bill and Trevor are together, flashing across eternal fields of green. I know I am richer, deeper, and stronger for what I've lived through. I can comfortably set my sights on my future, knowing I have the inner strength to see me through. I have friends and support when and where I need them. Anything is possible.

Learning to Love

Beth Sears

I looked at my hand, bandaged and braced, and wondered if I had made a mistake in buying Lily.

"That horse did a number on you," the doctor said as I was coming out of surgery. He'd inserted screws to hold the bone together. Days later, a physical therapy team molded a plastic form to protect the hand while giving it some range of motion.

"You'll be seeing a lot of us in the weeks and months to come," the physical therapist told me.

This was not what I had envisioned when I bought Lily a year earlier. After spending months researching horse breeds and test-riding horses, I had spent thousands of dollars on a fancy pony that I hoped would become my show mare. My friends called her beautiful, admired her luscious locks, her animated gaits, her look-at-me attitude. What would they think if I now said the three-year-old Lily may be wrong for me?

As a horse-crazy girl and young adult, I gratefully rode whatever equine was available—whether it be a pinto pony that tried to take me under trees or a herd-bound Anglo-Arabian endurance horse that spun in circles when nervous. I just wanted to be around horses and to ride. In my mid-twenties, when I bought my own horse, I didn't care that she was a grade gray mare of indeterminate breeding, that she would never win a confirmation class, that she had a big cresty neck and the barrel of a sixteen-hand horse plopped onto the legs of a large pony. My mare, Scuba, had personality, experience, and, best of all, she was mine.

Together we trekked around fields of alfalfa, corn, and beans and through the woods. She proved to be a great trail horse—popping over logs, nimbly stepping through briars, and even swimming across a river. She had the desire to gallop but willingly slowed when asked.

Around the barn, she was known for her personality—being patient with the cat who rubbed against her face and legs, ignoring the chicken roosting on her back, and carefully stepping around an inattentive dog. I welcomed the sound of her throaty whicker when I entered the barn and enjoyed her trustworthiness with farm visitors. Those big lips of hers tenderly lifted apples, carrots and treats from outstretched hands. Scuba stood patiently while children brushed her, picked up her feet, and climbed atop her. She adjusted her pace for her rider, walking slowly and deliberately for the timid and boldly cantering for the daring.

In times of honesty, I'd tell people that Scuba had her faults. She untied lead ropes and tested fences, leaning on ones that weren't electrified and jumping over ones that were too low. She knocked over water buckets and jumped into water tanks—thus earning her name. As a riding horse, I'd prefer one with more flexion, a softer mouth, and less sensitive feet. But I loved her.

As time went on, age started catching up with Scuba. She developed respiratory problems that limited her exercise tolerance, and navicular disease that limited her further. Our gallops became shorter, and then slowed to trots and, finally, mostly walks. I was in my mid-thirties then and not quite ready to settle for ambles. As we walked on our trail rides, I started dreaming of another horse.

For the first time in my life, my financial situation didn't limit me to a leased or bargain-basement horse. While I didn't have an unlimited budget, I had enough money to buy a young horse that could be competitive in the local show ring, somewhere I hadn't been since I was a child. Years of riding gave me confidence that I could train a young horse and experience the joy of growing up together. That young horse, I decided, would be a Haflinger. I loved their golden coats and blond manes and tails. Their pony size suited my shorter frame. Haflinger owners raved about the breed's sensible attitude, trainability, and hardiness. Plus, they made nice riding and driving horses. While I was still very much a rider, I realized that some day I might have to give in to those aching knees—and driving horses may be a way to stay involved with the animals I loved.

I dragged my husband to visit Haflinger farms where we looked at and rode horses, but I kept rejecting them. None of them was that perfect horse. After a few months of searching, I finally spotted her golden coat, her blond mane, and her white blaze. Her name was Lily, and she was a late two-year-old green broke to ride and drive. It was love at first sight, and I bought her immediately.

After Lily arrived in my barn, I couldn't stop looking at her and admiring her looks. It was winter in western Ohio. I had no indoor riding facilities and was limited in what work I could do with her. With warmer weather came the first signs that my love affair with Lily was in trouble and that the honeymoon period was over.

When I bought Lily, I saw everything she could become—an athletic competitor, a flashy show horse, a trail mount. Somehow, I didn't see what she was—a green horse who was pushy, nippy and spooked at cats, vehicles, blankets, and most everything else. Until I bought Lily, all of my riding horses had come to me trained and with basic ground manners. Sure, a few needed a tune-up in some areas, but overall, they stood for saddling and willingly headed out to the fields and pastures for rides.

Every training session with Lily seemed to end with a trip to my growing collection of horse training books or to the Internet. How do you teach a horse to stand quietly when you pick up its feet? How do you desensitize them to cars? How do you teach them about personal space? The list went on. Eventually, I realized that I needed more help and enrolled in riding lessons. At the time, I was naive enough to think that a few months of training could turn Lily into the lovely lady my old mare was. But as weeks turned to months, I realized what a project I'd taken on.

Lily

While Scuba wanted to go, Lily wanted to whoa. The filly was lazy. While the other horses raced around in the pastures, she grazed.

"Have you had blood work done on her?" my instructor asked. Thyroid problems could cause low energy. The vet drew and tested her blood.

When the results came in, my husband took the call. Later, he reported the news to me. "Her blood appears normal," he told me. "So it's probably LPD."

"L-P-D." I mouthed the initials and tried to remember what that stood for. Cholesterol levels? Respiratory woes?

"Lazy Pony Disease," my husband said. "There's nothing wrong with her. You just need to make her go."

And make her stop spooking, I thought. Lily's tendency to shy at objects equaled her insatiable curiosity. She noticed any movement or anything out of place. If I left my sweatshirt lying on the ground she stopped to look at it. Then slowly, with arched neck and pricked ears, she circled it before walking up to it, mouthing it, and leaping across the paddock out of harm's way. In the pasture, on lead and under saddle, she was constantly scaring herself with her curiosity. Because of this, I seldom ventured outside the confines of a fenced-in paddock. When I did, I could never relax and enjoy the scenery. I was tense and waiting for the next jump or sidestep. Riding Lily was nothing like my carefree ambles, often bareback, with Scuba. It was work, and I was starting to question if the work would ever pay off and if I could have the enjoyable, relaxing rides I dreamed of when I bought Lily.

"How do I teach a horse to be as nice as you?" I asked my gray mare. Frustrated with Lily, I'd hop on Scuba for an amble through the woods where I listened to birds, looked for wildlife, admired the flowers. Would Lily's personality ever allow her to be this calm on trails?

The answer seemed to be no.

On an early fall morning, she spooked at hay drying in the alfalfa field. The saddle slipped as Lily turned and bolted for home. I fell to the ground and was left lying there, assessing my injuries, alone. My entire left side—head, shoulder, hip and hand—throbbed. I stood up slowly and began the slow walk back to the barn where I could see Lily grazing, the saddle now underneath her.

On the walk back, I first noticed that my middle finger jutted at an unnatural angle toward my index finger. X-rays showed the finger had snapped right below the joint. Fixing it required cutting through a tendon and inserting screws into the bone. Months of physical therapy followed. My riding days with Lily were done for the year. I now had lots of time to question my decision and doubt my horse. Had I not realized the work starting a young horse would take? Was Lily a flake and just not the right horse for me? Should I cut my losses, sell her, and try again? I didn't like my golden girl much that fall, but I wasn't ready to give up on her. In my eyes, giving up on her would be giving up on myself and admitting that I might have been wrong in choosing Lily. I wasn't ready to face that fact just yet.

Thus began the determined journey that included horse trainers, riding lessons, horse shows, and hours upon hours in the saddle. I can't count the number of times I wanted to give up my pony or the number of times I doubted my decision.

"How can I trust her under saddle if I'm not sure I can hold on to her in hand?" I asked my husband. Lily was four years old, and she was entered in a confirmation class at a local horse show. When she came out of the horse trailer, she snorted, flared her nostrils, arched her neck, and flagged her tail. Her posture and animated gait caused several people to glance at her underside.

"She's a mare, not a stallion," I assured them.

When she started settling down some, I entered her in a walk-trot riding class. Completing the class and staying on my horse buoyed my spirits—as long as I didn't think about how hard it was to get her to trot.

"How am I ever going to get her to canter?" I asked my riding instructor. Lily was age five then and resisting the canter. When I asked her to go, she kicked out and bucked, knocking me off balance, unable to keep her in the canter for more than a few strides. In frustration, I hired a trainer to ride her for a month. It was money well spent. By the end of the year, she was cantering on command. It wasn't always balanced. She didn't often take the correct lead. But it was a canter.

"She's really starting to show improvement," my friend commented to me on a spring day when Lily turned six. She pointed out that Lily sometimes went on the bit, sometimes went forward, sometimes cantered with energy.

"But it's not consistent," I replied.

Over the summer, though, Lily started to change. When I took her to horse shows, she stood quietly at the trailer. During her dressage tests, she scored in the mid-60s. At home, she welcomed her weekly trail ride. When something spooked her, and something always did, she halted, looked, and went on. She learned to wait for treats and to give me space.

"I think she might be growing up," I told my husband. She was by no means perfect. We still weren't cantering consistently. I still worked, though not as hard, on forward. I still saw a lot of work ahead.

But during a riding lesson that fall, when my instructor told me to drop my stirrups and canter, I laughed when Lily leapt into a strong canter with very little encouragement. I yelled yee-haw, a word I reserved for when I was having a good time on my horse, a word I hadn't used atop Lily, ever.

"Ask for her to give to the bit," my instructor said.

After I did, I glanced in the mirror and was awed by my golden girl. Her mane flowed, her compact body glistened. As I brought her down to a trot, then a walk, I reached down and hugged her. This, finally, was the horse I envisioned when I bought her four years earlier. I was, after all these years, back in love with the golden girl.

I knew she wasn't perfect, that she'd always be a little lazy, a little spooky, and a little too curious for her own good. I loved her, though, for what she'd become, and for what we'd accomplished together. I was glad that I had persevered and hadn't given up on her. On that day, I knew that Lily and I would continue to work together for years to come.

I still have a faint scar that runs the length of my finger and provides a daily reminder of that time I was ready to give up on Lily and myself. Had I sold her and bought another horse, I'm sure that horse, too, would have revealed her imperfections over time.

My work with Lily developed me into a better rider and horsewoman. But it also reminded me the value of determination, patience, and belief in myself. As a director of a non-profit agency, I'm always faced with challenges of accomplishing goals with limited funding and adapting to changes around me. When I get frustrated,

I run my finger along that scar, think of my journey with Lily, and confidently set about working through the problem.

More importantly, Lily reminded that relationships—whether horse-to-human or human-to-human—take work. I fell in love with the two-year-old Lily because I liked the way she looked, not because I knew her. That love affair ended pretty quickly. But I fell in love with the six-year-old Lily after working with her for years. I know her imperfections and strengths, and I love her for both. At times in my adult life, both my husband and dear friends frustrate me. But we've developed a bond over the years that motivates us to work through our differences and grow stronger. And that, like my dear Lily, is golden.

Acknowledgments

Without horses, and the women who love them, this book would not have been possible. I would first like to thank the contributors who graciously opened their hearts and souls to share their intimate, funny, and memorable moments with me and, now, with the world. I feel quite fortunate to have the honor of Jane Smiley contributing a foreword to the anthology, sharing her own love of horses as well. I'm sure each of the contributors feels as honored as I do to share in this collection.

Thank you to my editor, Krista Lyons, who graciously offered me this opportunity to blend my love of writing and riding. It has been a pleasure working with you. I would also like to thank Tracy Saville, who assisted me in shaping and editing the collection of stories.

And behind every good woman is a wonderful family who shares and supports her success; thank you to my husband and my children. What I do, I am able to do because of your love, support, and encouragement. I love you dearly.

About the Editor

Verna Dreisbach is an author, educator, and literary agent. Her stories have been published in *EQUUS* magazine and Bernie Siegel's *Faith, Hope, and Healing: Inspiring Lessons Learned from People Living with Cancer.* Her essay "The Racehorse" won first place in the 2007 Dominic J. Bazzanella Literary Awards. She is the founder and president of Capitol City Young Writers, a national non-profit organization dedicated to the education and inspiration of young writers. She holds a bachelor's degree in English with honors from Phi Kappa Phi and Sigma Tau Delta International English Honor Society. Verna is currently pursuing a master's degree in English with a focus on creative writing at California State University, Sacramento. She lives in California with her husband, three kids, and myriad animals. Her website is www.vernadreisbach.com.

About Jane Smiley

 Jane Smiley is the author of many books, including *Horse Heaven, A Year at the Races, Barn Blind, The Georges and the Jewels,* and the forthcoming *A Good Horse.* Her novel *A Thousand Acres* won the Pulitzer Prize in 1992. She lives in California, where she has six horses and five trainers and shows as often as she dares at the Pebble Beach Horse Show.

About the Contributors

Dee Ambrose-Stahl lives in southwestern Pennsylvania with her husband of twenty-two years and their beloved corgis, a Maine coon cat, and paint horse, Sky. She teaches literature in the public secondary school setting and pursues non-fiction writing projects in her spare time. She has served as a reviewer and contributor for Holt, Rinehart and Winston. Dee's fiction and photography have both appeared in specialty corgi magazines.

Jane Ayres has been writing about her love of horses from a young age, with her first pony story published when she was fourteen. In addition to writing, Jane works at a performing arts college and teaches music and dance. Now living in Kent in the United Kingdom, she made the decision to give up riding several years ago after a bad fall. An animal lover, Jane supports a number of charities that are concerned with animal welfare issues.

Linda Ballou's pioneering parents took her when she was thirteen to Alaska, where she became firmly grounded in nature. From there she journeyed to California, where she obtained a degree in English Literature from Northridge University. Horses have always held a special place in her heart. Linda's articles have appeared in *Horse Illustrated* and *Equus* magazine. Today she is a freelance writer, based in Los Angeles and specializing in soft adventure travel. Her mission is to experience as many beautiful places on our planet as she can, before they are no more. Presently, she's having fun gathering stories for her travel collection, *Lost Angel Walkabout*. Visit her website at www.LindaBallouAuthor.com.

Chansonette Buck grew up as the stepchild of a Beat Generation poet, living all over the American West, in England, and in Spain. She spent those years dreaming of horses. When she was ten and eleven she lived on a ranch in Idaho, where she rode often. She came back to riding in middle age, volunteering, teaching, and riding at Wildcat Canyon Ranch, a horse program for at-risk inner-city high school students in Oakland, California. She rides rental string horses and is looking forward to the day when she has a horse of her own. Chansonette holds a PhD in English from the University of California, Berkeley, where she won awards for her poetry and her teaching. She has recently completed a memoir, *Unnecessary Turns: Growing Up Beat . . . A Love Story*. She lives in Berkeley with her daughter, three cats, and two dogs.

Lynda Fenneman was born and raised in Texas. "She went plumb horse nutty early on," her mother said. "I dressed her up in pretty little dresses only to see her running around in the front yard on all fours, whinnying and chasing the dogs, ripping her clothes, getting filthy, and she always had Band-Aids on her knees." Some things never change. Lynda got her first "real horse" at age forty-two and started living out her childhood fantasies, for real, in the mountains of Southern California. Working as an illustrator, aspiring to be a writer, and learning all about horses has opened many surprising doors for Lynda. She "obtained" a mule in 2001 and has written many short stories, which have been published in *Mules and More* magazine. At present, she is the writer and editor of ETI Corral 20 News, in Shadow Hills, California, and is still riding, the same first "real horse" and mule, at age sixty-seven.

Kara Gall is a poet, essayist, and singer-songwriter who writes about motherhood, food, and life on the Great Plains. Her writing has appeared in numerous anthologies, including *Breeder: Real-Life Stories from the New Generation of Mothers, Women Who Eat: A New Generation on the Glory of Food*, and *ReGeneration: Telling Stories from Our Twenties*. An English instructor at Southeast Community College, Kara lives in Lincoln, Nebraska, with her twelve-year-old daughter. She returns to her family's farm every May to work cattle and drive them to pasture.

Kathryn Hohmann competes her horses, Bourbon and Froglegs, in eventing and dressage. A former Washington lobbyist, she worked for a national environmental organization before relocating to Montana in 2000. Kathryn is co-author of a textbook on climate change and has been widely quoted in the *Washington Post, Time,* and the *New York Times,* and she has appeared before congressional panels and on network television. Currently, Kathryn is at work on a novel.

Dobie Houson has been in love with horses since she was eight. In eighth grade, she acquired her first horse, Pixie, a black and white paint retired from the Indian village attraction at Disneyland. Horses have been an integral part of her life ever since. At 38, she bought Bear and it was through coming to know him that she learned she could communicate with animals, a gift that she in turn used to help others more deeply understand their animal companions. Houson is an experienced writer, researcher, consultant, and communicator. For twenty-five years, she has worked for Ken Blanchard, founder of The Ken Blanchard Companies. During her time with Blanchard, Dobie has held dual roles as Director of Corporate Communications and Director of Marketing Research. Her expertise has helped the organization brand and differentiate itself as a leader in the field of global training and development.

Jacklyn Lee Lindstrom's love affair with horses surfaced with her first words, "Look, Mommy, oosie, oosie." A city girl for some thirty years, she finally realized her dream when she, her husband, Don, and their two young sons moved onto a small "ranchette" on ten acres— her goal, to raise and sell quality stock. One of the things she realized early on was how difficult it was to part with those baby foals—which is probably why she started out with two horses and ended up with nine in a four-stall barn. Now that she is a "Golden Ager," she's finally admitted that the ground is too hard and the bones too brittle to keep on riding, so she fosters her passion for those elegant creatures through writing and painting.

Diane Mapes grew up on a farm in the Pacific Northwest where she and her sisters often played tag with their Shetland pony, Prince. If you were able to climb under the electric fence and run to the side of the horse shed and back before Prince caught you, you won. If you were trapped inside the horse shed and repeatedly trampled, Prince won. Not surprisingly, Diane grew up with a great amount of respect for horses. Her essay "Horse Crazy" originally appeared in *The Seattle Times*. Other publishing credits include *Bust*, CNN, *Health*, the *Los Angeles Times*, MSN, MSNBC, and the late, great *Seattle Post-Intelligencer*. She is the author of *How To Date in a Post-Dating World* and the editor of the Seal Press anthology *Single State of the Union: Single Women Speak Out on Life, Love, and the Pursuit of Happiness*.

Janice Newton is an environmental consultant who lives in Portland, Oregon, with her husband, Rich. She is finishing up her first novel, *The Middle Girl*, about the lasting impact of war on women in the United States. She is also conducting a series of interviews for another book, *They Were Just Kids,* about the young men who disagreed with the Vietnam War and were instrumental in ending the military draft. Janice grew up riding on a girlfriend's Shetland pony farm and with her cowboy uncles. She never lost her love of horses, and started riding hunter-jumper several years ago. She still rides Stella.

Penny Porter, considered "one of the most successful storytellers ever to hit *Reader's Digest,*" has published in a wide range of national magazines, including *Arizona Highways, American Heritage, Catholic Digest, Range Magazine, Nevada Magazine,* and *Guideposts.* Penny's work appears in many *Chicken Soup for the Soul* books, *The Good Lord Made Them All* series by Joe Wheeler, anthologies, and textbooks in twenty-eight languages. The author of six books, Penny is the mother of six, grandmother of eight, and great-grandmother of two. Visit her website at http://pennyporter.com.

Andrea Richards is a writer and editor who, after a decade in publishing, finds herself working in a barn and wanting to be a cowgirl. She is a creative writing instructor at Taking the Reins, a Los Angeles–based nonprofit organization that teaches life skills to at-risk teenage girls principally through horse care and riding (www.takingthereins.org). Andrea has written articles and essays for publications such as *The Believer, Bitch: Feminist Response to Pop Culture,*

Bust, Helio, Hemispheres, make/shift, Los Angeles, LA Weekly, and the anthology *Bare Your Soul: The Thinking Girl's Guide to Spirituality* (Seal Press, 2002). She is also the author of the critically acclaimed book *Girl Director: A How-To Guide for the First-Time, Flat-Broke Film and Video Maker* (Ten Speed Press, 2005) and especially enjoys Westerns.

Valerie Riggs is a native San Diegan who has been a columnist for the *Del Mar Times* newspaper in the quaint seaside town of Del Mar, California. She graduated Magna Cum Laude from St. Mary's College in the San Francisco Bay Area. Valerie is a speaker and a volunteer for Voices for Children, a non-profit organization. Spending her childhood summers at the Del Mar Racetrack gave her a lifelong love of horses.

Lisa Romeo has always seen writing and riding as closely connected. After obtaining a journalism degree, Lisa wrote for many major (and a slew of minor) equestrian publications and handled public relations projects for equine businesses, all while competing on the hunter-jumper circuit. More recently, she worked in nonprofit PR before turning to memoir and personal essay, earning an MFA degree from the University of Maine's Stonecoast program. Lisa's work, on a variety of topics, has appeared in many venues, including the *New York Times, O-The Oprah Magazine, Tango*, and *skirt!*, and she is a frequent contributor to essay collections. Lisa lives in northern New Jersey and works as a freelance editor and creative writing teacher.

She is currently writing a memoir of linked essays. Visit her website, LisaRomeo.net, or her blog, LisaRomeoWrites.blogspot.com.

Sonia Saruba is an editor and writer working in the Silicon Valley. She is currently working on a full-length memoir about Trevor, a rescued paint horse. The rest of her time is spent with Sam, also a rescued paint horse, who smiles and gives kisses for a cookie.

Michele Scott is the author of *Murder Uncorked,* the *Wine Lover's Mystery Series* as well as the *Horse Lover's Mystery Series,* published by Berkley Prime Crime (Penguin). Michele began writing at nine years old as has never stopped. After twelve years of pursuing her passion, she signed her first book deal with Berkley. Her debut novel, *Murder Uncorked,* nominated for a best first mystery award by Romantic Times BookClub, hit the Barnes & Nobles mystery bestseller list and the Independent Mystery Bestseller list. Her third book in her equine series, *Tacked to Death,* was released in February 2008. She is currently under contract for eight books with Berkley. Michele has been featured in *The Writer, Romantic Times, San Diego Magazine,* and *Touring & Tasting.* She graduated with a degree in communications from the University of Southern California, where she studied journalism and hoped to be a reporter. Michele lives in San Diego, California, with her husband and three children.

Beth Sears and her husband live on a farm in western Ohio with horses, Katahdin sheep, Buckeye chickens, and rescued Border collies. She writes a weekly newspaper column and blogs about farm life at www.ewechicksandallama.blogspot.com. Among her publication credits are articles in *EQUUS* and *WHY*.

Kate St. Vincent Vogl reveals what happens when her birthmother finds her through her mom's obituary in *Lost & Found: A Memoir of Mothers*. Her writing has been honored in international competition. She teaches creative writing at the Loft, the country's largest literary center, and she serves as Distinguished Faculty at the University of Phoenix.

Emily Alexander Strong's essays about motherhood and family have been published in *It's a Girl: Women Writers on Raising Daughters* (Seal Press, 2006), *A Cup of Comfort for Mothers to Be,* and *A Cup of Comfort for Dog Lovers*. Other contributions include essays in *The Bark* and *Angel Tails* magazines and online in *Mothering* magazine. Emily lives in Ashland, Oregon, with husband Eric (her *real* enchanted prince) and budding young riders Eliza and Harper.

Samantha Ducloux Waltz is an award-winning freelance writer and teacher of writing in Portland, Oregon. Her essays appear in the *Chicken Soup for the Soul* series, the *A Cup of Comfort* series, the *Ultimate* series, and a number of other anthologies, as well as the *Christian Science Monitor, The Rambler,* and Seal Press's *Ask Me About My Divorce.* Other writing includes an adult nonfiction book, *Parenting: Four Patterns in Child Rearing,* and a young adult novel, *Young Rebel,* written under the name Samellyn Wood. Read more at www.pathsofthought.com.

Jill Widner was the recipient of a 2007 Artist Trust/Washington State Arts Commission fellowship in literature and a 2009 Artist Trust grant for artist projects. She has been awarded residencies at Yaddo and the Virginia Center for the Creative Arts and is a graduate of the Iowa Writers' Workshop. Excerpts from her novel in progress, which fictionalizes her experience growing up in Indonesia in the 1960s as the daughter of a petroleum engineer, have appeared or will appear soon in *North American Review, Hobart, Kartika Review, Kyoto Journal, Asia Literary Review,* and *Bamboo Ridge: The Hawai'i Writers' Quarterly.* A longer excerpt was one of two equal runners-up in the 2009 *Willesden Herald* international short story competition and appeared in *New Short Stories 3,* an anthology published by pretend genius press in the United Kingdom. "Akualele," an excerpt from her novella *Before the Rain,* is set on the island of Lana'i, where Jill lived and taught in the early 1980s.

Jacqueline Winspear was born and grew up in the county of Kent, England. Following higher education at the University of London's Institute of Education, Jacqueline worked in academic publishing, higher education, and marketing communications before emigrating to the United States, where she continued her career in marketing and as a personal/professional (life) coach while embarking upon her dream to be a writer. Jacqueline published her first novel, *Maisie Dobbs*, in 2003, and it was subsequently nominated for seven awards, including the Edgar Award for Best Novel. Subsequent novels garnered more nominations and awards. Jacqueline divides her time between homes in Northern and Southern California, and is a frequent visitor to the United Kingdom and the rest of Europe. When she is not writing, Jacqueline enjoys the equestrian sport of dressage. She has two horses and is at the barn almost every day.

Vanessa Wright is an award-winning author, teacher, and photographer whose work celebrates the human-equine bond. Her internationally touring equestrian exhibit, *The Literary Horse: When Legends Come to Life* (www.theliteraryhorse.com), pairs photos of today's horses and horse-people with quotations from the world's great books. More than three hundred of her photos and writings on horses have also been published through organizations ranging from Personal Ponies to HCI Books. Vanessa holds an MEd from Harvard, a BA from the University of Chicago, and certification from the American Riding Instructors Association.

Therese Zink, MD, MPH, and her younger sisters acquired their first horse, Tex, a Shetland pony, when Therese was seven years old. Horses have been part of her life ever since. When she is not riding or cleaning out the barn, she is a family medicine physician who sees patients in Zumbrota, Minnesota. She also does research and teaches medical students and family medicine residents. Her medical work has allowed her to care for patients around the world. These experiences inspire her writing, and her stories have been published in medical journals and magazines. She won the *Minnesota Medicine* writing contest in 2009 and the *Pilgrimage Journal* Writing Award in 2007. *The Country Doctor Revisited*, an anthology of stories, poems, and essays about rural health care in the twenty-first century, will be published by Kent State University Press in 2010. She is working on a memoir and a collection of stories about doctoring.

Selected Titles from Seal Press

For more than thirty years, Seal Press has published groundbreaking books. By women. For women. Visit our website at www.sealpress.com. Check out the Seal Press blog at www.sealpress.com/blog.

Woman's Best Friend: Women Writers on the Dogs in Their Lives, edited by Megan McMorris. $14.95, 978-1-58005-163-7. An offbeat and poignant collection about those four-legged friends girls can't do without.

Cat Women: Female Writers on Their Feline Friends, by Megan McMorris. $14.95, 978-1-58005-203-0. From a tale about how rescuing a stray cat ended up saving a friendship to an unapologetic piece by a confirmed—and proud!—crazy cat lady, this collection of essays ranges from thought-provoking and heartrending to laugh-out-loud funny, delving into the many ways these often aloof little divas touch our lives.

DIRT: The Quirks, Habits, and Passions of Keeping House, edited by Mindy Lewis. $15.95, 978-1-58005-261-0. From grime, to clutter, to spit-clean—writers share their amusing relationships with dirt.

Marie's Home Improvement Guide, by Marie L. Leonard. $16.95, 978-1-58005-292-4. A practical how-to guide for women with to-do lists, *Marie's Home Improvement Guide* offers all the tips you need to tackle home repair projects … yourself!

Dirty Sugar Cookies: Culinary Observations, Questionable Taste, by Ayun Halliday. $14.95, 978-1-58005-150-7. Ayun Halliday is back with comical and unpredictable essays about her disastrous track record in the kitchen and her culinary observations.

She's Such a Geek: Women Write About Science, Technology, and Other Nerdy Stuff, edited by Annalee Newitz and Charlie Anders. $14.95, 978-1-58005-190-3. From comic books and gaming to science fiction and blogging, nerdy women have their say in this witty collection that takes on the "boys only" clubs and celebrates a woman's geek spirit.